BROTHERS AT WAR

BROTHERS AT WAR

Dissidence and Rebellion in Southern Africa

Abiodun Alao

BLOOMSBURY ACADEMIC
LONDON • NEW YORK • OXFORD • NEW DELHI • SYDNEY

This book is dedicated to the memory of my mother
Mrs A.M. Alao
whose life was rich, not because of its duration but because of its donation, and who did everything during her life to make me proud today to be called her son.

BLOOMSBURY ACADEMIC
Bloomsbury Publishing Plc
50 Bedford Square, London, WC1B 3DP, UK
1385 Broadway, New York, NY 10018, USA
29 Earlsfort Terrace, Dublin 2, Ireland

BLOOMSBURY, BLOOMSBURY ACADEMIC and the Diana logo are trademarks of Bloomsbury Publishing Plc

First published in 1994 by I. B. Tauris, British Academic Press
This paperback edition published in 2021

Copyright © Abiodum Alao, 1994

Abiodum Alao has asserted his right under the Copyright, Designs and Patents Act, 1988, to be identified as Author of this work.

For legal purposes the Acknowledgements on p. xi constitute an extension of this copyright page.

All rights reserved. No part of this publication may be reproduced or transmitted in any form or by any means, electronic or mechanical, including photocopying, recording, or any information storage or retrieval system, without prior permission in writing from the publishers.

Bloomsbury Publishing Plc does not have any control over, or responsibility for, any third-party websites referred to or in this book. All internet addresses given in this book were correct at the time of going to press. The author and publisher regret any inconvenience caused if addresses have changed or sites have ceased to exist, but can accept no responsibility for any such changes.

A catalogue record for this book is available from the British Library.

A catalog record for this book is available from the Library of Congress.

ISBN: HB: 9 78-1-8504-3816-8
PB: 978-1-3501-8388-9

Typeset by the Author

To find out more about our authors and books visit www.bloomsbury.com and sign up for our newsletters.

"And brother has shut out brother, and from the same womb they have come."

Alan Paton, *Cry The Beloved Country*

"It seems essential to move to the road of dialogue for reconciliation which will end the shedding of blood between brothers and purify the environment of hatred and lack of love."

Pope John Paul II,
Maputo, September 1988

Contents

Preface	ix
Acknowledgements	xi
Foreword	xv
Chronology of Anti-government Activities in Southern Africa	xvii
1 Introduction: In the Beginning, there were Wars...	1
2 Angola: From Bullet Through Ballot to an Uncertain Future	14
3 Mozambicans at War: Renamo Against the Frelimo Government	45
4 Anti-Government Forces in Zimbabwe: ZIPRA Dissidents and Muzorewa Auxiliaries	82
5 Ethnicity and Anti-Government Activities in Southern Africa	108
6 Counting the Economic Cost	125
7 Conclusion	138
Notes	152
Appendices	172
Bibiography	188
Index	197

Preface

There is a tendency to think that there is nothing new again to be discussed on southern Africa's recent past — not with the enormous attention the region has received from academics, journalists and other interested observers from all walks of life. This position has, however, left a number of important factors unconsidered. First, most of the major issues that have accounted for the attention the region has received in the past still remain contentious, bringing out different patterns on an almost regular basis. Thus, events may need to be considered afresh, when developments hitherto unexpected introduce scenarios which throw overboard some of the earlier assumptions and predictions. Second, the issues involved in southern African affairs are such that they appear virtually inexhaustible, and as in most troubled regions, new issues have kept emerging to require attention. Third, even some of the issues that have been discussed in isolation may need to be regrouped and reconsidered under a wider sub-regional theme.

This book is written against the background of all the above three reasons. I feel that detailed and exclusive attention should be given to why some people in some southern African countries have launched attacks on their comrades and brothers alongside whom they had fought the liberation war. The need for such a study has become all the more necessary now, as recent sub-regional and global developments have introduced changes to events in this regard. In seeking to address these objectives, however, I do not claim to have done a complete dissection of these conflicts, neither do I pretend to have catered for all the growing kaleidoscope of interest and research on the subject, neither still do I claim to have broken many new grounds. My apparently modest intention is thus to synthesise some of the factors that have accounted for and explained dissidence and rebellion in southern Africa, and in the process to attempt two things: first: to provide a comparative study of the civil tensions in these countries; and second: to update the literature in this regard according to changes brought about by regional and global developments. This modest contribution will have achieved one of its main objectives, if it sets more people thinking about the problems in these countries with a view to finding permanent solutions to them.

Like most studies on contemporary politics, there is the inevitable problem of where to place the cut-off for the discussion in this book. Although by the end of 1992, anti-government activities in southern Africa had reached a stage different from that when the bulk of the published works on the issues were written, events were still unfolding in rapid, albeit somewhat predictable, ways. In this book, events and developments are updated till December 1993, while in the conclusion, possible future options for the protagonists in the on-going conflicts and the implications of these options are identified and discussed.

The decision to write this book was taken shortly before my first visit to southern Africa in early 1990. My good fortune of being in the sub-continent when a number of important developments occurred (like the un-banning of the ANC, the release of Nelson Mandela and the independence of Namibia) strengthened this decision. It was my hope then — as it still is now — that the "peace epidemic" that invaded southern Africa with these developments may percolate into other unresolved conflicts in the region. Thus, here, I can only hope, nay pray, that a book of this nature may not have to be written on the new South Africa, as I hope that there will be no conflict to write about.

Writing on the political situation in southern Africa is faced with the problem of objectivity. This becomes all the more profound where one has to consider why blacks fight one another — as against where one is faced with the choice of either justifying or condemning the Republic of South Africa's internal or regional policies. Although I have tried to be neutral in each of the conflicts discussed in this book, I still feel it is advisable to follow Fred Bridgland's example in his two books on the Angolan civil war, and thus quote George Orwell's comment in his book on the Spanish civil war, *Homage to Catalonia:*

> It is difficult to be certain about anything except what you have seen with your own eyes, and consciously or unconsciously everyone writes as a partisan. In case I have not said it earlier, I will say this now: beware of my partisanship, my mistakes of fact and distortion... And beware of exactly the same when you read any other book of this period.

As it was with Spain, so it is with southern Africa.

Acknowledgements

It is practically impossible for me to list the names of all those who have assisted in getting this book out. Thus, I must start by apologising to those whose help I can not acknowledge here for obvious lack of space. In general terms, my interest in southern Africa is the outgrowth of friendship and academic opportunities that have taken place over the years. In this regard, perhaps the first debt I should acknowledge is that to two former teachers, colleagues and friends — the late Professor Olajide Aluko and Dr Layiwola Abegunrin. Their works served as my "Rosetta Stone". It was, in fact, with Professor Aluko that I first discussed the idea of this book. It is unfortunate that he died before its completion. I can only hope that the book merits his judgement.

A Ford Foundation scholarship for a Doctorate programme in War Studies at King's College, University of London, provided a number of opportunities, one of which was the extensive field trip it sponsored to southern Africa. I am thus grateful to the Ford Foundation. At King's College London, I was a beneficiary of enormous kindness and consideration. The Head of War Studies Department, Professor Lawrence Freedman, has given me so many opportunities that I cannot hope to ever repay him for what he has done for me. I hope this book will express a little of that appreciation. Another inexpressible gratitude goes to Dr Barrie Paskins and Dr Martin Navias. Barrie supervised a Ph.D. thesis I wrote on another aspect of southern African security while Martin invited me to deliver a number of lectures to his undergraduate class on southern Africa. This book has benefited a lot from these two opportunities.

I have also been fortunate to enjoy the wisdom, advice and friendship of Professor Jack Spence, of the Royal Institute of International Affairs, while Professor Terence Ranger and Dr Phyllis Fergusson, both of St Antony's College, Oxford University, have encouraged my interest in southern Africa. I thank them. Professor

Spence should be further thanked for agreeing to write a foreword to this book. I must also mention some of the numerous friends and colleagues with whom I have shared the idea of this book. They include Professor Adebayo Olukoshi, Drs Sola Akinrinade, Kunle Lawal, Tajudeen Abdulraheem and Remi Ajibewa. Drs Adeola Olorunnisola and Samuel Tesunbi, both of Howard University, Washington DC, offered editorial assistance. I thank them all for the interest they showed.

It has been my good fortune to complete this book while I am a Research Associate at the Centre for Defence Studies, University of London. The friendship and encouragement I have received from the Centre have been tremendous. I want to thank the Director, Mr Michael Clarke, and all the staff of the Centre, especially my colleagues in the North-South Defence and Security Programme, Dr Chris Smith and Mrs Frances Evans, for the kindness and consideration they extended to me.

It is my privilege to thank the staff of the British Academic Press, especially Dr Lester Crook and Helen Simpson, for being so kind and helpful in seeing my manuscript through to publication. Dr. Edgar Whitley and Mrs Liz Dada both of the London School of Economics did a lot to assist in the technical production of this book. A lot of thanks goes to them.

I have decided to leave out the names of all the southern Africans who assisted me in this study. This step I took with the greatest possible regret, but I would want to disassociate them (in all forms) from my positions in this book. This becomes all the more necessary when I do not have their permissions to identify them personally. I hope they will be content with this general expression of gratitude, and with my assurance that I share with them the hope and prayer for a more peaceful sub-region.

I am profoundly grateful to a number of friends and families who have shown tremendous friendship while I was working on this book. At the top of this list is the family that hosted me throughout the period — that of Dr and Mrs Adebayo Bello. The family did a lot to make life comfortable for me. To Adebayo, Faramade and little Busola Bello, this is a public apology for the "hardship" I brought upon them, and a public thanks for their unfathomable affection. Thanks are also due to Olakunle and Bola Kunle-Lawal, Olusola and Rita Akinrinade, Remi and Remi Ajibewa, my "son", Olabode Esan, Funmi Olonisakin,

ACKNOWLEDGEMENTS

Adewunmi Oyemade, Sina and Bola Gbadamosi, Kenny and Augusta Alowoesin, Col Ade Ajibade, Oladapo and Tope Ali, Dr Segun Obafemi, Tony and Kemi Adeoye, Adebayo Olowoake, Jimi Peters, Jullyette Ukabiala, Doyin and Wemimo Sheyindemi, Kayode and Bisi Fayemi, and many others who offered friendship and consideration.

At the early stage of my writing, I was fortunate to share the "labour ward" with other friends and researchers who were also undergoing "labour pain" about the same time as me. With their friendship, comradeship and through their "confidential gossips", they lightened the burden of research. Thus, I want to put on record my thanks to Dr Ladipo Ogunlana, Mohammed Umar, Lanre Okikiola, Kofi Oteng Kufuor, Ugochukwu Uche, John Mgbere, and all those who shared with me life at the London School of Economics computer room. Finally, I thank Oyeronke, for showing remarkable understanding when some circumstances made me stay on in London longer than we had both anticipated, and all the members of my family for the same understanding.

One last note: I do not wish — by name-dropping in this acknowledgement — to give the impression that every word has gone through the vetting of one expert or the other. Far from it. Thus, if I have got it wrong anywhere in this book, it is my own fault.

Abiodun Alao
Centre for Defence Studies
University of London

Foreword

It is a pleasure to recommend this book. The author - Dr Abiodun Alao - brings a fresh and sensitive perception to the civil wars that have wracked southern Africa over the last two decades. His poignant title - *Brothers at War* - is a potent and depressing reminder of the destruction the region has suffered as those united in the struggle for independence (particularly in Angola and Mozambique) went to war against each other.

What is especially impressive is the detached tone of this analysis. Equally notable is the author's attempt at comparative analysis of war and revolution in southern Africa. Much of the existing literature is country-specific and Dr Alao has skilfully disentangled the strands of a complex regional conflict.

No doubt his Nigerian background was helpful in this context. No reader of this book can doubt his profound commitment to a peaceful and prosperous southern Africa. Yet precisely because he comes from "another country" he is able to examine southern Africa with a reasonably objective eye. It is entirely to his credit that he recognises the force of George Orwell's comment: "...beware of my partisanship, my mistakes of fact and distortion..." Happily, he has given little cause for complaint in this, his first major and pioneering work.

J.E. Spence
Director of Studies,
Royal Institute of International Affairs (Chatham House), London.

Chronology of Anti-government Activities in Southern Africa

Some points are necessary of note about the chronology presented here. The first is that it centres only on the anti-government activities in post-independence Angola, Mozambique and Zimbabwe and not on all the countries in southern Africa. Second, as the nature of the post-independence activities in these countries can only be understood against the background of their pre-independence antecedents, the chronology is divided into two parts. The first covers the period before 1974, when most of the events that determined the post-independence activities in these countries occurred, while the second lists the events after the 1974 coup in Portugal resulted in many fundamental changes in southern Africa. The final point of note is that, while attention is focused largely on anti-government activities within these countries, essential mention is sometimes made of South Africa's direct destabilization of these countries, especially where such actions bear directly on anti-government activities in the region.

Part One

1956 **December** The Popular Movement for the Liberation of Angola (MPLA) founded.
1961 **April** South West African People's Organisation (SWAPO) founded in South West Africa (Namibia). **17 December** The Zimbabwean African People's Union (ZAPU) launched in Rhodesia.
1962 **25 June** Frelimo founded in Mozambique. **20 September** ZAPU banned in Rhodesia.

1963	**5 August** ZAPU split and a breakaway group headed by Revd. Ndabaningi Sithole formed the Zimbabwean African National Union (ZANU). **25 September** Armed struggle began in Mozambique.
1965	**5 November** Ian Smith announced the Unilateral Declaration of Independence (UDI) in Rhodesia.
1966	**March** Jonas Savimbi formed the Union for the Total Independence of Angola (UNITA). **26 August** SWAPO launched armed struggle in Namibia.
1969	**3 February** Eduardo Mondlane, FRELIMO leader, assassinated.
1974	**24 April** Coup in Portugal. The new government promised a policy of decolonization. **17 June** Jonas Savimbi declared a unilateral ceasefire binding UNITA forces in Angola **15 December** The MPLA announced the expulsion of Daniel Chipenda who had earlier led an anti-Neto campaign within the MPLA.

Part Two

1975	**January** An agreement was signed by Portugal, MPLA, FNLA and UNITA, establishing a transitional government, and setting November 11 as a date of independence. The agreement is known as the Alvor of Algarve Agreement. **2 5 June** Independence of Mozambique under FRELIMO. **October** South Africa invaded Angola from Namibia. **October** Cuba sent military advisers to Angola at the invitation of MPLA. **5 November** Cuba initiated "Operation Carlota" - the sending of regular troops to assist the MPLA government. **11 November** MPLA announced the establishment of Independent Republic of Angola. **19 December** The United States Senate voted by 54 to 22 to prohibit further U.S. covert aid to the anti-MPLA forces in Angola.
1976	**1 January** MPLA/Cuban force went on counter offensive. **16 January** MPLA/Cuban force retook Cela and Santa Comba from South Africa. **8 February** Huambo, the UNITA "capital" abandoned in favour of Savimbi's military stronghold at Bie. **11 February** The Organisation of African Unity (OAU)

CHRONOLOGY

recognised MPLA. **3 March** Mozambique imposed sanction on Rhodesia. **5 April** The United State Secretary of States, Henry Kissinger, announced that the U.S. would not normalise relations with Angola as long as the Cuban forces are in the country. **16 June** Soweto riots in South Africa. **23 June** U.S. vetoed Cuba's nomination of Angola to the U.N.

1978 **13 February** Ian Smith announced the "internal settlement" agreement in Rhodesia. **29 September** UN Security Council Resolution 435 on Namibia and the recognition of SWAPO as the legitimate representative of the Namibian people.

1979 **17 December** The Lancaster House Agreement ended the Rhodesian war.

1980 **18 April** Zimbabwe became independent under ZANU headed by Robert Mugabe. **27 November** The first Southern African Development Coordination Conferences (SADCC) conference held in Maputo.

1981 **June** The United States introduced the "linkage" theory, linking the independence of Namibia to the withdrawal of Cuban troops from Angola. **August** South African troops occupied southern Angola. **31 August** U.S vetoed a Security Council resolution condemning the South Africa invasion of Angola. **November** A second invasion of Angola by South Africa.

1982 **February** Arm caches discovered on some sites in Matabele province of Zimbabwe. **4 March** Machel appointed Provincial Military Commanders in Mozambique. **26 July** Castro announced Cuba's readiness to defend Angola against any attack by South Africa.

1983 **11 January** First summary execution of captured RENAMO men in Mozambique. **December** South African raid on Angola.

1984 **January** The Lusaka Agreement signed between Angola and South Africa. **February** South Africa failed to honour the Lusaka Agreement.

1985 **15 April** South Africa agreed to complete the withdrawal of its forces from Angola

1986 **18 February** The U.S. Assistant Secretary of State for African Affairs, Chester Croker, admitted openly that the U.S. has decided to provide covert military aid of at least $15 million to UNITA. **10 September** Castro announced that Cubans would remain in Angola until the withdrawal of South African leaves Namibia and Angola. **20 October** President Samora Machel of Mozambique killed in a plane crash. Joaquim Chissano succeeded as President.

1987 **June** Negotiation between Angola and the United States began. **July** South Africa came to the aid of UNITA forces trying to defend a key UNITA base at Mavinga, south-east of Angola from MPLA forces. Before this, South Africa had always claimed that its incursions into Angola were aimed at SWAPO forces. **11 November** Cuba decided to reinforce its troops in Angola because of South Africa's repeated attempts to take Cuito Cuanavale in south-eastern Angola. **15 December** Captured UNITA soldiers said U.S. personnel were piloting supply flights from Zaire to southeastern Angola.

1988 **13 January** South Africa attacked Cuito Cuanavale. **28-29 January** Cuba officially joined negotiation on Namibia. **8 March** South Africa declared it would not withdraw from Angola until Cuban troops did. **9 March** Angola, Cuba and the U.S. held further rounds of talks on Namibia. **23 March** Further South Africa attacks on Cuito Cuanavale repealed by the Angola/Cuban forces. **3 May** South Africa joined the Angola, Cuban, U.S. negotiations on the future of Angola and Namibia. **June-August** Various rounds of talks on the Angola/Namibian problem in New York and Geneva. **8 August**: Angola, Cuba, and South Africa announced ceasefire agreement in Angola and Namibia. **22 December** Angola and Namibian accord signed at the United Nations in New York

1989 **10 January** First Cuban troops withdrew from Angola. **4 February** Amnesty law declared for UNITA rebels in Angola. **26 April** Soviet Union sent diplomatic mission to South Africa for the first time since 1956 to discuss the implementation of the Namibian peace agreement. **14 August** Botha resigned as President. De Klerk became Acting President. **14 September** De Klerk elected President for a five years term.

1990 **January-February** Fierce fighting in Angola. Savimbi reported wounded. **2 February** De Klerk announced the unbanning of the ANC, SACP and PAC. **11 February** Nelson Mandela released. **5 March** Savimbi agreed to a ceasefire in

CHRONOLOGY

Angola. **21 March** Namibia became independent. **March** Seven-Point peace document on Mozambique provided by the United States. **April** Power lines sabotaged 5 times by Renamo. **8-10 July** First direct talk between Renamo and the Frelimo government in Rome. **12-14 August** Second direct talks between Renamo and the Frelimo government in Rome. **August** Offensive against Renamo base. **November** Continued Peace talks on Mozambique after initial delay. **30 November** Adoption of multi-party system in Mozambique. **1 December** Partial ceasefire announced in Mozambique. **December** MPLA government ended one-party rule.

1991 17 March UNITA's 7th Congress ended with a call for Free elections. **1 April** Estoril Accord signed between UNITA and MPLA. **28 April** MPLA party rejects Marxism-Leninism in favour of Democracy. **1 May** MPLA government and UNITA signed peace accord in Portugal. **15 May** Ceasefire commenced in Angola. **31 May** UNITA and MPLA signed the Estoril Agreement. **27 September** Savimbi returned to Luanda. **November** Angolan Government confirmed election for September 1992. **November** Angolan Government asked the Portuguese to assist in negotiating to resolve the on-going conflict with FLEC.

1992 14 January MPLA's organised multi-party Conference opened in Luanda to draw up proposals for a future constitution. Twenty six political parties were represented. UNITA declined invitation. **February** The US Under-Secretary of State for Africa, Mr Jeffery Davidow, visited Angola and held talks with President Dos Santos and Savimbi. **March** Two senior members of UNITA - Miguel N'Zau Puma and Tony da Costa Fernandes - deflected. **July** Mugabe, Masire, and Tiny Rowland met Dhalakhama in Gaborone. **August** Chissano and Dhalakhama met for the first time. **30 September** Election held in Angola. **4 October** UNITA rejected the speculated election result. UNITA troops undergoing integration into the new national army asked to withdraw. **5 October** Chissano and Dhalakhama signed peace agreement in Mozambique. **17 October** Angolan election result officially released. Dos Santos of MPLA won. **November** Conflicts broke out in Luanda between UNITA and the MPLA government.

1993 **3 January** Government troops attacks UNITA forces in the Southern city of Lubango. **4 January** Violence erupted in Benguela. **7 January** Savimbi calls on US to broker a ceasefire in Angola. **11 January** Intense figting in Angola. Government troops took Luena and Huambo. **19 January** UNITA captured Soyo oil base. 17 Foreign oil workers also captured. **27 January** Addis Ababa Peace Talks on Angola failed. **21 February** UNITA fails to turn up for another Peace Talks on Angola. **9 March** UNITA broght up new demands and insists that peace talks should be in Geneva and not in Addis Ababa. **15 April** Zimbabwe troops started withdrawing from Mozambique. **April** Angolan Peace Talks began in Abidjan. **May** US recognises the MPLA govenment in Angola. **19 May** UN announced 12,000 government soldiers demobilised in Mozambique.

1 Introduction: In the Beginning, There were Wars

The conflicts in southern Africa have become all too familiar to the entire world. Familiarity in this respect has, however, not bred contempt, as the events in the sub-continent have never ceased to attract considerable attention. The world woke up to the problem of the region in 1948, when the policy of racial discrimination that had long been in practice inside South Africa received official endorsement, but more in 1960, when the South African government demonstrated its determination to preserve this policy by brutal suppression — as exemplified by the killing of protesters at Sharpeville. In the neighbouring countries, too, the refusal of the colonial regimes to accept the inevitability of the ephemeral nature of colonialism resulted in wars of liberation in Angola, Mozambique, Namibia and Zimbabwe. Although these liberation wars achieved the basic objectives of their prosecution, the legacies they bequeathed combined with other subregional peculiarities as well as external interference to result in other wars which engulfed virtually all of these countries shortly after their independence.

Writing on southern Africa often generates more heat than light. This is understandable for a region that has been in turmoil for more than three decades. The consolation, however, is that, unlike conflicts in most other regions of the world, southern African conflicts often reach landmarks which may be taken as "the end" of one of numerous and interwoven conflicts. Such landmarks include the resolutions of the liberation wars in some of the dependent countries, and more recently, the removal of apartheid which resulted in the cessation of the ANC's armed struggle. However, like most conflicts that have so far defied complete solution, new conflicts — often, but not always, related to the resolved ones — do emerge to return the sub-region into a vicious circle of wars, controversies, and tension.

In considering the roots of anti-government activities in southern Africa, one inevitably has to look into the history of the region, as this represents the antecedent to contemporary problems. Two phenomena are particularly relevant here. The first is the vicissitudes of colonial division, which grouped people of different ethnic, social and cultural traits together in redrawn national boundaries. This factor, which was originally taken to ease the colonial administrative problems, was exploited in later years by other internal and external forces that were determined to cause or inflame unrest in the sub-region. A second impact of colonialism on post-independence conflicts in some of the southern African countries, emerged from the colonial policies pursued in these colonies. In most of the countries, the colonial powers established systems of government that were not only racist but fundamentally authoritarian. It is not the intention of this chapter to discuss in detail what colonialism meant for the people of southern Africa. This has been the subject of many other studies.[1] Thus, all that the remainder of this introduction does is to extract and discuss aspects of southern African history that were to prove relevant to post-independence dissident and rebel activities in the region.

Perhaps a convenient point to start the required "extraction" in this regard is with the agitation of the countries in the region for independence from colonial control. When this started, it took the same pattern as elsewhere in the continent — formation of liberal political associations and the pursuit of peaceful demands for constitutional dialogue. When, afterwards, the colonial/minority authorities in these countries "criminalised" all the legal avenues opened to the colonial agitators, the black nationalists resorted to armed struggle. More than any other single factor, the armed struggles that inevitably ensued in these countries proved to be the most important factor in the emergence of post-independence conflict in some of the countries in the region.

The history of the liberation struggles in southern African countries is also one that is adequately documented, such that one only needs to extract portions relevant to any discussion.[2] In Angola, three movements — the *Movimento Popular de Libertacao de Angola* (MPLA), the *Frente de Libertacao de Mocambique* (FNLA), and the *Uniao Nacional para Independencia Total de Angola* (UNITA) —

INTRODUCTION

respectively under Augustino Neto, Holden Roberto, and Jonas Savimbi — fought the Portuguese in a war of liberation, but also one in which they devoted as much energy to fighting one another as they did against their common enemy.[3] Two features of the liberation war are relevant. These are the ethnic and ideological divisions of the liberation movements and the inevitable internationalisation of the war. The MPLA had its membership drawn largely from the Mbundu ethnic group in the middle belt of Angola, a group that formed about 26 per cent of the country's population. The movement had an ideological tendency (although often overblown for propaganda purposes) towards socialism. UNITA, ideologically confused initially but later opting for capitalism, was largely dominated by the Ovimbundus in southern Angola, with an estimated ethnic percentage of 38 per cent, while FNLA held sway among the Bakongo group in northern Angola — close to the border with Congo. The Bakongos formed about 17 per cent of the Angolan population.[4] These ethnic and ideological divisions were to play a significant role in the post-independence conflict.

The second relevant feature — the internationalisation of the Angolan war of independence — could be linked to the ideological commitment of the parties mentioned above. As the war progressed, the movements sought external support both in their conflict against the Portuguese and against each other. In the intricate international politics that ensued, the United States initially supported FNLA, but later changed to UNITA, with the CIA providing military and intelligence support for the organisation largely through South Africa.[5] The MPLA obtained its main support from the Soviet Union and Cuba. The issue of foreign support for the Angolan liberation movements has remained a controversial one, as the questions of who did what, and at what time among the external actors, remain sources of major dispute. Due largely to the inseparable line between the end of the liberation war and the beginning of the country's civil war, all the foreign actors in the Angolan liberation struggle were always at pain to deny the allegation levelled by others of being the country that provoked the internationalization of the independence war and the subsequent civil unrest in Angola. However, while the issue of who did what and when may be in dispute, what is certain is that the internationalization that started during the liberation war continued into the affairs of post-independence Angola, and it combined with other factors to determine the nature and scope of the country's civil war.

Mozambique's liberation war evoked a lesser complication — both in terms of ethnic percolation into the conflict and the degree of external involvement. Although many movements initially emerged to fight for independence,[6] they had all come together by 1962 under the *Frente de Libertacao de Mocambique* (FRELIMO). This movement was under the leadership of Eduardo Mondlane. After his death in 1968, the party was administered by a triumvirate, comprising Samora Machel, Uria Simango and Marcelimo dos Santos. Simango, shortly afterwards, defected to the Portuguese, and in the party restructuring that followed, Samora Machel became the Frelimo head. He was to lead the country into independence in 1975. A factor that is worth noting, however, is that, while Frelimo was the only liberation movement, not all Mozambicans actually supported the organisation. There were those who refused to support it on the ground that they saw the party as dominated by people from a particular ethnic group. This resulted in a situation where Frelimo's activities could not reach some parts of Mozambique, and it was to prove vital in post-independence years.

The situation in Zimbabwe was different, and more complex than in Angola or Mozambique. Unlike the case in those countries, where the colonial headquarters was in a far away "mother-state", Zimbabwe's liberation movements had to contend with a colonial regime that was internally entrenched. This gave the country's liberation war some shades of a civil war, and further compounded the legacies it bequeathed to Zimbabwe at independence.

As far back as 1923, whites in southern Rhodesia had obtained concession to make policies with little or no interference from the British colonial government. However, in 1965, the Rhodesian Prime Minister, Ian Smith, made the unilateral declaration of independence (UDI), which withdrew Rhodesia from British imperial control. Expectedly, the UDI evoked global reactions,[7] but the most relevant here is that it increased the militancy that was already emerging among black Rhodesian nationalists. Shortly after the declaration, a full scale war of independence began in the country.

The aspect of the Zimbabwean liberation war that has the strongest link with post-independence civil unrest in the country was the ethnic politics that enmeshed the struggle at a later stage. The first major liberation movement — the African National Congress (ANC) —

INTRODUCTION

formed in 1957 under Joshua Nkomo, enveloped African opposition to white rule.[8] When the organisation was banned and a new one, the National Democratic Party (NDP), was formed in 1960, the united forum continued, though in a somewhat weakened form. The eventual banning of the NDP marked the end of this unified opposition. By the time the party metamorphosed into the Zimbabwean African People's Union (ZAPU) in 1962, some of its members had found reasons to defect. These people later formed the Zimbabwean African National Union (ZANU), under the Revd Ndabaningi Sithole.[9] When it later became apparent that force was needed to bring about independence, the two parties developed armed wings which prosecuted their war of liberation against the Rhodesian security force. ZANU had the Zimbabwean African National Liberation Army (ZANLA), while ZAPU controlled the Zimbabwean People's Revolutionary Army (ZIPRA). Internal crisis soon erupted in ZANU and Sithole lost the leadership of the party to Robert Mugabe.[10]

It may be a bit difficult to know the exact extent to which ethnicity played a role in the split-up of ZAPU in 1963. However, what can be said with complete ease is that, shortly after the break-up, it became noticeable that ZAPU was dominated largely by the Ndebele ethnic group, while ZANU was constituted largely of Shona people. The Ndebeles inhabit the western part of the country, and they constitute about 20 per cent of the total Zimbabwean population. The Shonas, on the other hand, had a strong majority of about 70 per cent. The ethnic division in the political parties inevitably extended to the armed wings, where ZIPRA had largely Ndebele combatants and ZANLA comprised mostly Shona guerrillas. In post-independence Zimbabwe, this division became one of the most important factor used to determine, explain or rationalise action and inactions.

Apart from the ethnic politics in all these countries and foreign support for the liberation movements, another factor that should be considered in any effort to understand anti-government activities in southern Africa is the place of the Republic of South Africa in the region.

South Africa in southern Africa

South Africa is no stranger to controversy. The Republic has lived with it (in one form or the other) for more than half a century, as the internal and external ramifications of its apartheid policy have been the crux of criticism since 1948. A major area where South Africa's activities has attracted much criticism until recently is its sub-regional policies, one of which manifested in the support given to dissidents and anti-government activities in some of the neighbouring countries. This aspect of southern African politics has again been the subject of numerous studies such that a capsule summary will suffice here.[11]

Since the 1950s, the Republic of South Africa's relation with its immediate neighbours has been characterised by a "big-brother" syndrome, as every attempt has been made by the country to carve for itself a sphere of sub-regional influence. This is the tendency Hyan described as South Africa's "sub-regional manifest destiny".[12] The neighbours which became engulfed in this relationship were Rhodesia, South West Africa, the Portuguese dependencies of Angola and Mozambique, and the British protectorates of Botswana, Lesotho and Swaziland. In fact, as far back as 1952, it had been observed that the natural boundary of South Africa, considered geographically, was the Zambezi, which contained the Union, South West Africa, Rhodesia, most of the Portuguese African dependencies and Swaziland.[13] By the mid-1960s, South Africa had started trying to weld the white-ruled countries of the region into an economic and military block, as its Prime Minister, Hendrick Verwoerd, had, as early as 1964, spoken of a Southern African Common Market. At least two reasons accounted for South Africa's desire to consolidate its grip on the region. First, was to create economic partners, a situation made more necessary by the closure of African markets against the Republic,[14] and second was to ensure that these neighbouring countries served to shield South Africa from the hostilities of the independent black states of central Africa.[15]

When the decolonization efforts in Angola, Mozambique and Zimbabwe resulted in wars, South Africa's interest in these countries increased astronomically. In two interwoven ways, Pretoria saw the upsurge of revolutionary militancy in the region as being inimical to its apartheid policy. First, it was realised that such a development could radicalise the blacks inside the Republic, and second, the support the then Communist world was extending to the liberation movements in these countries was seen as an opportunity for the communists to establish a foothold in the region. All these spelt ominous signals for the future of apartheid, and South Africa began its military involvement in the region. Regular consultations were held between the

INTRODUCTION 7

heads of security police of South Africa, Rhodesia, and Portugal.[16] As will be seen in subsequent chapters, South Africa's involvement in these liberation wars served as the antecedents to its post-independence destabilization policy in these countries.

The degree and pattern of South Africa's involvements in the liberation wars of its neighbours differed from one country to another. Ironically, the Angolan war of liberation, whose repercussions turned out to be one of the most expensive outside engagements for South Africa, did not attract much of the Republic's attention at the outbreak. Although South Africa watched the developments with concern, it did not make any serious attempt to interfere in the war. Pretoria's concern during the early stages of the Angolan liberation war was to prevent it from having serious impact on Namibia — the territory it then controlled. However, it is known that in the pursuit of the war in Angola, Portugal depended on South Africa for certain categories of military equipments, especially helicopters, and by 1970, the MPLA had reported the presence of South African helicopters at the Lumege base.[17] In Mozambique, Frelimo, in 1968, reported the presence of South African troops in the Chioco, Chicoa, Magua, Zumbo and the strategic province of Tete.[18] Pretoria also kept the developments in Rhodesia under close monitor right from the time of the UDI, but the country got directly involved in the Rhodesian war in July 1967, when the South African ANC and ZAPU launched an unsuccessful military attack on Rhodesia. The following month, the ZAPU Vice President, James Chikerena, and the Acting President of the ANC, Oliver Tambo, announced a military alliance between the two organisations. From that time, Pretoria took the affairs of neighbouring countries seriously, such that by 1970, a German military magazine had claimed that one-third of the South African army was stationed outside the country.[19]

The impacts of the 1974 coup in Portugal are such that many writers consider it a landmark in the history of southern Africa. For a number of reasons, not the least of which was the extensive colonial wars it was then prosecuting simultaneously, the regime that was committed to the perpetuation of Portuguese colonial empire was overthrown in Lisbon.[20] The new leadership in the country was not long in announcing its disengagement from the country's colonies all over the world.[21] The somewhat hasty transfer of power that ensued was successful in some of these countries, especially those that had only one liberation movement. For Angola, however, it was the beginning of post-independence crisis, as conflict began between the three movements. The internationalization that ensued with this conflict inevitably brought South Africa into the struggle for the future of Angola.

South Africa's involvement in the Zimbabwean liberation war was more complex, due largely to the important place Rhodesia occupied in South Africa's geo-strategic thinking.[22] Although South Africa was opposed to the UDI,[23] it gave Rhodesia the assistance needed to circumvent its effects.[24] When eventually the blacks in Rhodesia took up arms, South Africa felt obliged to support the cause of the white Rhodesians for two main reasons. First was to express racial solidarity, and second was to prevent a victory of the guerrillas, which Pretoria believed could have implications on the blacks inside the republic. Against this background, South Africa got involved in the military activities against Zimbabwean guerrillas, such that, by 1975, the Rhodesian war had cost Pretoria a staggering sum of about $300 million.[25]

South Africa's involvement in the Rhodesian liberation struggle was forced to change largely by sub-regional developments. The collapse of the Portuguese colonial empire resulted in the establishment of Marxist governments in Angola and Mozambique. This, in turn, had an attendant consequence in the intensification of the guerrilla activities in Rhodesia and Namibia, and brought home to the South African government the inevitable radicalization that could engulf the region if the Rhodesian crisis was allowed to escalate further. In Vorster's estimation, white rule in Rhodesia was ultimately doomed, and the best option open to South Africa was to reduce the hitherto unqualified support it had given Smith. Thus, as Jack Spence rightly noted, "white rule in Rhodesia was expendable, if the price was a breathing space for South Africa."[26]

The Pauline conversion of South Africa resulted in the country putting pressure on Ian Smith to embark on negotiations with black leaders considered to be "moderates". This they found best in Abel Muzorewa, the leader of the United African National Congress (UANC). He was thus to receive financial and military backing from South Africa when, in subsequent years, efforts to solve the Rhodesian problem resulted in an election that included all the country's nationalist movements. Thus, in all the countries, South Africa had become sufficiently involved to make it interested in which party eventually took over after the independence of these countries.

The dawn of independence: The sowing of the seeds of discontent
The internal and external forces that played roles in ending southern Africa's cataclysmic liberation wars equally played important roles in shaping the post-independence unrest that engulfed some of the countries. The sudden exit of the Portuguese resulted in an unorganised transfer of power in its colonies. This worked out fairly well in Mozambique, where Frelimo was the only liberation movement. Independence was thus granted to the country with relative ease. The lack of consensus among the Angolan nationalists made a neat transition difficult for the Portuguese. Efforts made by the OAU to organise a transfer of power failed, and renewed conflict ensued between the movements. An agreement reached between all the sides to cease fire in June 1975 failed, and by the following month, Angola was splitting up into areas controlled by the various movements. It was at this stage that South Africa launched its ill-fated attack to support anti-MPLA forces. With Cuban and Soviet support, the MPLA launched a counter attack, and by the end of August 1975, 11 of the 15 provincial capitals had fallen under the movement's control. Angola thus became independent under the MPLA. This, however, turned out to be the end of a scene and not that of the drama of the Angolan crisis.

In Rhodesia, Vorster's urging that Smith should embark on dialogue with "moderate" black nationalists resulted in the infamous Internal Settlement administration. Under this arrangement, Smith agreed to transfer "power" to the "moderates" among the Rhodesian nationalists. Included in this pact were Bishop Abel Muzorewa, the Revd Ndabaningi Sithole (the deposed leader of ZANU), and a local chief, Jeremiah Chirau. Although, the constitution conceded a black Prime Minister, it was nothing more than white leadership in black skin, as all the powers were still concentrated in the hands of the whites. Smith expected, or perhaps wished, that this "transfer of power" would make the international community remove sanctions. He also hoped that it would end guerrilla infiltration — or at least, remove the local basis of guerrilla support. In the resultant elections, Bishop Muzorewa's party, the United African National Congress (UANC), won, and the clergyman became the first (and last) Prime Minister of the hyphenated state of Zimbabwe-Rhodesia. The transfer of power did not, however, bring the outcome Smith desired, as sanctions were not lifted and the moderate politicians could not make the guerrillas moderate their offensives. The new country again did not receive the expected official recognition. The failure of this initiative, as well as the increase in guerrilla activities, combined with other global developments (not the least of which were pressures from African Commonwealth governments on the new Tory government in London) to lead to the Lancaster House Conference in 1979.[27] This conference brokered the Rhodesian crisis, and in the election it proposed, ZANU won 57 of the 80 seats reserved for the blacks, and its leader, Robert Mugabe, became the Prime Minister of independent Zimbabwe. Nkomo's ZAPU won 20 seats, while the 20 seats the constitution reserved for the whites were won by Ian Smith's Republican Front.

The "interpretation" these new nations gave to their new-found independence, and the consequences that emerged from such interpretation, also had bearing on the subsequent emergence of rebel activities in some of the countries. These expectations brought them into conflict with South Africa and in some cases, they also brought attendant strains on these societies that ordinarily should be recovering from the effects of the liberation wars. Mozambique, under the late Samora Machel, for example, interpreted the country's independence more as a sub-regional sacrifice for the eradication of colonialism. The country immediately supported the Zimbabwean nationalists, and ZANLA was given military bases inside Mozambique. This support made Mozambique the target of Rhodesia's "hot-pursuit" attacks. According to the late President Machel, 1,338 Mozambicans were killed in Rhodesian raids, with another 1,538 wounded and 751 people missing.[28] Apart from the human cost, Mozambique implemented the United Nations imposed sanctions on Rhodesia, resulting in considerable financial loss for the new country. For example, the closure of the Mozambican ports cost the country between $110-135 million annually, and accounted for almost $200 million of Mozambique's $430 million balance of trade deficit. Between 1976 and 1980, about $46 million in damage was inflicted on Mozambique's economic targets.[29] Most importantly, however, the minority regime in Rhodesia established a fifth column in Mozambique. This movement was created to infiltrate the ZANLA ranks operating from the country, as well as to destabilise Mozambique, and thus detract the attention of its government from supporting ZANLA. This organisation, which was to become a household name in subsequent years, was the *Resistencia de Nacionale de Mocambique* (RENAMO).[30]

The leadership that took over in Harare had a far less ambitious interpretation of the country's independence. Despite the professed radicalism of its leaders during the liberation war, the government made it clear at independence that, beyond the general support through verbal condemnation and the payment of OAU liberation dues, the country would not provide any military assistance to the liberation movements in southern Africa. In a blunt policy statement, Mugabe confirmed that the fear of retaliatory attacks from South Africa predicated this position. However, there was still an aspect of Zimbabwe's interpretation of its independence that later created problems in its relationship with South Africa. This was the extent of its condemnation of South Africa's internal and sub-regional policies, in language more vitriolic than that of other weaker neighbours.

Although immediately engulfed in a civil war after its independence, Angola too tried to carve for itself a sub-regional assignment. The country found this in the struggle for the liberation of Namibia, where the South West Africa People's Organisation, (SWAPO) had earlier taken up arms to liberate the country from South Africa's illegal control. Independent Angola provided assistance in later years for SWAPO, and this was to add more to the conflict between South Africa and the new country.

South Africa saw the developments in most of these countries in different light. The emergence of Marxist professed regimes in the countries created in the republic a "siege" mentality. Pretoria thus wanted to keep at bay the wind of revolutionary militancy that had started threatening the country. In 1976, a new phase emerged in South Africa's perception of sub-regional events, when Prime Minister John Vorster lost the leadership to P.W. Botha, the erstwhile Defence Minister. In later years, Botha was to bring into his cabinet party members with extreme views of internal and regional events. These people were to reinforce South Africa's "siege" perception of sub-regional developments. A foremost individual in this respect was Magnus Malan, the Defence Minister.

Angola presented a major problem for South Africa, largely because of the Soviet involvement. After the initial South African invasion failed, the country continued opposing the new MPLA government. The affairs of the other Portuguese colony, Mozambique, did not attract Pretoria's attention initially. This was largely because the new country did not challenge the apartheid regime in any significant way. Mozambique's post-independence "regional patriotism" was targeted largely towards Rhodesia. It was only in the latter years that South Africa changed its policy towards Mozambique.

The development in Zimbabwe was seen in a different light. The pressure Vorster had put on Smith to embark on dialogue with black nationalists had brought unintended consequence in the election victory of Robert Mugabe. South Africa's expectation was that Muzorewa would win the election. However, although Pretoria hated a Mugabe victory, the enormous goodwill that greeted the Lancaster House proceedings and Mugabe's election victory ruled out violent opposition as an option South Africa would want to contemplate initially. Thus, all that the Republic did was to warn that "any neighbour which allowed its territory to be used against South Africa and its interest would bear the full brunt of the Republic's strength".[31]

Other peculiar considerations equally emerged soon after the independence of these countries to give signals of possible future unrest. For example, the new Frelimo government in Mozambique embarked on an extensive nationalisation, which was to affect the economy of the country. These drastic attempts to "revolutionise" the country created problems that were exploited for anti-government activities. The war in Zimbabwe also left legacies that could be exploited by those who might want to destabilise the country. First, although ZANU won the elections with a convincing majority, the results showed some ethnic bias. ZAPU got its 20 seats from Matabeleland, while ZANU's 57 seats were from the Shona section of the country. This pattern of electoral support also coincided with the operational areas of ZANLA and ZIPRA during the liberation war. Second, the war in Zimbabwe left a number of embittered groups. These included members of the former Rhodesian army who preferred to go to South Africa and the armed units of the other parties ZANU defeated at the poll. There were also whites who feared for their safety under a black majority rule, especially one led by an "avowed Marxist" like Robert Mugabe. All these people carried with them their hatred for the new leadership in Harare as they fled. Finally there were those whites who stayed behind, not out of love for the new country but to destabilise and frustrate its leadership.

The Mugabe administration formed a Government of National

INTRODUCTION

Unity, with representatives from the two ethnic groups and from the white minority. ZAPU was invited into the government, with its leader, Joshua Nkomo, receiving a senior cabinet post — after having rejected the largely ceremonial office of president. This policy of reconciliation and prudence launched Zimbabwe on a good start by putting some of the differences that had hitherto characterised the relationship among all the motley lot on board under the carpet. In Angola, the MPLA government was not allowed to settle down and arrange its priorities before having to start another war to establish its legitimacy, while Mozambique, too, soon became engulfed in a war with the fifth column the Rhodesian minority regime had created to undermine Mozambican support for Zimbabwean guerrillas.

There were also wider sub-regional and global considerations which, even at the independence of most of these countries, gave indications of possible unease in their domestic and sub-regional affairs. The first again came from South Africa. The gradual disintegration of the "cordon-sanitaire" that had protected the Republic was viewed with disquiet. It was in fact, the case that the decade that followed Zimbabwe's independence was one of considerable sub-regional tension, as Pretoria was determined to prevent the countries in the region from providing support for South Africa's liberation movements. Another major sub-regional issue which was to get South Africa interested in the internal affairs of these countries was the creation, in 1980, of the Southern African Development and Coordinating Conferences (SADCC). This union was created to coordinate regional resources against South Africa's economic domination. Pretoria saw this as a threat, and the desire to frustrate the activities of the union was to underline some of Pretoria's involvement in the internal affairs of these countries. Finally, South Africa was determined to contain the SWAPO forces believed to be obtaining sanctuary and military support from the MPLA government in Angola.

2 Angola: From Bullet Through Ballot to an Uncertain Future

The Angolan civil war is one of Africa's most publicised conflicts. This is due as much to the length of the war, as to the intricate international politics it has evoked. Writing on the Angolan civil war at this time is, however, fraught with a number of difficulties. First, the war is still in progress — a factor which makes it impossible to put a tone of finality to any discussion as regards the outcome. Second, the complexities of the war are such that writing on its past is made somewhat difficult. This is because, quite unintentionally, one may end up discussing the history of an Angolan/South African war; or an Angolan-Cuban war against a UNITA-South Africa coalition; or, worse still, an American/Soviet war fought by surrogates. The Angolan civil war is, in a way, all of these, but yet, in another way, none of these. Although, at one stage, the war had the hallmarks of the former cold war in abundance, it nevertheless had other features which made it detachable from the international ramifications that influenced it. In this chapter, a capsule summary of the Angolan conflict is provided; from its outbreak through the disputed October 1992 election to the resumption of conflict afterwards. The chapter identifies some of the dynamics that have governed the war as well as the peculiarities and similarities with other civil conflicts in the region.

In at least two geo-strategic considerations, Angola is somewhat different from Mozambique and Zimbabwe, and these differences affect the nature of the country's civil war. First, Angola is geographically situated in southern and central Africa, a factor which makes it possible for the country to influence the events in both regions. As these two regions were undergoing important developments during the period after 1970, the situation in Angola became one of significant interest in southern and central Africa. Second, unlike Mozambique and Zimbabwe, Angola shares no direct border with South Africa. The link between the two countries is Namibia, which South Africa controlled (in defiance of international opinion) until April 1990.

As shown in the preceding chapter, the post-independence civil war in Angola is deeply intertwined with its war of liberation. At the exit of the Portuguese, the three liberation movements were not only at war with one another, but also within themselves. For example, the MPLA's internal squabble resulted in the organisation breaking into three, with far-reaching implications extending into post-independence years. One of the factions — led by Daniel Chipenda — was to create a fairly sustained opposition to the Neto leadership. Other parties were in no better shape. Holden Roberto's autocratic tendencies were later to destroy the FNLA, as many members left the party in protest. Jonas Savimbi of UNITA was much like Roberto. Although his party was still comparatively young, he had started showing the dictatorial tendencies that were to manifest fully in subsequent years.

It was in this prevailing general confusion that the internationalization of the civil war started. Shortly after Portugal announced the withdrawal of its troops from Angola in September 1975, South Africa launched an invasion from Namibia, in order to prevent the MPLA from assuming office. By 21 October 1975, armoured motorised columns of the SADF had invaded Angola from Namibia. The little resistance the MPLA presented was easily defeated, and a number of Angolan towns fell to the invading South African force. At about the same time, too, the FNLA, supported by Zaire, organised a march into Luanda. It was against the background of this two pronged attack that the MPLA sought and received Cuban assistance.

The Cuban military mission in Angola (named Operation Carlota[1]) started with the arrival of Cuban troops on 9 November 1975, and by 20 November, "the airlift of the full reinforced special forces battalion" had been completed.[2] Although, pro-MPLA writers, like Wilfred Burchett, are wont to stress the "battle-tempered hard core" MPLA troops (implicitly to reduce the tendency of overblowing the extent of Cuban support),[3] there can be no doubt that the support given to the MPLA by the Cubans was the single most important factor that drove the South African and Zairian forces out of Angola and secured victory for the MPLA. Apart from turning the tide of the war in favour of the

MPLA, the entrance of the Cubans marked a turning point in southern African history, as it marked the beginning of a factor that was to be a reference point in the resolution of a number of sub-regional conflicts.

On 11 November 1975, two sovereign governments were proclaimed almost simultaneously in Angola. In Luanda, the MPLA proclaimed the People's Republic of Angola, with Augustino Neto as the President, while in Ambriz, north of Luanda, FNLA and UNITA jointly proclaimed the Popular and Democratic Republic of Angola under Roberto. To counter the independence declared by the MPLA, both UNITA and the FNLA agreed to form a joint government which they said would be tentative.[4] This, however, did not work, and both continued separate opposition to the new government. At the time independence was declared by the MPLA in Luanda, the FNLA forces were said to have gone as far as Quifandongo (about 20 kilometres from Luanda)[5] while the UNITA forces were about 200 kilometres away from the capital.

The Position of the Opposition

It could be taken that the UNITA is the main anti-government group in Angola, as FNLA soon faded out as an effective opposition movement. UNITA based its opposition on a number of different but related grounds. Fred Bridgland's detailed (though sympathetic) biography of Jonas Savimbi enumerates some of these grounds. First is UNITA's belief that the haphazard process of Portuguese decolonization was responsible for the problems that confronted Angola after independence. Very few students of Angolan affairs would dispute the fact that a more orderly process of power transfer in Angola would have had greater chances of bringing about post-independence peace, than the method Portugal adopted. Savimbi further extended the argument that this style of decolonization was deliberately undertaken by the Portuguese to impose the MPLA leadership on the country. He put this problem thus:

> ...the only one responsible for the situation that we face today is Portugal. If Portugal had the firmness to guide the process, today we would not have war. But Portugal wished to decolonise by leaving us here with its god-child named Antonio Augustino Neto,

and today we find ourselves in a civil war.[6]

UNITA's perception of the MPLA and its ideology provided another reason for opposition. At the outbreak of the war, UNITA believed that MPLA had no legitimacy to rule, since the party was not democratically elected. This was the core issue on which UNITA rested its case, and it was one that was exploited to attract western sympathy to its cause. Again Savimbi puts this position thus:

> The day MPLA decides to consider other liberation movements as patriots... then we will say to MPLA: "Come here brother ..." Only through general election, when peace returns to the country will we be able to decide definitely who will be leaders of the nation. Anything other than this we cannot accept.[7]

The assistance Cuba and the Soviets gave MPLA led UNITA into believing that MPLA was determined to impose communist ideology on the country. Savimbi was quoted to have said "while the MPLA goes on thinking that only through Russian arms can they offer an ideology, we will say 'no' and will continue to fight". Understandably this resulted in intense opposition to the presence of the Cubans in Angola. The Cuban troops in the country were seen as an occupation force, brought to sustain what UNITA saw as an illegitimate government. In this stance against Cuba, UNITA had the support (at least initially) of some of countries like Zambia and Zaire who also believed that the Cuban involvement was unnecessary and could destabilize moderate governments in the region. President Kenneth Kaunda was particularly vociferous in supporting a government of national unity that would bring all Angolan parties together.

Sometime in March 1977, UNITA abandoned the previous policy of forcing MPLA to concede to a government of national unity, and the organisation started clamouring for a separate state called "Black African and Socialist Republic of Angola". This was to be located mostly south of the 11th parallel, running from Novo Redondo on the coast of Texeira de Sousa in the east, taking in the Benguela railway. Savimbi sent Jorge Sanguiba to seek support for the new "nation" in Europe.[8] At a later stage, however, the desire faded out, and the original, and perhaps more realistic, desire of forcing MPLA to grant concession to UNITA again became the organisation's main objective.

The MPLA government, on its part, ruled out any form of concession to UNITA or FNLA, insisting instead, on "driving FNLA into Zaire and UNITA into South Africa". UNITA's link with South Africa became a strong weapon used by the MPLA to gather African support, since opposition to Pretoria's racial policy was one of the few unifying factors in the continent. The neighbouring countries like Tanzania, Mozambique, and Botswana gave the MPLA government psychological and military backing, while Nigeria, then with substantial oil wealth, became the main African financial supporter of the Neto government.[9] The extent of Nigeria's support was to lead later to UNITA's claim that the country's troops were fighting alongside MPLA,[10] an allegation emphatically denied by the Nigerian government.

Writers have criticised MPLA's resolve of adopting military solution to address the war from the outset. A representative of this school of thought, Assis Malaquias, attributed this to three "strategic miscalculations" on the part of the MPLA, viz (a) miscalculation of UNITA's strength and ability to re-emerge as a powerful military and political force; (b) underestimation of the commitment of South Africa and the US to support UNITA; and (c) overestimation of its own ability to end the civil war by military means with the help of the Cubans and the Soviet Union.[11] These positions, valid as they may appear, were taken with the advantage of hindsight, with little consideration for the tides that were prevailing at the time the civil war started. Even despite this advantage of hindsight, there is nothing now to conclude with certainty that adopting a less militant approach would have brought a result different from what eventually happened in Angola, although his position on the impact of foreign involvement is particularly valid.

Sub-regional and Global Undercurrents of the Angolan Civil War

Politically and militarily, the civil war in Angola could be better understood against the background of the wider sub-regional and, in a way, global developments. Within the sub-region, the Angolan civil war got deeply entangled with the then controversy over the future of

Namibia and, to a lesser extent, with the internal politics in neighbouring Zaire. South Africa's support for UNITA was calculated to prevent the South West African People's Organisation (SWAPO) from launching any serious operation from south-eastern Angola.[12] Indeed, at one stage in the Angolan civil war, it became difficult to separate South Africa's support for UNITA from the country's war against SWAPO. The support for UNITA became all the more convenient for Pretoria, because, as will be shown in subsequent chapters, the organisation was far more organised than any of the anti-government forces in the region. Again, by the late 1970s, UNITA had shown itself as being "anti-communist", at a time Pretoria and the Western world were getting increasingly apprehensive at the Communist successes in the region. Furthermore, Savimbi supported South Africa's internal and sub-regional interests. For example, he confirmed that one of UNITA's military objectives was to fight SWAPO in Namibia.

Zaire's connection with the military activities in the Angolan civil war was far less significant (compared to that of South Africa) but it was also one that manifested constantly both in the war and in the numerous attempts to bring peace to Angola, especially after 1978. Mobutu has always desired to prevent the MPLA from gaining control of Angola. As early as September 1974, he had met secretly with Spinola of Portugal on the Island of Sal in the Cape Verde Archipelago, where the two men agreed that the Neto faction of the MPLA should be prevented from assuming office. They were willing, instead, to accept the faction led by Daniel Chipenda.[13] Zaire's initial involvement in Angolan affairs started in the support the country gave to Holden Roberto during the liberation war and immediately after the exit of the Portuguese.[14] When eventually FNLA became too weak to organise any sustained opposition, Mobutu transferred his support to UNITA. The internal crisis inside Zaire gave the MPLA government an opportunity to repay Mobutu for any assistance to either Roberto or Savimbi. Since the attempted secession of the Katanga province from Zaire in 1963, there had been a substantial number of Zairian refugees in Angola. Some of these had taken part in Portuguese insurgence against the MPLA. After the collapse of Portuguese rule, these refugees refused Lisbon's advice of moving them to South Africa. Instead, they stayed back in Angola where they supported MPLA.[15] The number of Zairian exiles in Angola increased considerably after the March 1977 uprising in Zaire, and they remained a credible anti-government force against the Mobutu regime.

The global undercurrent that influenced the Angolan civil war was the then prevailing cold war politics. The US opposed the MPLA government, citing the support it received from the Cubans and its inability to assume office through a "free and fair election" as reasons for the objection. Both the MPLA government and writers sympathetic to its cause have offered "explanations" to address these two grounds. The Angolan Foreign Minister, Paulo Jorge, pointed out that there were more American military instructors in Saudi Arabia and Iran (during the time of the Shah) than Cubans in Angola.[16] Jake Miller, in his article in *Transafrica Forum*, argued that America's objection to MPLA's process of assuming office, "demanded far more from Angola than from many of America's allies including the Philippines (under Marcos), El Salvador, Kuwait and a host of African dictatorships".[17]

The extent to which successive US administrations supported anti-government activities in Angola differs. As the crisis erupted under Gerald Ford, his administration's stand was as unequivocal as was his interpretation of Soviet threat. In June 1976, the US vetoed Angola's application for membership of the UN Security Council on the basis that the Cuban troops were still in the country. This position received considerable criticism, especially from African states, and the former Tanzanian Ambassador to the United Nations, Salim Ahmed Salim, condemned it as "politically unjust, legally untenable and morally unsound". He was to pay for this criticism a few years later, when the US (then under another administration that shared Ford's perception of global affairs), vetoed his nomination for the position of the United Nations Secretary General. The Ford administration also made attempts to influence "moderate" African leaders against the MPLA government. Zaire, Zambia, Senegal and Ivory Coast were among those used in this regard. In Zambia, the former US ambassador to Lusaka, Jean Wilkowski, was believed to be the key influence on Kenneth Kaunda in his initial reluctance to accept MPLA victory.[18] Again, as early as December 1975, the US State Department had exerted sufficient pressure on Gulf Oil, which operated the oil fields in Cabinda, to persuade it to suspend royalty and tax payment to the new MPLA government in Luanda.

The Carter administration was initially in a dilemma as to what should be the policy towards Angola. In his campaign, Jimmy Carter had declared that his administration would reconsider policy towards Angola. He said:

> ... the United States position in Angola should be one which admits that we missed the opportunity to be a positive and creative force for good in Angola... We should realise that the Russian and Cuban presence in Angola, while regrettable and counter-productive to peace, need not constitute a threat to the United States interest nor does that presence mean the existence of a satellite on the continent.[19]

Circumstances, however, prevented Jimmy Carter from pursuing this course of action when eventually he became the President, as Soviet moves in the Horn of Africa (where they supported Ethiopia against Somalia in the Ogaden war) and the American belief that Cuba was behind the invasion of the Shaba province of Zaire by Katangese refugees in Angola, dictated caution to any move to consider the Angolan crisis as an isolated event. It is, however, believed that there was a subtle division in the Carter administration regarding what should be the policy towards Angola after the new Soviet moves in the Horn of Africa. The Secretary of State, Cyrus Vance, and a number of others in the administration were believed to have insisted that the issue of the Horn of Africa was separable from Angola, and as such, should not be used to determine US-Soviet relations in Africa. However, the National Security Adviser, Zbigniew Brzezinski, argued that some form of concession should be sought from the Soviet Union before relations could be established with the new Angolan government. The Soviet Union, however, denied any Cuban involvement in the Shaba invasion. As it turned out, the United States was wrong in its allegation, and Cyrus Vance was to concede later that the United States had "some ambiguous, and as it turned out, not very good intelligence" on Cuban involvement in the Shaba crisis.[20]

The Soviet Union joined Cuba in sustaining the MPLA government in office. Why the Soviet Union intervened decisively in Angola has been widely debated, and a number of reasons have been proffered: ranging from the desire to bring Sino-Soviet rivalry to Africa, and the hope of exploiting the advantage of the Vietnam failure and the Watergate scandal to embarrass the US; to the Soviets' realisation of the strategic significance of southern Africa and the combination of multiple factors, of which all those listed above were parts. However, whichever it was that underlined the Soviet action, the United States reacted with concern to this major shift in Soviet foreign policy in Africa, and successive US governments saw in the Angolan civil war, perhaps, the best manifestation of the cold war in Africa. The US interpreted the Soviet move as a danger to South Africa and other "moderate" governments in Zambia and Zaire. The impact of the Soviet move on America's interpretation of the events in Angola could be seen in the statement by Helmut Sonnenfeld, a Counsellor in the US State Department and one of Henry Kissinger's closest advisers. He noted:

> [the US] had no intrinsic interest in Angola as such [but] once a locale, no matter how remote and unimportant for us, becomes a focal point for Soviet, and in this instance Soviet supported Cuban military action, the United States acquires a derivative interest which we simply cannot avoid.[21]

From 1976, the Soviet Union started supplying Angola with a sophisticated array of weapons. These include a squadron of MIG-23 Fighters, MI-24 Hind attack helicopters, an air defence network south of the Benguela rail-road using SAM-8 missile, and an assortment of battle-tested tanks, artillery pieces and logistical/communications equipments.[22] In October 1976 both Angola and the Soviet Union signed a Treaty of Friendship and Cooperation which stipulated that the Soviet Union would come to the assistance of Angola in time of crisis.

The extent of Soviet and American support for MPLA and UNITA respectively has obscured certain features of the roots of international alignment in the civil war. First, contrary to what the post-independence demonstration of affection might reflect, the relationship between Moscow and the MPLA before Angola's independence was not one that was completely harmonious. In fact, the United States has to be thanked for the deep closeness that later ensued between the two sides. There are at least two reasons why Moscow did not get on well with the MPLA under the late Augustino Neto. First, Moscow considered the MPLA leader "rather secretive and prickly".[23] A former Soviet diplomat who defected to the West, Arkady Shevchenko, did confirm that Moscow never trusted Neto, and went further to quote a Soviet Foreign Ministry specialist who allegedly said that the Soviet Union was behind "several assassination attempts on Neto before independence".[24] A second reason why Neto was not particularly loved by the Soviet Union was his stand on the Marxist ideology. Neto had always made it clear that the MPLA was not a Marxist-Leninist organisation, and that the party's leadership was not Marxist-Leninist. He personally confessed that he had never read a book on Karl Marx.[25]

On the other hand, too, although the US had, as far back as the early 1960s, become involved in the provision of military support to the FNLA in Angola, there are also evidences to support the fact that America's policy towards Angolan independence movements was equally confused initially. Just a few days after his election as the MPLA leader in December 1962, Augustino Neto paid a visit to the US to appeal for American sympathy for his organisation, stressing that the extremists in the party had been removed.[26] This appeal had considerable impact, as the CIA special report issued after the visit favoured a more even-handed approach towards the MPLA and FNLA. The report further confirmed that the MPLA under Neto favoured "genuine neutrality". Gerald Bender quoted a State Department circular issued in July 1973, expressing a similar stand.[27] The outbreak of the civil war, however, removed all the shades of confusion and contradiction in the Soviet and American policies.

The Civil War
In February 1976, three months after the MPLA's declaration of independence, Savimbi announced that UNITA forces would revert to guerrilla warfare, and the following month he led his force to the bush. This move was an acceptance of failure as well as an expectation of hope. The failure was the remarkable advance made by the MPLA, which resulted in it being recognised by the Organisation of African Unity (OAU) in February 1976, as the sole and legitimate government in Angola; while the expectation of hope was the belief that, with some foreign support, and with the ethnic base UNITA had among the Ovimbundus, the movement could at least force the MPLA government to concede to some of its basic demands. As was the case during the liberation war, UNITA was still militarily weak at the time it declared war on the MPLA government. The South African support that was

later to be UNITA's basic source of strength had not come, as the SADF had withdrawn to the Namibian border with Angola after their October 1975 invasion. UNITA further suffered a fundamental setback in 1976, when it was banned by the Zambian government from operating from the country. The MPLA government, on the other hand, was relatively well consolidated, with the presence of the Cuban troops.

Apart from the US and South Africa, UNITA obtained support from a number of countries in Africa and the Middle East. These include Morocco, Senegal and Saudi Arabia. The former Senegalese President, Leopold Senghor, was alleged to have provided diplomatic passports for UNITA officials.[28] Morocco's involvement too was particularly pronounced. In October 1977, Senghor arranged a meeting between King Hassan of Morocco and Savimbi. This meeting marked a turning point in the affairs of UNITA, as Savimbi himself confirmed later that "the meeting ... changed completely the situation in UNITA because King Hassan conducted our diplomatic struggle. From there UNITA was no longer isolated. The King made his friends our friends".[29] UNITA established an external headquarters in Rabat, while its officers also went to Morocco for military training at the country's military base at Benguerir, near Marrakesh. Morocco also gave UNITA arms. In 1978, for example, Morocco sent 10,000 uniforms to Angola for UNITA's semi regular army.[30] Finally, the country stood as UNITA's link with the Western and Middle Eastern governments "who either wanted to help UNITA or gather intelligence about the situation in the country".[31] Contacts like this earned UNITA some US$10 million between 1977 and 1979.[32]

UNITA believed that the realisation of its objectives could only come with the military defeat of the MPLA government, or after sufficient pressure has been mounted to force the government to negotiate. Against the background of its military and numerical weakness, UNITA started its campaigns by using local recruits among the Ovimbundus and the people from Cuanhama and other central parts of Angola. Most of the early recruits from these areas were won by UNITA propaganda that the MPLA was planning a widespread massacre in the region. Although, this propaganda was successful, the resultant military activities of UNITA in the first few years were weak and carelessly planned. Their largely hit-and-run tactics were ineffective. By 1978, the MPLA government believed that the main striking strength of UNITA had been crippled, with only a few remnants left to be mopped up. This launched the government on a feeling of euphoria, such that some Cuban troops were sent back home. UNITA, however, bounced back. Bridgland noted that, up till the end of 1979, the military strategy of UNITA was to overrun MPLA-held towns, and "destroy their infrastructures before surrendering them again to the enemy".[33] This appears unconvincing, as it would be unwise to surrender voluntarily to the enemy territories already captured. One is thus left to wonder what UNITA would use to negotiate any deal that could force the MPLA into conceding to any of its demands. What appears to be the true situation during this period was that UNITA did not make any major threat to the MPLA controlled territories, and it was not until after 1979 that UNITA started making significant inroads into the MPLA held parts of the country.[34]

Some of the traits of UNITA — which were to become more visible in subsequent years — were, however, noticeable at the early stage. An example of this was concentration of attack on economic installations, with the Benguela railway being a major target. Like other dissident movements, UNITA forces often resort to banditry and looting, in the effort to feed themselves. An aspect of UNITA war strategy, which was not employed in any of the sub-regional civil wars, was the employment of mercenaries. This was largely due to the extent of the internationalisation of the country's civil war and the degree of the intensification. UNITA mercenaries were largely from western Europe, as the 13 captured mercenaries arraigned before the "People's Revolutionary Court" in June 1976 were mainly from Britain and the United States. UNITA later confirmed that British professional soldiers were fighting for them.[35]

UNITA's military strategy changed considerably from the end of 1980, due largely to the increase in support from the US and South Africa, and the acquisition of more bases in southern Angola. It was about this time, too, that the organisation manifested more clearly most of its strategies. The first of these was its propaganda method. Foreigners were often kidnapped and taken to Jamba, UNITA's declared capital, where they would later be released (amidst propaganda) to the official representatives of their respective countries. For example in March 1983, 63 Czechs working in a paper factory at Alto Katumbala in central Angola were kidnapped only to be later released. Again, in May 1984, Britain had to send Foreign Office Deputy Under-Secretary, Sir John Leahy, to Savimbi's Jamba headquarters to negotiate the release of 16 British workers captured from the Kafunfo diamond mines. As Victoria Brittain observed, kidnapping was extraordinarily successful propaganda for UNITA, and curiously, it brought little hostile comment to the organisation as the practice did in other places — especially in the Middle East. Not even when a kidnapped Swedish aid worker was killed in late 1987 was there any sustained critical comment from the western world against UNITA's strategy of kidnapping.[36] The attacks against economic installations also increased considerably after 1980, with enormous implications for the national and sub-regional economy. All these are discussed in Chapter Six.

From 1981 onwards, the United States and South African support for UNITA became pronounced. In the United States, Ronald Reagan became the President, and no sooner had he assumed office that he came up with what later became known as the "Reagan Doctrine", the primary objective of which was to give American support to all movements that opposed Soviet backed governments in the Third World. The MPLA government in Angola, alongside the governments in Afghanistan, Ethiopia, Nicaragua and Cambodia, fell under the governments so identified as targets for the Reagan doctrine.

The Reagan administration was unequivocal in its support for UNITA. In December 1981, Savimbi was invited to the United States, where he met Secretary of State Alexander Haig. From this time, the CIA started the provision of money, arms and equipments for UNITA.[37] The Reagan administration made clear its determination that the recognition of the MPLA government would only come if the government would negotiate with UNITA. The refusal of the MPLA necessitated the extent of destabilization the US injected into the country. For example by 1984, the US Information Agency Daily Report (Middle East and Africa) increased by more than 300 per cent, its broadcasts of destabilization propaganda from UNITA sources.[38] Again, as an attempt to inflate the international credibility of UNITA, a pro-Reagan US lobbying group "Citizens for America" organised a meeting of anti-government groups from Nicaragua, Laos and Afghanistan. The meeting was hosted by Savimbi in his Jamba headquarters. Although the organiser of the meeting stated that he was not Reagan's envoy, he nevertheless read a letter supporting the meeting which he said came from President Reagan.[39]

America's ideological fixations appeared a stronger determinant of its policy towards Angola than the actual perception of events in the country. For example, Washington continues to oppose the MPLA government because it is perceived to be a socialist country, forgetting that Angola has always clamoured for Western (in particular American) investment. The country hired Arthur Little of Boston, Massachusetts, as its principal Economic Consultant, and many of the American companies trading with the country testified before the African subcommittee that they enjoyed trading with Angola.[40]

What, perhaps, assisted UNITA most were the series of independent raids Pretoria made against Angola, ostensibly to eliminate SWAPO forces. It also assisted UNITA's propaganda strategy, as the organisation was allowed to claim military successes of South Africa's exploits. As early as 1978, South Africa had started serious attacks on Angolan territories, especially in the Cunene and Cuando Cubango provinces. In 1978, the biggest South African operation for three decades was launched against Angola. This operation was code-named "Operation Reindeer", and the purposes were basically three: an airborne assault on Cassinga, some 250 kilometres inside Angola; overall assault on a series of SWAPO bases near Chetequera, 25 kilometres north of the Angolan border; and a helicopter-borne sweep through a series of small SWAPO bases 17 to 21 kilometres east of Chetequera.[41] Although, South Africa claimed that the attacks were against SWAPO bases, it was equally confirmed that some Angolan soldiers were killed. Another decisive attack was launched in July/August 1981. This operation was code-named "Protea", and it involved more than 10,000 men, 36 tanks, 70 armoured cars, 250 troop carriers with 155 mm guns, 127 Kenton missiles and around 90 airplanes and helicopters. The attack resulted in South Africa's occupation of a number of Angolan towns, including Mulemba, Nehoma, Ndovu, Mupa and Evlao, with a South African command post established at Mulemba. By the end of the operation, South African troops were able to hold on to about 55,000 sq. kilometres of Angolan territory.

Operation "Askari", the third in the series of South African attacks on Angola ostensibly against SWAPO forces, was launched between December 1983 and January 1984. In the words of the South African military commander of South West Africa, Major General George Meiring, the military aim of the operation was "to disrupt the planned infiltration of SWAPO's special unit into South West Africa".[42] This attack was launched from Xangongo in the Cunene province of Angola, which the South Africa force had not vacated since the "Protea" raid of 1981. The invading South African force directed attacks largely on the north-east at Cahama and Caiundo and further east on Mulondo and Cuvelai. The degree of success that attended "Askari" was, however, not as profound as its predecessors, especially "Protea". With the assistance of the Cubans, the MPLA forces succeeded in repelling the attack. The air superiority that had accounted (at least to a large extent) for the previous SADF successes had started diminishing. This was to become more pronounced in subsequent years. All these South African attacks on Angola served a basic purpose in the country's civil war between the MPLA government and UNITA, as they militarily weakened the MPLA forces and further diverted its attention from the war. This obviously made UNITA's military objectives easier to accomplish. Initially, UNITA did not acknowledge that it was receiving military assistance from South Africa. However, when this became difficult to deny, Pretoria's support was acknowledged.

After Operation "Askari", there was an effort towards peace between the MPLA government in Angola and South Africa. Morgan Norval's somewhat biased account of the war attributed this initiative to the Angolans and Cubans. He noted thus: "as is common with communist regimes, when facing a military setback, they resort to a well-orchestrated propaganda campaign to recoup their losses by means of diplomacy".[43] This is inaccurate, as the initiative that eventually led to temporary peace between Angola and South Africa was not at Angolan instance, and neither did the country negotiate from the position of weakness. Paul Moorcraft was thus more accurate to note that the military setback suffered by the SADF and larger global developments underlined the detente.[44]

When South Africa first proclaimed a cease-fire after "Askari", Angola accepted on three basic conditions viz: that SWAPO's consent be obtained; that South Africa withdraw from Angola; and that the UN Resolution 435 granting independence to Namibia be implemented. An agreement (tagged the Lusaka Accord) was eventually signed between South Africa and Angola, under which the SADF was to withdraw from the Cunene region it had occupied since 1981, while Angola was to end SWAPO's incursions from this zone. The two countries further agreed to jointly patrol some 400 miles of the Angolan/Namibian border. Both UNITA and SWAPO were excluded from the agreement.

UNITA's reaction to the accord was that of rejection, and the movement declared that any peace effort that failed to take adequate notice of it as a major force was bound to fail.

A great dent to South Africa's reputation and intention in the accord came with the failure of a sabotage mission organised by 4 Recce Commando Unit of the SADF on the Cabinda enclave of Angola in May 1985. Fifteen men from this unit launched the ill-fated attack on the oil storage tanks in Cabinda. The team left Saldanha Bay on the night of 13/14 May in an Israeli-built destroyer, the *Jean Fouchier*, with two 76 mm rapid firing guns and six Scorpion ground to air missiles as well as three Zodiac inflatable speedboats. At some stage in the operation, things went wrong. Two of the attackers, Louis Pister van Broder and Rowland Ridgaw Lieberbeirg, were killed and another member of the team, Wynand Petrus du Troit, a captain in the SADF, was captured. The captive confessed that their operation had nothing to do with looking for ANC or SWAPO guerrillas, but aimed to destroy the storage tanks at Cabinda Gulf.[45] On further interrogation, he confirmed that he had taken part in an earlier sabotage activities against Angola, the responsibility for which was claimed by UNITA. Finally, he confessed that if their ill-fated attack on Cabinda had been successful, UNITA would have claimed the success.[46] At first, South Africa denied any responsibility, but later, General Constand Viljoen, the SADF Commander, confirmed the operation. Effectively, it could be taken that from this time on, the Lusaka Agreement was dead.

Most of 1986 and 1987 were devoted to the continuation of the Angolan civil war, with both sides — especially UNITA — inflating the extent of the other's external support in order to get increasing sympathy. In 1986, Savimbi paid another high profile visit to the US, where he was received by President Reagan and Secretary of State Shultz, at the White House, and was the keynote speaker for the annual Republican dinner in Washington. During the visit, he received promises of military assistance, and in March 1986, hardware worth $10 million, including Stinger missiles was given to UNITA.[47] The US also promised to send TOW anti-tank weapons to UNITA. In September 1986, further assistance worth $15 million was extended by the Congress to UNITA in the form of covert assistance, while in late 1987, a further $15 million was given to Savimbi.

As military support for UNITA continued, so did pressure on the diplomatic front. The most pronounced of these was the introduction of what later became known as the "Constructive Engagement". On the broad level, it links the independence of Namibia with the withdrawal of Cuban troops from Angola. The extent of the controversy the Constructive Engagement has generated could be seen in the series of twists that has been given to the concept, ranging from "Destructive" and "Obstructive" engagement to "Constructive instigation".[48]

In reality, the announcement of the constructive engagement did nothing more than to give a tag to a policy that had long been in operation — at least implicitly. The underlined consideration of America's policy in southern Africa during this time was that most of the black organisations in the region — especially, the ANC in South Africa, SWAPO in Namibia and the MPLA in Angola — were more of Soviet proxies than the legitimate representatives of their peoples.[49] The United States shared South Africa's interpretation of sub-regional affairs that the Cubans and the Soviets were responsible for the problems in the region. In a secret memorandum, Chester Crocker, who was credited with the creation of the Constructive Engagement, was quoted to have requested his boss, Alexander Haig, to tell South African Foreign Minister Botha that "we [the US] share your [South Africa's] view that Namibia must not be turned over to the Soviets and their allies. A Russian flag in Windhoek is as unacceptable to us as it is to you".[50]

Chester Crocker first outlined the policy later incorporated into the Constructive Engagement in an article he wrote in *Foreign Affairs*, in late 1980, but was more explicit in a speech at the Congressional hearing in 1981. He said:

> South Africa is a region of unquestioned importance to US and Western economic and strategic interest. Its potential as a focal point of African economic progress warrants a substantial effort on our part to reinforce these projects and to forestall heightened conflict and polarization. Second, this region has a tragic potential to become a magnet for internationalised conflicts and a cockpit for East-West tension. It contains an explosive combination of forces — Soviet Cuban military involvement, African guerrilla operations across and within borders, and a politically isolated and economically strong South

ANGOLA

Africa. It is imperative that we play our proper role in fostering regional security, countering Soviet influence and bolstering a climate that makes peaceful change possible.[51]

The introduction of the Constructive Engagement had profound implications for southern Africa. Here, its impact on the civil war in Angola is considered. The Reagan administration attempted to convince the MPLA government in Angola of the need to accept the Constructive Engagement. For example, the Assistant Secretary of State for Africa during the Reagan administration, Chester Crocker, went to Angola in 1981 to discuss the linkage; and in 1983, Vice President Bush conferred in Washington with Angola's Interior Minister, Manuel Alexandre Rodriques.[52] As would be expected, the Angolan government found the terms unacceptable, not only because they infringed on its sovereignty by imposing terms on it, but largely because any attempt to send home the Cubans at that time would have almost certainly marked the end of the MPLA's rule in Angola, as UNITA would receive military reinforcements from South Africa to launch attacks on Angola. In the MPLA's perception, the Constructive Engagement was only a pretext to get the Cubans out and then enable the western backed UNITA to take over in Angola. SWAPO in Namibia also opposed the deal. Once it was announced, South Africa held the Constructive Engagement as the basic deal with which to solve the problems in the region. All that the Constructive Engagement offered were those conditions needed to alleviate South African fears: departure of the Cubans and almost implicitly (in Pretoria's belief) the reduction in Soviet grip of the region; the independence of Namibia (most likely under a government that would be inevitably sympathetic towards South Africa).

UNITA also used the opportunity to step up its public relations propaganda both in the US and in South Africa. For example, shortly after the 1987 whites the only election in South Africa, Savimbi praised President Botha for the "changes" the latter had introduced to the apartheid system. Without mentioning the ANC by name, he criticised "those black leaders" who refuse to negotiate with Pretoria.[53] The South African Foreign Minister, "Pik" Botha, joined this stance when he said (in response to Savimbi's position) that the future battle in

South Africa would have nothing to do with colour but ideology.[54] The MPLA, too, ruled out any talk with UNITA. A member of the ruling Politburo, Mr Van Dunem, said the Angolan government would prefer to negotiate with South Africa instead.[55] In this refusal to negotiate with UNITA, the MPLA government had the support of the Soviet Union, as the Soviet Deputy Foreign Minister, Mr Anatoly Adamishin, agreed that such a talk would be "pointless".[56]

In 1986, the Soviet Union sent a general in the army, Konstantin Shaganovitch, to Angola. He was the highest ranking officer ever to be posted outside Europe or Afghanistan. He was assisted by another general, Mikhail Petrov, who is believed to be a counter insurgency expert. The extent of all the military support given by the Soviet Union could be seen in the elimination of South African air superiority at the battle of Cuito Cuanavale (discussed below). The Soviet position on Angola and the extent of America's support for UNITA placed Moscow on the side of virtually all African states. This thus made the Soviets more committed to a cause they realised attracted affection from most of the African countries. Another factor which made Moscow's commitment strong was the apparent loss of face it suffered in Zimbabwe to China. The involvement of the Soviet Union in the country's liberation had not yielded the desired result, as ZAPU, the party it had supported, lost the independence election to the Chinese backed ZANU.[57]

By 1987, evidence of a split had been noticed in the UNITA ranks. This was to become more glaring in subsequent years, although it never moved near threatening Savimbi's leadership. Allegations of Savimbi's hard grip on both the UNITA ranks and the civilians living in UNITA-controlled territories, have always been rife. Malaquias described it as "one of fear and horrifying atrocities ... combining the worst aspects of Chinese cultural revolution and Stalinism" to control the region.[58] There were several cases of "witch-burning", in which individuals and families were thrown into massive bonfires, on the grounds that they were witches. Many UNITA leaders, including Jorge Sangumba, Antonio Vakulula and Pires Chindondo, were believed to have been killed for allegedly holding contrary opinions to Savimbi. However, it was the execution of Tito Chingunji and Wilson dos Santos — two former top members of UNITA — that brought the extent of Savimbi's hard grip on UNITA to international attention. The men were killed after more than two years in detention in Jamba for allegedly trying to undermine Savimbi. The allegation that these men had been executed was first made by the former "Interior Minister" of UNITA, Miguel Nzau Puma, and the former "Foreign Minister", Tony de Costa Fernandes, after they deflected from UNITA. The allegation was first denied, with UNITA's London representative, Isaias Samakuva, maintaining that it was unproven that the men were dead.[59] Savimbi was to admit the following week that the two men had been executed, but that it was Puma (as the "Interior Minister") that was responsible for the "gross abuse of human rights that occurred". However, as Lisa Alfred has pointed out, it is difficult to accept that such gross violation purportedly perpetrated by Puma could have occurred without Savimbi's knowledge, more so when the latter had often described Puma as his close friend.[60] The farthest extent the dissension within UNITA ever moved towards rebellion against Savimbi was the creation, in June 1987, of the UNITA-D (Democratic UNITA). The breakaway organisation claimed that Savimbi was "tired", and that his deputy, Jeremias Chitunda, was a United States "man". They also accused the organisation of gross human-rights abuse and concluded that Angola wanted peace.[61] Nothing however, came out of this, and Savimbi maintained his leadership of the party.

UNITA concentrated its main activities on the northern frontier with Zaire, the southern provinces of Cunene and Cuando Cubango and the central province of Huambo, Bie and Kwanza Zul. Cabinda, which produced more than 60 per cent of the country's oil also had some form of UNITA presence. The government embarked on the recruitment of regional defence force among local people in the provinces to help the regular army in its fight against UNITA. The war, however, continued until the decisive Cuito Cuanavale debacle.

Cuito Cuanavale and its Aftermath
Cuito Cuanavale has always been a geo-strategically important town in Angola. For the MPLA government, it was one of the bases from where air attack could be launched on the UNITA headquarters of Jamba. It is also at a point from where the whole south-eastern corner of Angola could best be controlled. Beyond these, however, there was little indication before 1988 that Cuito Cuanavale would become a reference point (although sometimes overblown) in the history of Angola and southern Africa. The military engagement that took place in the town has been described "the largest battle to be fought in sub-

saharan Africa since world war II".[62] Although, controversy surrounds the casualty figures, it is estimated that close to 4,000 people were killed and thousands of others injured. What is presented here is a summary of the battle, especially as it resulted in policy changes on the part of all the sides in the Angolan conflict.

The roots of the battle in Cuito Cuanavale could be traced to early-1987, when MPLA government forces launched a major offensive to capture Mavinga in south east Angola. With its strategic air strip, Mavinga served as supply route to UNITA headquarters at Jamba.[63] Furthermore, the $15 million arms the US gave UNITA were being flown from Kamina in southern Zaire to Mavinga, from where they were later taken to Jamba. All these made Mavinga a military target for the MPLA. Fourteen brigades of the Angolan army were involved in the offensive, and the military objective was to attack Mavinga and Jamba with Cuito Cuanavale as the main forward base.

The offensive was launched in August 1988, but by the following month, it had come to a halt due to South Africa's intervention on the side of UNITA. The South African supporting team were from the 32 and 101 battalions of the SADF, regular troops and units from the South West African Territorial Force, and they deployed Mirage ground attack jets, AML-90 armoured cars, heavy artillery and Scorpion tanks. The South African and the UNITA ground forces pursued the MPLA forces in the latter's retreat to Cuito Cuanavale. At Cuito Cuanavale, however, the MPLA forces stood up against the combined UNITA/SADF forces and succeeded in blunting all attempts to seize the town. As the war was becoming one of attrition, South Africa considered direct infantry assault politically unacceptable.[64] Cuito Cuanavale thus showed the South Africans that the MPLA forces could take on the SADF on terms approaching equality.[65] Later, in November 1987, Cuba agreed to send an additional force of combat soldiers to Angola. This reinforcement had a dual mission: to relieve the garrison in Cuito Cuanavale; and to engage the SADF forces directly in South Africa. With the protection offered by advance radar systems and a more effective air arm, South Africa's perception of military victory in Angola had changed.[66] The impasse continued for most of October and November 1977, while reinforcement around the town continued till March 1988. UNITA had about 4,000 troops around Cuito Cuanavale, while South Africa had more than 6,000 troops backed with more than 300 tanks, 600 field artillery pieces, and a

ANGOLA

variety of other armoured vehicles. After the initial loss of ground, the SADF and UNITA launched another attack against the Angolan force installations in March 1988. This was mainly to the north of Cuando Cubango, Bie and Moxico provinces. The strategic intention of this move was to take Cuemba, which would have made control of the Benguela railway easy for UNITA, and would have further made it possible to capture the Moxico province capital of Luena.[67] Later on 8 June 1988, the Chief of SADF, General Jannie Geldenhuys, called up SADF reserves.

Initial successes attended the UNITA/SADF attacks, but the MPLA/Cuban forces later forced them to withdraw to Mavinga. It was also at about this time that SWAPO forces joined the MPLA/Cuban blockade of the UNITA/SADF invasion. Further reinforcement against UNITA and South Africa came from the sea and from the Angolan forces on the Benguela front. All these were developments that ran against South Africa's strategic calculations.

The outcome of the Cuito Cuanavale battle has been variously interpreted by the two sides — each giving interpretations that advance its own interest and that confer victory on it. The MPLA/Cuban side considered it a victory, and interpreted the South African peaceful gesture after it to be the manifestation of Pretoria's implicit acceptance of defeat. To say that South Africa lost at Cuito Cuanavale may not be an accurate assessment of the events that took place in the war. What probably happened was that the war showed Pretoria that there had been some reversal of strategic tides which dictated the need for a re-assessment of sub-regional events. This manifested in at least two ways. First, it became evident that the MPLA soldiers in Angola had attained some level of confidence previously absent in their prosecution of the war. The country's acquisition of MIG-23s and its sophisticated air defence, including a radar screen and SAM missiles, meant that South Africa's military superiority had been reduced considerably. Further confidence for Angola had come with the rising oil production and new economic reform that improved Angola's war-torn economy. Second, and consequent on the first, South Africa's military invincibility had been removed. Some evidences of Cuito Cuanavale confirmed this. First, South Africa's unchallenged air superiority had been eliminated. Thus, the relative ease with which the SADF and UNITA had patrolled a large part of southern Angola was no longer possible. This was to have impact that transcended Angola to Namibia.

Second, the rate of white casualties was getting significant. South Africa admitted 31 killed and 90 wounded. Again, there were considerable equipment losses, including one Mirage, one spotter aircraft, three Olifant MBTs, four Ratels as well as a number of military vehicles.[68] The fact that the SADF was then being overstretched by the global arms embargo and the stepped-up security at home to address internal uprising, further compounded the implications.[69] The Cuito Cuanavale debacle thus further convinced the advocates of arms embargo that the strategy could work, if effectively applied against South Africa.

The Cuito Cuanavale battle brought out a major lesson for South Africa which affected the future of the region in general and Angola in particular. First, public opinion against adventurous foreign policy that had committed South Africa troops in foreign countries became pronounced to the level the government could no longer ignore. In August 1988, almost 150 white conscripts publicly refused to accept the SADF call-up order. A public opinion poll conducted by the South African Institute of International Affairs in the same month, showed that 57 per cent of white South African adults would prefer direct dialogue with SWAPO in Namibia, while three out of every four white adults opposed any increase in defence spending. Even giving allowance for several variables that influence opinion polls, these were not figures that would satisfy the hawks in the South African government. It was this realisation on the part of Pretoria, coupled with the MPLA's belief that some form of give-and-take was inevitable and the larger global tilt in the super-power relations, that started Angola on the path of peace.

Peace Moves
Efforts at bringing peace to Angola have proved particularly difficult because of the number of interests that have become entangled in the country's civil war. After the debacle at Cuito Cuanavale, efforts towards peaceful resolution of the conflicts concerning Angola and South Africa started. The first in what was to become a series of meetings took place in London in May 1988, between Angola, Cuba, and South Africa, with the US participating as an observer. The efforts centred basically on three main themes: (a) the implementation of United Nations Resolution 435 on Namibian independence; (b) the withdrawal of South African troops from southern Angola; and (c) the

ANGOLA

withdrawal of Cuban troops from Angola. Meetings to agree on these proposals took place throughout 1988, with successive rounds of talks in Geneva, Brazzaville, Rucana, and New York. At the end of all these, a number of agreements were reached, including the implementation of Resolution 435 on Namibia; South Africa's withdrawal from southern Angola into Namibia; the setting up of a Joint Military Monitoring Committee (comprising Angolan, Cuban, and South African officers) to monitor the decisions; and the withdrawal of Cuban troops from Angola within 24 to 30 months. In a tripartite accord signed in Brazzaville by Angola, Cuba, and South Africa, 1 April 1989, was set as the date for Namibian independence.

One noticeable thing about the package of the tripartite agreement signed in Brazzaville was the conspicuous absence of UNITA's role in Angola. This decision was largely at the insistence of the MPLA government, who argued that UNITA had no international legal status to make it a credible negotiating partner. A clearer position on the MPLA's stand in this regard was made on 1 August 1988, when the party's political bureau statement said: "UNITA and its chief lost the legitimacy of being considered an integral part of Angolan nationalism by allying themselves with South Africa and reactionary force in the world which support colonialism and apartheid".[70] It is, however, ironical that some of the countries these descriptions fitted were those with whom the MPLA government was negotiating. There is, nevertheless, a military undertone to the MPLA government's decision to ignore UNITA in the rounds of peace talks. Implicit in this position is its belief that, even without the Cuban assistance, it could effectively take on UNITA, if South African support for the organisation could be made to stop.

While efforts towards Namibian independence continued — albeit amidst hiccups — the relationship between UNITA and the MPLA government did not show any remarkable positive development. Despite their participation in the Namibian independence package, both the US and South Africa openly continued their support for UNITA. As late as November 1988, the South African Foreign Minister "Pik" Botha still promised that relations with UNITA would remain based on "good neighbourliness and friendship",[71] while the US maintained in December 1988 that it would continue sending aid to UNITA, until a deal could be struck between the rebel organisation and the MPLA government.

By early 1989, the MPLA government had started giving positive indications towards ending the conflict. In February, an amnesty law was decreed by the government for UNITA members. The sudden change of heart on the part of the government was more clearly manifested in May 1989, when President dos Santos put forward his proposal for peace. Although, this proposal still did not countenance any idea of power-sharing with UNITA or alteration in the country's one-party system, it gave sufficient indications that the party could, in future, make more concrete concession. The opportunity in this regard was seized by Zairian President Mobutu, and through his efforts, dos Santos and Jonas Savimbi met and signed a cease-fire agreement on 22 June 1989, in Gbadolite, Zaire.[72] The meeting attracted the presence of many African leaders, and a number of agreements were said to have been accomplished. The least controversial of these was a cease-fire, which was to take effect on 24 June 1989. It was further reported that Savimbi recognised dos Santos as the Angolan Head of State and further agreed to go into exile from the country, while dos Santos was said to have promised to work on a government of national unity. Even a cursory look would show this to be a curious set of agreements. Almost immediately after the agreement were signed, Savimbi denied having agreed to the clause putting him into exile. The clause recognising dos Santos as the President was also denied. In the end, Savimbi rejected all peaceful calls except a joint MPLA-UNITA transitional government and a free election.

Renewed fighting started after the collapse of the Gbadolite Agreement. On 23 July 1989, an aircraft carrying many government officials was shot down by a UNITA missile. The government forces replied with a large scale offensive against UNITA. This was however halted on 15 January 1990 (allegedly at the request of the Soviet Union). Few days later, UNITA forces killed four Cubans and three Angolan soldiers, resulting in the suspension of the Cuban withdrawal and a renewed attack on UNITA. Fierce fighting continued throughout January and February 1990, with considerable casualties for UNITA. Savimbi himself was allegedly wounded in an air raid on Jamba on 24 February. The success of these raids was further attributed to the absence of air cover occasioned by the reduction in South African commitment to the war after President de Klerk assumed office. On 5 March 1990, Savimbi said on UNITA radio that he was ready to sign a cease-fire, if the MPLA force would evacuate the territories recently

ANGOLA

taken. This was rejected by President dos Santos.

Disagreement soon emerged on the credibility of the external mediators. UNITA wanted President Mobutu of Zaire to continue his mediatory role, and suggested that a transitional government should be set up under "a man of integrity". Joaquim Pinto de Andrade, a Roman Catholic priest, was suggested.[73] President dos Santos had, however, become dissatisfied with President Mobutu's initiative and by early March 1990, he had indicated his intention of finding alternative mediators.

The independence of Namibia in March 1990, provided an opportunity for President dos Santos to meet US Secretary of State James Baker to discuss the future of Angola. The opportunity was also seized by the US and Soviet governments to hold more talks on Angola. The outcome of these meetings was not disclosed. However, a more fruitful outcome came from the regular meetings of Lusophone African countries, which started in 1989, and which had always discussed the Angolan war. It was this forum that arranged meetings between UNITA and the government. On 19 April 1990, UNITA offered an immediate truce and direct talks without the earlier condition that MPLA forces must withdraw from territory then occupied. A secret meeting was held between the government and UNITA representatives on April 24/25 1990, in Evora, Portugal.

A major step towards peace was attained on 3 July 1990, when the MPLA Central Committee agreed for the first time to change to a multi-party system. This, however, was almost derailed, when war was again renewed. Later, however, there was another truce, and new rounds of peace talks on peace began on 16 June, 1990. There were again problems after the talks, owing largely to continued US support for UNITA which encouraged the latter's intransigence. In December 1990, the MPLA held a Congress which ended the single party system and also gave up Marxism-Leninism in favour of democratic socialism as its ideology. UNITA's reaction to this was, however, negative, as it claimed that it was not impressed by the changes.[74] The year 1991 opened with a mixture of hope and trepidation. Early in January, diplomats from Portugal, the US, and the Soviet Union finalised plans to end the civil war in Angola. The details of these plans were not made known, but on 23 January, the MPLA government announced its acceptance of the proposal with "slight amendments". Later it became obvious that there were still disagreements over the timing of the cease-fire and election. UNITA wanted the election within a year after the cease-fire, while the MPLA wanted about 36 months gap. The disagreements in this regard was however resolved, and in April 1991, an agreement was signed between the two warring sides in Bicesse, near Estoril, Portugal. The agreement provided for a cease-fire which was to be monitored by a joint military and political committee, made up of representatives from MPLA, UNITA, UN, Portugal, the US and the Soviet Union. Foreign military aid, too, was to stop, and efforts to create a new national army — composed of equal representatives from UNITA and MPLA forces — were to begin. Free and democratic elections were scheduled for the end of 1992. Those in exile were given a year within which to return. On 31 May 1991, both UNITA and the MPLA government met in Lisbon to sign the Estoril Agreement.

Although continued UNITA and MPLA offensives initially cautioned against any optimism of lasting peace, the cease-fire agreement was respected by both sides. There were initial difficulties in the implementation of some of the other sides of the agreement, and UNITA announced that it was temporarily withdrawing from the negotiation. This, according to the organisation, was to express dissatisfaction over alleged violation of the agreement by the MPLA. The government denied the allegation and went further to accuse UNITA of "obstructionist" tendency.[75] UNITA returned to the peace table later the same month, and on 27 September, Jonas Savimbi finally came back to Luanda after 16 years. In the spirit of the peace agreement, he was met at the airport by government representatives.[76] The following month, Savimbi announced that UNITA headquarters was being transferred from Jamba to Luanda, and by November 1991, the government was able to confirm that elections would take place during the second week of September 1992.

Political activities in the country increased considerably, and several political parties — with varying degrees of seriousness — emerged to contest. Horace Campbell grouped the parties into three categories. First were those with histories dating back to the independence struggles. These were MPLA, UNITA, and FNLA. With the exception of the MPLA, where Eduardo dos Santos had replaced the late Augustino Neto, all these parties were led by the same leaders they had during the liberation struggle. The second category were parties with "national and international standing". Three parties were identified in this regard. These were: the Party for the Renewal of Democracy

(PRD), led by Luis dos Pasos; the National Democratic Party of Angola (PNDA), led by Daniel Chipenda; and the Democratic Party of Angola, under Dr Antonio Neto, a member of the executive of the African Jurist.[77] The third category Campbell identified were parties with "leaders which are aligned to one or more of the major parties". Again, here, three parties were identified, and all were believed to be supporting the campaign of Jonas Savimbi. These were the Convention for National Democracy in Angola (CNDA), under Pinto Joas, a former Minister and Director General of Information of the MPLA; the Social Democratic Party of Angola (PSDA), led by Andre Kilandamoko; and the Democratic Party for Progress and the National Alliance of Angola (PDP-ANA) of Professor Nflumpinga Nlando.[78] All other parties were poorly organised with no clear positions. Legislation stipulated that political parties must enjoy support in at least 14 of Angola's 18 provinces. This was basically to discourage ethnically based movements, especially the FLEC advocating the secession of the Cabinda province.

UNITA's campaign followed a predictable pattern. Savimbi opposed virtually everything for which the MPLA stood, going as far as promising to disband the police trained by the Spanish. He also promised to cut Angola's link with Cuba and to expel all Cubans from Angola. Savimbi was specifically blunt that the decision to sever diplomatic links with Cuba was due largely to the role the country played in the country's civil war.[79] There was also the issue of the intention of the FLEC to secede Cabinda from the country. Both UNITA and MPLA promised to give the people of Cabinda a better deal. FLEC, however, turned down the overtures from the two parties, and maintained that nothing short of secession was acceptable. Of all the registered political parties, the relationship between UNITA and MPLA was the only one that was contentious. There were reported clashes between the two groups, emanating from accusations and counter accusations that both sides were trying to impede the road to democracy. All these resulted in Savimbi and dos Santos meeting to resolve some of the issues in dispute.

Despite the preparation, many people believed that the elections could be stalled. Not the least among these was the UN Secretary General, Boutrous Boutrous-Ghali. His fears were based on the fact that some parts of the agreement reached in 1991 to make way for a free and fair election had not been implemented. Foremost among these were the confinement of troops and weapons as well as demobilization and formation of a new national army and police to accommodate UNITA.[80] It was only a day before the voting started that the commander of the MPLA force, General Antonio dos Santos Frances (N'dau), and UNITA's General Arlindo Chenda Pena Ben-Ben, were sworn in as Deputy Chiefs of Staff of the new national army. As of the time, only 110,000 soldiers of the combined total of 150,000 had been demobilised, while less than 9,000 of the projected 40,000 members of the new army had been trained.[81] The election was held in September 1992. The MPLA won, but UNITA rejected the outcome.

Resumption of War
Renewed tension soon started after the election, and by the first week of January 1993, full scale civil war had broken out again in Angola between UNITA and the MPLA government. The government forces made initial successes. In fact, by the second week of January, the government had announced that Savimbi's headquarters, Huambo, had been captured, and that the UNITA leader had escaped to Zaire. This was, however, denied by UNITA. Initial fighting was particularly fierce in the southern part of the country, with casualties heaviest in towns like Lubango, Cuito Cuanavale and Huambo. By the middle of the month, however, there had been a major reversal of tides for the government, and UNITA was able to record a number of military successes, the most significant being the capture, on 19 January, of the oil rich town of Soyo, the location of one-third of Angolan oil production. This was both a military and an economic loss for the MPLA government. Later in the month, UNITA also succeeded in cutting off Luanda's water supplies.

Talks to end the renewed conflict began in Addis Ababa, Ethiopia, between UNITA and the MPLA government, on 27 January 1993, with the ambassadors of Portugal, Russia and the USA as observers. The talks centred on four main issues: (a) the establishment of a ceasefire; (b) the implementation of the Bicesse peace accords; (c) the definition of the UN's role regarding the ceasefire accords and the second round of presidential elections; and (d) the release of prisoners. Subsequent meetings, however, failed to hold, as UNITA refused to cooperate with the UN brokered peace talks. The UN Security Council, on 12 March 1993, adopted the Resolution 811 (1993) accusing UNITA of being responsible for the renewed conflict in Angola, and ordered the

ANGOLA

organisation to accept the result of the September 1992 election. Other clauses of the resolution include an immediate ceasefire and a condemnation of UNITA's decision to withdraw from the new Angolan Army. UNITA condemned the resolution as "treacherous backstabbing" and insisted that the UN representative in Angola, Margaret Anstee, must be replaced before UNITA could take part in any peace talk.

The major objective of the government still remains to contain UNITA in the central highlands. Presently, UNITA controls about 75 per cent of the country, including key cities like Huambo, Uige, Negage and Caxito, while the government still holds on to many of the cities along the Atlantic coast — Luanda, Simibe, Lobito and Benguela. Should the rebels break through the coast, attack on Luanda would be easy as it would not be difficult for the organisation to rearm.

Allegations of foreign involvement and employment of mercenaries by both sides continue. The government alleged that Zairian and South African troops are supporting UNITA. The Zairian government denied official involvement, although it confirmed that Zairian officials could be supporting UNITA in their individual capacities. The government also claimed that it brought down a South African C130 transport aircraft, near Jamba, implying that South Africa was still giving support for UNITA. Accusations were also made against a South Africa charter airline (Wonder Air) of flying secret supply missions to UNITA. The owner of this charter airline, Gert de Klerk (no relation of F. W. de Klerk), is said to be a close associate of the South African Foreign Minister, "Pik" Botha, and former Defence Minister, Magnus Malan.[82] On its part, UNITA, too, claimed that Namibia was supporting the Angolan government, and that the organisation had already captured a Namibian soldier. This again was denied by the authorities in Windhoeck.

The military situation is still unstable. The oil rich town of Soyo was recaptured by the government in March 1993, but control was again lost to UNITA in May, by which time the destruction of storage facilities had been completed. Since the beginning of 1993, it is believed that the government problem has not been with the availability of weapons (as it is believed that there are massive stocks of military equipment at airport in Cabinda), but volunteers for military service. All the government forces demobilised under the 1991 peace agreement are being drafted back, and in March 1993, the parliament passed a new law introducing compulsory military service.

In May 1993, the Clinton administration recognised the MPLA government, and immediately established diplomatic relations with it. UNITA expectedly condemned this and accused the US administration of being completely confused. It further accused Portugal of supplying military assistance to the MPLA.[83] The government called up conscripts between 20 and 22 years on 1 June 1993, with the expectation of having 50,000 men capable of attacking Huambo. The casualties in the war have kept on increasing at an alarming rate, with figures quoting up to a thousand people dying every day in Angola. It is difficult to verify this figure, partly because reliable information on the progress of the fighting in many areas is somewhat difficult to get, and partly because the areas where the civilian population are most vulnerable are inaccessible.[84] What is, however, certain is that virtually everyone in the country carries a tragedy of the war, as death, starvation and epidemic spread across the entire population.

Between November and December 1993, efforts to resolve the conflict made some progress. This followed the efforts of the new UN Secretary General's Special Representative, Maitre Alioune Blondin Beye, which took him to Namibia, Gabon, Zaire, Zimbabwe, and Zambia, in search of broad regional support for a peace deal.

3 Mozambicans at War: Renamo Against the Frelimo Government

Renamo's name rings more than a bell. It evokes a reaction. Very few of those who have followed the affairs of post-independence Mozambique would be indifferent to the organisation. One is either completely against its objectives or sympathetic towards them. Those against Renamo's objectives are so largely because of their objection to the method being employed to achieve them, while most of those sympathetic towards the organisation's cause often pause to disassociate themselves from its method. In short, whether one is for or against Renamo's objectives, its method has always remained a target of considerable controversy, and often criticism. However, Renamo has always been a peculiar organisation. Unlike the movements that took up arms in post-independence Angola and Zimbabwe, Renamo did not exist during the Mozambican war of liberation. Thus, it did not participate (in its present form) in the war that brought independence. Secondly, and again unlike other movements, the organisation was formed by outsiders. It is, however, ironical that these two features, which ordinarily should serve as the organisation's weakness, turned out to be some of the sources of its greatest strength.

Though not without subtle controversy, the creation of Renamo has been linked to Ken Flower, the former Head of the Rhodesian Central Intelligence Organisation (CIO).[1] The increase in guerrilla activities from the Mozambican borders after the country's independence, as well as its implementation of the UN-imposed sanctions against Rhodesia both impelled Ian Smith's minority government to create a Mozambican-based dissident movement.[2] The primary objectives in this regard were to spy on ZANLA combatants and to destabilise Mozambique. Although, the shape Renamo eventually took was determined by its major sponsor (South Africa), the core of the recruits Rhodesia got to start the organisation, too, went some way to determine the ultimate form of the movement. The first set of converts were Mozambicans and Portuguese who had an axe to grind with the new leadership in Mozambique. Most of these Portuguese were those who lost property in the wake of the nationalisation exercise the Frelimo government adopted after independence, while the Mozambicans were former Frelimo guerrillas expelled from the party, or serving terms of imprisonment in Frelimo-organised prisons.

Not much of the actions that later became the characteristics of Renamo were actually carried out while the organisation was under Rhodesian control. Their activities then were limited, and Ken Flower put their numerical strength at about a thousand.[3] In fact, it was the intention of Rhodesia to keep the organisation "small and clandestinely manageable".[4] It is likely that the Rhodesian CIO actually expected Renamo to work perpetually in conjunction with units of the Rhodesian army, as the possibility of a future independent existence was not considered either by the Rhodesians or even by Renamo. In fact, Rhodesian assistance for Renamo was limited to the supply of military materials and the provision of propaganda machinery.[5] In return for all these, the new Renamo recruits assisted the Rhodesian security force in gathering information on ZANLA forces, while they also accompanied the Selous Scouts (a special counter-insurgence unit of the Rhodesian army) on attacks on ZANLA guerrillas.

The efforts to resolve the war in Rhodesia brought a major turn of events in the country's link with Renamo. Shortly after the Lancaster House Conference, the Rhodesian Intelligence signified its intention of cutting links with the organisation. Flower claimed that he gave Renamo members the option of either reverting to civilian life or alternatively, being transferred to South African control. According to him, most of the members preferred the latter option, and "within days" he (Flower) transferred Renamo "lock, stock and barrel" to South Africa, with the latter accepting "immediately and enthusiastically".[6]

With the change of sponsors also came changes in style and objectives of Renamo, and in a number of ways, what Renamo ultimately became was what South Africa made of it. The first thing Pretoria did after Renamo came under its control was to create some aims and objectives for the organisation. This was in order to give Renamo some international credibility and thus prepare it for independent existence. A new military strategy was also drawn up, allegedly by Alfonso Dhalakhama and Van Nierkerk, the Renamo leader and an official of the SADF Military Intelligence respectively. The latter was to become a recurring name in South Africa's link with Renamo.[7] International credibility was also enhanced by Pretoria's assistance for Renamo in opening offices in Europe. Along the military lines, South Africa ensured that Renamo membership swelled considerably, resulting in the organisation having sufficient strength to challenge the Frelimo government in Maputo. This diplomatic and military support was again complemented by direct military raids on Mozambique. The first of these was launched in January 1991 — ostensibly against the ANC installation — and it continued with intensity in subsequent years, contributing to the weakening of Mozambican economic and social life.[8]

Mozambican society at the Outbreak of Dissident Activities

The cataclysm that befell Mozambique through Renamo, fed on the social, economic, and political situation in the country shortly after its independence. For example, the literacy rate at independence was about 10 per cent, with less than a hundred medical doctors, six economists, and only a few thousand higher school graduates. The years of colonial rule had disrupted the Mozambican economy, and, unlike Angola with its considerable agricultural and mineral resources, Mozambique lacked the endowment that could replenish the economy. This was made worse by the several years of drought that confronted the country almost immediately after independence.

Apart from the inherited handicaps, independence, too, brought its own demands. Economically, efforts at reconstructing the country after the liberation war brought further strain on the rather slender budget of the country. This was further compounded by the mass exit of the Portuguese, with their skills and financial capital, undermining the production and industrial investment. Again, as mentioned in the introduction, some initial policies of the Frelimo government, too, made the country vulnerable to dissident operation. For example, the foreign policy decision to close the border with Rhodesia, though commendable for African solidarity, had an adverse impact on the Mozambican economy. Furthermore, the speed with which the government moved towards the establishment of socialism in the country was such that it could have encouraged the growth of opposition. Apart from the far-reaching nationalisation of property, a number of traditional institutions were abolished. A group that was particularly affected in this regard was the *regulos* — the colonial-appointed chiefs, who later became powerful in the pre-independence power structure in the country. All these dissatisfactions were exploited by Renamo to attract sympathy and to establish legitimacy among the people in subsequent years. President Samora Machel was to concede later that Renamo success could be attributed to two factors — support from South Africa and the failure and mistakes of his own party.[9] While the factors that underlined Renamo activities are exactly identifiable, not quite the same could be said of the workings of the organisation.

The more you look, the less you see: Attempt to understand Renamo

Possibly nobody fully understands Renamo. In fact, when one considers the often contradictory policies and actions of the organisation, especially during its early years, the extent to which its leaders understand the organisation may equally be in doubt. This is as much due to the nature of its evolution as to the policy of almost complete secrecy under which its leaders lived, especially during the early years of the organisation. The latter reason initially resulted in a situation where, for most of the time, spokesmen for the organisation made conflicting and often inconsistent statements which ended up confusing the outside world as well as the rank and file of the organisation itself.

Throughout the time Renamo was under Rhodesian control, there seemed to be no attempt to give the organisation any clearly defined objectives. This, as mentioned earlier, was largely because the Rhodesians had a very limited and specific assignment for Renamo. Thus, the organisation only attacked specified targets. In one of his few interviews, the Renamo leader, Alfonso Dhalakhama, was quoted as saying that all their targets during this time were determined by the "English", apparently referring to the white Rhodesians.

Even after the organisation was passed on to South Africa, and concerted efforts were made to evolve for it some clearly defined aims and objectives, Renamo, for some time, still remained an ill-understood movement. It has been suggested that part of the reasons why Renamo lacked a clearly defined political focus at this stage was that, at the time South Africa inherited the organisation, internal problems within the South African Bureau of State Security (BOSS) and the then recent demise of its head, General Hendrik van den Bergh, meant that it was the South African military authorities (and not the Pretorian Intelligence service) that initially administered the organisation. This may, in a way, account for Renamo's total lack of political skill and a reliance, instead, on the purely military approach.

It is, however, possible to extract some of the aims of the organisation from the declared positions of its key leaders. During the early attempts to carve an independent image for Renamo, the most consistent of the organisation's positions was to get rid of what it called "communist oppression", and thus revert to "traditional arrangement", which its leaders claimed the Frelimo government had disregarded in its ambition to revolutionise Mozambique. While it is true that some of the immediate post-independence policies of the Frelimo government gave justification for these aims, Renamo specifically selected them for propaganda purposes. Its "anti-communist" stance, for example, was to attract support from the Western world which, after the events in Angola, was getting highly critical at the speed with which the Soviets were making inroads into southern Africa. Renamo's second policy of wanting to revert to "traditional life" was basically aimed at getting sympathy from Mozambicans whose conservatism made it difficult for them to cope with the speed at which Frelimo was transforming Mozambican society.

Another early "objective" of Renamo was its claim of wanting to return the country to the path envisaged for it by the founding leader of Frelimo, Eduardo Mondlane, a path from which they claimed Mondlane's successor, Samora Machel, had deviated. This again was an objective richer in propaganda than in intention. At the time of independence, Eduardo Mondlane had come to be highly revered as the father of the Mozambican nation. It is, however, ironical, that it was against the Frelimo party — which did much to mystify Mondlane — that the propaganda was directed and successfully exploited. However, after Renamo had attracted sufficient international attention, it came up with the much more respectable objective of aiming for a general, free and fair elections in Mozambique.

Much like its aims and objectives, the organisational structure of Renamo is equally shrouded in secrecy. However, in one of the most authoritative books on Renamo to date, Alex Vines attested to some form of organisation along conventional military structure.[10] This had earlier been affirmed by William Minter.[11] It is, nevertheless, strange that the degree of order and discipline presented by these two sources was not reflected in most of the activities of Renamo. From the accounts, Renamo is believed to have a hierarchical military structure, with Alfonso Dhalakhama as the Commander-in-Chief, followed by the army generals who have under them regional commanders, sector commanders, and zonal commanders in that descending order. The basic operational unit of Renamo is said to comprise about 100 to 150 men, with smaller units attached for special functions. Almost every company is believed to be equipped with radio-transmission facilities, and a communication officer who is regularly in touch with the provincial base and the headquarters. Two or three companies reportedly make up a battalion with 450 men at full strength, while a provincial base may have two, three or more battalions in its immediate vicinity. A company is divided into platoons and sections as well as groups selected for specific operations.

Recruitment into Renamo was largely forced, with most of the conscripts responding to their predicament with fatalistic acceptance.[12] The initial recruits were subjected to severe forms of control which deterred them from contemplating escape, the most prominent being the fear of execution. Another strategy to ensure permanent membership was to make sure that a new recruit performed one of his earliest operations against his own village (under the leadership of a senior officer). Having done this, the recruit was then told he could not return home without facing retribution from his people. All these, coupled with the excitement of roaming about the country, made most of the recruits stay on in the organisation. The economic situation in the country also explained why some stayed on — since membership of the organisation guaranteed them daily food. It is, however, possible that some people actually joined the organisation voluntarily. These could be those embittered by some of the post-independence activities of the Mozambican government who thus felt that the government should be replaced. These, however, formed a smaller percentage than those conscripted or forced by economic circumstances to join the organisation.

Renamo owes most of what it later became to the extent of the external support it has received over the years. Although, many of its sponsors later found it damaging to ally themselves openly with the organisation, external assistance from certain sources was later established beyond reasonable doubt. Apart from South Africa, whose support has been more or less confirmed, many Portuguese businessmen who incurred huge financial losses in the wake of Frelimo's economic policies after independence, offered tremendous assistance to Renamo. Some prominent names in this regard include Jorge Jadin, a controversial millionaire with enormous investment in Mozambique, and Orlando Martin.[13] Beyond the activities of the disaffected individuals, there seems to be no concrete proof that the Portuguese government was involved in any form of assistance to Renamo. In the United States, the Heritage Foundation, a right-wing organisation in Washington D.C., assisted in spreading Renamo propaganda. In the main, these groups worked with Renamo officials in the United States.

A fairly reliable, but as yet unconfirmed, report alleged Saudi Arabian support for Renamo. A journalist, Godwin Matatu, claimed that he personally witnessed a secret airlift of Saudi military assistance to Renamo.[14] The reason for Saudi support (if true) is not clear. It is, however, known that the Saudis occasionally give money to movements claiming to be fighting "Marxist oppression" of Muslims. Although, Renamo lays no claim to Islamic religion, the organisation uses Frelimo's communist tendencies and the presence of the Muslim population in Northern Mozambique to inflame passion.

Malawi is alleged to have given (at one stage or the other) support to Renamo. This is particularly intriguing, as Malawi, too, has always been a victim of Renamo attacks. For example, the organisation was always attacking the 640 kilometre railroad cutting across northern Mozambique to link landlocked Malawi to the Indian Ocean port of Nakala. The attack forced Malawi to use alternative routes via South Africa and Tanzania with an extra millage cost of about US$100 million a year — which was approximately one-third of the total value of exports.[15] Paul Moorcraft has, however, espoused some reasons to explain Malawian support. First is the cultural ties between the dissidents in the Zambezia and the Tete provinces of Mozambique and the southern Malawian communities. Second, Pretoria could have manipulated its economic leverage to force Malawi to provide support for Renamo.[16] Furthermore, the Malawian President Banda might want to use his support for Renamo to re-launch his long-standing claim that northern Mozambique was historically part of Malawi. Allen Issacman noted that as far back as the early 1960s, President Banda had proposed to the former Tanzanian President Julius Nyerere, that they should divide the northern part of Mozambique.[17] This would have given Malawi access to the sea. In the end, Malawian support for Renamo attracted the attention of Mozambique as well as other Frontline State, and a delegation was sent to Banda who was said to have promised to withdraw his support for the dissident movement.[18]

Renamo has equally secured offices in Western European capitals. These offices are largely to assist in its propaganda as well as to raise money for its activities. The propaganda work was particularly important, as some of the activities (alleged and proven) of the organisation brought images considered unsuitable for a movement that required assistance from the "free" world. At the initial stage, most of the people assigned to these offices were often unclear about the activities of the organisation, as most of them had little or no link with Renamo central leadership. This resulted in the issuance of many confusing policy statements about the organisation, a situation which became apparent when the war became full blown.

The civil war
The Frelimo government did not initially take Renamo seriously. The organisation was seen more or less as an ad-hoc dissident movement that would fade out with the independence of Zimbabwe. Thus, rather than address the organisation with the necessary political and military attention, efforts were directed, instead, towards the independence of Zimbabwe. It was never envisaged then that South Africa could take over and transform Renamo into a strong destabilisation force. Despite the advantage of hindsight, Frelimo's initial underestimation of Renamo could be understood, as Renamo's early activities were few, and were largely sporadic and carelessly executed. In short, during this time, Renamo was more of a nuisance than a serious military threat to the government in Maputo. The fact that it took some time before South African control had an impact on Renamo could also justify Frelimo's euphoria.

By 1982, Renamo had up to 5,000 armed men operating inside Mozambique, and by the middle of the decade, this number had more than doubled. Renamo started its operation around the local suburbs. It was only afterwards that the organisation extended its activities. Basically, Renamo activities may be grouped under three rough headings. First is the physical attacks on civilians, both in Mozambique and the neighbouring states. This was one of the earliest activities of Renamo, and one which gave it the reputation it later had. Second was its raids on houses, shops, etc. in Mozambique and other states — carried out to obtain foodstuff and other things needed for day-to-day survival. The third was the attacks on economic installations in which Mozambique and other neighbouring states had considerable stake. All these brought Renamo into the limelight of international attention.

The usual style of Renamo attacks on civilians was to invade villages in the middle of the night in small groups of between 15 and 20 men. During such attacks, civilians were often killed, raped or maimed. Houses, farmlands, and shops were also often destroyed. This resulted in an enormous refugee crisis for the country. It is impossible to get the exact number of those killed in Renamo attacks, but conservative estimates put it at hundreds of thousands. So serious has this been that a US State Department publication described Renamo activities as one of "the most brutal holocaust against ordinary human beings since World War 11", while former British Prime Minister, Margaret Thatcher, described Renamo as the "most brutal terrorist movement that there is".[19] Renamo's attacks on civilians may have been carried out to create panic and disaffection necessary to destabilize and discredit the central government. This position becomes more credible when one considers the propaganda that came along with most Renamo activities. For example, after attacking a village, maimed people were often told to go and show themselves to the Frelimo government in Maputo.[20] Renamo also organised large-scale attacks on unarmed civilians. The worst of these was its attack on Homoine, in southern Mozambique, where up to 500 civilians were killed. In its military operation, the organisation relied considerably on charms, and it claims to have the support of the ancestral spirit. This, in a way, also brought many people into its fold.[21]

Renamo's attack on economic installations was by far the most extensive and damaging. It was also the one that attracted as much attention as its attacks on unarmed civilians. A number of key targets were at the fore of Renamo hit list. These include:

(a) The rail-line from Maputo in Mozambique to Chikualakuala in Zimbabwe.

(b) The oil pipe-line from Beira in Mozambique to the Zimbabwean border town of Mutare.

(c) The main road linking Malawi to the Indian Ocean port of Nakala.
(d) The main paved roads in the centre of the country and along the coastal routes.

In various ways, these routes, especially the first three, are necessary for regional survival, and any desire to reduce dependency on South Africa (as it is the wish of the states in the regions) depends largely on them. The economic significance of these routes is expatiated in Chapter Six.

This leads to the consideration of the sub-regional implications of Renamo activities. Renamo actions had ramifications that transcended Mozambique, and this resulted in a situation where Renamo became a "factor" in the domestic politics of most of the neighbouring countries. Foremost in this regard is Zimbabwe. The Mugabe administration has at least four reasons to get concerned about Renamo activities. The first arose out of the refugee problem the war in Mozambique created for Zimbabwe. This problem started immediately after Renamo began its activities, but it was not until much later that the gravity of the situation dawned on Zimbabwe. Mozambican refugees found it relatively easy to enter and settle in Zimbabwe, as the colonial division of the region left people on both sides of the border with similar historical and cultural traits. When the influx became difficult to manage, the Zimbabwean government, in 1983, invited the United Nations High Commission for Refugees (UNHCR) to assist, and in 1984, the Commission established four camps in Zimbabwe. These camps are in Manicaland and Mashonaland, and as at April 1990, there were about 80,000 Mozambican refugees in Zimbabwe.[22]

The second reason why Zimbabwe got involved in the war was the desire to express appreciation and solidarity to the Frelimo government. The ruling party in Harare appeared not to have forgotten the friendship demonstrated by the Frelimo leadership and the Mozambican people during their war of liberation. Among numerous other sacrifices was the provision of military bases for ZANLA and the contribution of a day's wage every month to the liberation of Zimbabwe. So much were these appreciated that Mugabe swore that he would do everything possible to ensure that Renamo does not defeat the Frelimo government in Mozambique.

Renamo's attack on Zimbabwean villages along the border presented Zimbabwe with a third reason to get involved in the Mozambican civil war. Not long after the outbreak of the war, Renamo extended its raids to Zimbabwe. The raids later became frequent, such that the Zimbabwean authorities estimated a Renamo attack every second day.[23] Thus, urged by the legitimate expectation of a government to protect its citizens, the Mugabe government began to take the Renamo activities seriously. But by far the greatest reason for Zimbabwe's decision to intervene in the war was Renamo raids on the major rail and road links between the landlocked state and Mozambique. In fact, the first set of Zimbabwean troops sent to Mozambique were basically to protect the trade routes linking the two countries, although in subsequent years, the desire to defeat Renamo became Zimbabwe's military objective in Mozambique. The Zimbabwean involvement later became a major political issue inside the country, with a percentage of the population questioning the rationale of the country's involvement inside Mozambique. Alex Vines quoted some Zimbabweans describing the war as "our Vietnam".[24] As would be expected, this has been exploited by opposition parties in the country, with Sithole's party (ZANU Ndoga) and Tekere's Zimbabwe Unity Movement (ZUM) condemning the involvement and calling for the complete withdrawal of Zimbabwean troops from Mozambique. This is further discussed in Chapter Four.

For Mozambique, the implications of Renamo activities fell into three categories — military, economic and political. The military dimension was the desire of the organisation to destabilise the country and overthrow its government; the economic implications accrued from Renamo's attack on economic routes and its disruption of internal economic life; while the political implications stemmed basically from the propaganda activities of Renamo as well as its attacks on civilians. Renamo propaganda was often broadcast on its radio, and was aimed at discrediting the Frelimo government, with a view to encouraging local insurrection.

Against this background the Frelimo government too responded with military attack. It was, however, the case that not much success attended the military response of the government. This is so for a number of reasons. First, the Mozambican army at the time was weak and somewhat disorganised. Colin Legum quoted a Mozambican official admitting that shortly after the independence of the country, the army went to sleep.[25] The poor shape of the army at the outbreak of Renamo activities may have been due to the strain it had undergone in the preceding two decades — having fought successive wars against

Portuguese colonial rule and the Rhodesian minority regime. A second reason for the ineffectiveness could have been due to the tactics adopted against Renamo. The government used conventional tactics, which proved to be of little help against the largely guerrilla tactics of the Renamo forces. Finally, the extent of external — especially South African — support for Renamo should be mentioned in any consideration of the Mozambican government's ineffectiveness against the dissident movement.

Zimbabwe's involvement in the war assisted in the recapture of some Mozambican towns from Renamo control. Such towns include Sena, Mutara, Vila Nova, Bade and Vilacara. However, the turning point in Zimbabwe's involvement was in 1985, when the country assisted in the recapture of Renamo headquarters in Gorongosa. During the successful attack, diaries, minutes of meetings, and other documents implicating South Africa of supporting Renamo were uncovered. The documents remain, to date, the most convincing evidence of South Africa's support for Renamo. To enhance the performance of the Mozambican troops in the war, the Zimbabwean government also coordinated an arrangement through which the British Military Advisory and Training Team (BMATT), then training members of the Zimbabwean National Army, assisted in the training of Mozambican soldiers.

In 1987, the Tanzanian army got involved in the combined military operation against Renamo. At the outset, the troops were meant to spend just six months in Mozambique, but they ended up staying about two years, during which time they were deployed to the north to protect the Nakala railway line. Malawi, too, sent in a small contingent in 1988, but this was more to express solidarity with the desire to defeat Renamo (and thus reduce the negative impression other neighbours had of Malawi's commitment in this regard) than to contribute any substantial force to genuinely assist in the military operation. The Malawian contingents withdrew the following year.

Apart from this military assistance, all the Frontline States extended enormous diplomatic support to the Frelimo government. This came largely in the form of condemnation of Renamo activities and of South African support, as well as assurance of solidarity for the Frelimo government. Zimbabwe coupled this with the establishment, in April 1986, of the Zimbabwe-Mozambique Friendship Association (ZIMOFA). This was an economic programme through which the

Zimbabwean army and civilians contributed economic aid to assist Mozambican victims of Renamo activities. All these, apparently, did not solve the Renamo problem, as South Africa kept providing the organisation with military and financial support. The failure of the military option forced the Mozambican leadership to consider another solution to the crisis. This resulted in the now infamous Nkomati Accord with South Africa.

The Nkomati Accord and its aftermath
A lot has been written on the accord of "friendship" and "good neighbourliness" signed between Mozambique and South Africa at the border town of Nkomati in March 1984. Most of these have centred largely on what could have motivated the two signatories (especially Mozambique) and the aftermath of the accord. Some have also considered the ideological implications for the Mozambican state, investigating whether the signing of the accord contradicts the professed Marxist ideology of the Frelimo government. Most of these will be considered here.

By 1983, Renamo was driving Mozambique to a halt. Militarily, it had not been defeated, and the prospect of a military defeat appeared slim. Economically, the organisation had aggravated the Mozambican problems. Mohammed Mawani put the problem succinctly:

> The MNR (Renamo) has always paid close attention to economic side of the war. By concentrating much of their effort on economic targets, they have played an important role in bringing the country's inept economy to a virtual collapse. This has helped consolidate public attention to a government and economic system which even, at the best of times, was never able to feed its people.[26]

All these resulted in a situation where the economy was near total collapse. The country had to reschedule some $14 billion debt owed Western financial institutions. By the end of 1983, Mozambique was $150 million in arrears on its debt repayments, with a further $242 million falling due in 1984.[27] The desperate economic situation necessitated an extensive tour by President Machel to Belgium, Holland, Portugal, Yugoslavia, France, and Britain in February 1984.

The tour was largely to request investment and military assistance. Beyond Britain's decision to waive the £22.5 million debt Mozambique owed, not much success attended Machel's tour.

It may be necessary at this stage to consider how the Frelimo government saw Renamo, and why it preferred to negotiate with South Africa instead. Frelimo's perception of Renamo was fixed, and the vicissitudes of sub-regional developments appeared not to have affected it in any significant way. To Frelimo, Renamo was an organisation created externally to cause problems for the country. In fact, the government did not see the war in the country as a civil war. It was seen instead as an externally sponsored aggression. Implicit in this perception is the fact that the Frelimo government saw the Renamo problem under a wider sub-regional context. However, while possibly not denying the inevitable role which internal problems within Mozambique could have added to the situation, the government believed that the crisis was a part of Pretoria's wider intention to destabilise the region and frustrate all economic and political initiatives aimed at escaping from South African domination.

Ideologically, Frelimo did not consider Renamo as having any ideological direction. Even the anticommunist position it tried to espouse was not, in Frelimo's perception, presented in any sustained and intelligible manner. Frelimo's perception of Renamo's military strength was not better. The organisation, in itself alone, was not seen as constituting any serious threat to the government. Although the Mozambican army was as of then new and relatively inexperienced, it was still strong enough to handle Renamo (especially, in the early stages). In short, the government believed, somewhat justifiably, that it could effectively handled the Renamo problem, if only the South African military support for the organisation could be made to cease. It was against the background of this belief that the Frelimo government in Maputo believed that talks should be held with the "real" and not the surrogate problem. In the words of the Mozambican Security Minister, Sergio, "why talk to the corporal, when you can go to the general".[28]

It would appear that many Mozambicans at home also supported the idea of a dialogue on the Renamo problem. Beyond this, however, many seemed not to care with whom the dialogue was held. A durable solution was needed to end the war, and a dialogue was believed by many to be the answer. The government was thus given a free hand to determine with whom to talk. Thus, when it came up with the position that the dialogue would be with South Africa, most Mozambicans welcomed it. This was further influenced by the propaganda the government gave — both before and immediately after the signing of the accord — that the Nkomati Agreement held the key to the Renamo problem.[29]

Another reason for the preference for direct discussions with South Africa (instead of talking with Renamo) was that any direct negotiation with Renamo was seen as implicitly granting the organisation some sort of legitimacy, which the government was then not ready to concede. A lot of unprintable names like "bandits", "hyena" etc, had been used by government officials to describe Renamo to the Mozambican people. Thus, the government felt that coming up with an idea of direct dialogue with Renamo would not only be contradictory but could also affect the government's subsequent stands on the management of the crisis. On the whole, Mozambique saw an accord with South Africa as a way of getting peace with some honour — if perhaps little.

South Africa had a number of interwoven reasons for going into the accord. First, Pretoria wanted to present the image of a Pariah that wanted peace. This, it was envisaged, would signal to other African countries that pragmatism had prevailed on both sides of the signatories. It was also envisaged that the accord would end ANC activities from Mozambique, or alternatively, provide the legal basis for dealing with such activities. Again for South Africa, the accord had its international targets, as the country wanted to show its Western clients that it was committed to peace, and also that one of the communist strongholds in the region had been coerced into signing an accord. South Africa saw the Nkomati Accord as a vindication of the Total Strategy. The fact that "Marxist" Mozambique was forced to seek peace would show that destabilization as a tool of regional policies had worked.

The approach of the accord necessitated a major rethinking of South African strategy. Attempts were made to make South African support more covert, as the overt support hitherto demonstrated would not be in the interest of the accord. In this regard, a link man, Charles van Nierkerk of the South African Military Intelligence, was appointed to coordinate affairs with Renamo. Before this appointment, he had been in charge of monitoring SADF's involvement in Portugal's military campaigns against the colonies.[30]

A number of clandestine meetings took place before the official signing of the accord, and it was during these that the seeds that eventually destroyed the accord were sown. Both countries agreed during the period immediately preceding the signing of the accord not to infiltrate men and equipment or carry out reprisal attacks against each other. But it was at this time that South Africa prepared the transition of Renamo from an extension of the SADF into a force apparently independent of Pretoria. In an attempt to reorganise Renamo for the post-accord phase, arms and ammunition sufficient to last for some months were given to Renamo, and a clandestine liaison between the organisation and the SADF was established. All these were not known by the Mozambican leadership, and the country entered into what turned out to be a trap.

The crux of the eleven-article accord is article 11, which states thus:

> The High Contracting Powers shall not allow their respective territories, territorial waters or air space to be used as a base, through fare or in any other way by another state, government, foreign military forces, organisations or individuals which plan or prepare to commit acts of violence against the territorial integrity or political independence of the other or may threaten the security of its inhabitants.

This article basically had the ANC and Renamo in mind. In short, Mozambique agreed to stop all forms of support for the ANC, while South Africa promised to cut off all assistance to Renamo. Another core article is article 4, which created individual and collective efforts to police and stamp out dissident elements within the territorial borders of both parties. To effectively address this, a joint security commission was established between the two countries. This was to meet regularly to review the security situation on both sides.

It was obvious that the accord was not in Mozambique's long-term interest, and, as it eventually turned out, it was not even to pay in the short term. First, the accord was basically between unequal partners, as Mozambique had neither the military nor the economic strength to ensure compliance. All it thus had to rely on was that South Africa would act in good faith. Pretoria, on the other hand, had everything to ensure Mozambique's total and perpetual respect of the agreement. Second, the fact that it was obvious that Mozambique was forced to sign the accord because of its precarious economic situation reduces the extent to which the country could seize any initiative in the entire process. Finally, Mozambique would have to strain its army too far before it could prevent ANC activities in the country. This is because Mozambique's long and porous borders with South Africa made it easier for guerrillas to infiltrate.

In a rather curious way, Mozambique — at least outwardly — saw the accord as a victory. It is not certain whether the leadership genuinely believed this or presented the impression to cushion the domestic opposition to what was obviously an unequal agreement. However, there may be some truth in Frelimo's claim that the accord was "an instrument for the defence of (the country's) national sovereignty [as] it creates the condition for the economic development and the building of the socialist state".[31] The ruling party newspaper, *Noticias,* drew historical analogies between the Nkomati Accord and the Brest-Litovsk Treaty, which the Soviet Union signed with Germany to buy some relief so as to consolidate the then enfeebled Russian revolution. In South Africa, the accord was seen as a diplomatic victory, more so when Mozambique's acquiescence in signing the accord was largely a product of South Africa's destabilization measures.

The accord generated mixed reactions, most of which went along predictable patterns. The ANC was naturally disappointed that Mozambique had fallen under Pretoria's pressure.[32] Among the members of the Frontline States, the reaction was a cautious "wait and see" attitude. Shortly before the signing, Machel dispatched his foreign minister, Joachim Chissano, to break the news of his decision to the governments of Zambia, Zimbabwe, and Tanzania. After the deliberation of the accord at their meeting in Arusha, Tanzania, the Frontline States gave a qualified endorsement of Mozambique's action. They realised the disabilities under which Mozambique existed, but they were equally sceptical of South Africa's intention. However, some members of the Frontline States, Zimbabwe in particular, had a mild rebuke for Mozambique's isolated diplomacy. In North America and Europe, the accord was seen as a triumph for Western diplomacy over Soviet policy in the region.

When, eventually, the Nkomati Accord was signed, van Nierkerk continued to ensure that South African arms went on reaching Renamo through clandestine means, while South African instructions to the organisation equally went through him. South Africa had shown that it had no regard for agreement signed with its neighbours, judging from the May 1985 ill-fated commando raid against Angolan oil installations in Cabinda, discussed in Chapter Two. This raid was organised despite the ceasefire agreement signed with Angola the previous year. It might be appropriate to do a comparison of the two accords. The Nkomati Accord differs from the Lusaka Accord discussed in the last chapter in a number of ways. First, while Angola insisted in the Lusaka Accord that it would not discontinue its support for SWAPO, Mozambique, more or less, abandoned the ANC. In fact, the MPLA government claimed that SWAPO was adequately informed before the signing of the Lusaka Accord.[33] Stephen Chan noted three other differences. First, the Lusaka Accord was signed in the territory of a third party; second, the accord was a treaty between two states who could both dispose of considerable military resources; and third, Angola's military strength and the extent of support for SWAPO was greater than Mozambique's and its support for the ANC.[34]

In a number of irredeemable ways, the signing of the accord dented Mozambique's reputation. As Robert Jaster noted, it was a violation of two long-standing policies of the Frontline States — signing a non-aggression pact with South Africa and the establishment of official links with Pretoria.[35] More serious, however, was the impact the accord had on the relationship between the ANC and the Mozambican government. Understandably bitter and disappointed, an ANC spokesman contemptuously compared Mozambique to one of the nominally independent South African "Homeland States". To this, the Mozambican government reacted by denouncing the ANC as suffering from ideological and organisational weakness, and asserted that the organisation was conducting a feckless military campaign which was bound to fail.[36] This marked an unprecedented low point in the Mozambican/ANC relations.

The signing of the accord launched Mozambique on a feeling of euphoria. Machel declared after the signing that "what Nkomati means for the bandits is that the spring where the water rises has run dry. It leaves the water that was already pumped up here to evaporate". Still operating under this euphoria, Mozambique demonstrated remarkable zeal and determination in fulfilling its own side of the bargain. The government forces made a number of raids on houses belonging to ANC supporters, and in April 1984, "the government delivered an ultimatum to ANC members obliging them either to live in controlled refugee camps inside Mozambique or leave the country". By October 1984, it was estimated that up to 800 ANC members had left Mozambique. In the characteristics that would be expected of a weakling wanting to satisfy an aggressive powerful neighbour, Mozambique demonstrated remarkable high-handedness and over-zealousness in trying to persuade South Africa to honour its own side of the accord.

The rest of the Nkomati Accord is now history. The accord did not give any of the hopes Mozambique had anticipated. Julie Frederikse, who witnessed the signing of the accord in March 1984, went back to Mozambique a year later and concluded that the "peace and prosperity seemed further away than ever before". She wrote:

> The railway line to the South African border has been repeatedly sabotaged, and cars and buses attacked on the road. (Renamo) has infiltrated the southern province of Maputo, previously unaffected by war, and the capital has been blacked out seven times over the past three months by Renamo saboteurs .... Since the Nkomati Accord, they have developed a variety of new tactics. When arms and ammunition stocks run low — in between periodic re-supplies, in violation of the agreement — rural residents are butchered with knives and bayonets.[37]

South Africa initially denied violating the terms of the agreement. President Botha, in fact, categorically stated that the "government will not allow South African territory to be used for the planning or perpetration of acts of violence against neighbouring states",[38] whereas, within three weeks of the accord, there had been reports of its violation by South Africa.[39] Even when it became obvious that South Africa was unfaithful to the accord, Mozambique still tried to ensure that the agreement did not collapse altogether. There were at least three reasons for this. First, the breakdown of the agreement would give South Africa a freer hand to support the dissident activities. Second, Mozambique wanted to avoid the loss of face that would attend the failure of the accord. The signing of the agreement was portrayed to Mozambicans at home as the "death warrant" of Renamo. Thus, coming up shortly afterwards to admit that the accord could no longer "kill" Renamo was something the Frelimo government was not willing to do easily. Third, there was the sub-regional dimension to the decision to cling on to the accord. The zeal with which Mozambique expelled the ANC from the country was remarkably unique, such that the Frelimo government could not come out easily to acknowledged that the accord whose agreement they had carried out with the fury of an old testament prophet was a fraud, and that they would want to back out of it. However, in September 1984, Mozambique's main negotiator, Major General Jacinto Veloso, issued a public statement that the accord was not working. The South African government, however, maintained that "not a single bit of evidence has been produced" to implicate the government or any of its departments.[40]

When the evidence eventually came, it was in a way that could not be denied. In September 1985, members of the Zimbabwean National Army operating with the Mozambican Armed Forces overran the Renamo headquarters of Cassa Banana, and uncovered documents incriminating South Africa. The documents showed clearly that after the Nkomati Accord, South African support for Renamo had continued. The Foreign Minister, "Pik" Botha, was forced to confess some "technical breaches" on the part of South Africa. Attempts made later by the SADF chief, General Constand Viljoen, to discredit the documents as Soviet forgeries were not successful. Commenting after examining the documents, a South African columnist wrote:

> ... if they are concocted forgeries, they are remarkably well done. It would have taken a brilliant propagandist with an intimate knowledge of matters in both South Africa and Mozambique to have compiled the notes ... if it were to come to a credibility contest between Maputo and Pretoria, then Maputo would have a head start in overseas eyes. Against South Africa's record of reversed accounts of international operations, Mozambique has a clean sheet.[41]

A few months after the diaries were published, on 6 February 1986,

"Pik" Botha confirmed to the parliament that the documents were genuine. "One can go through all those entries in the diary ... the information tallies with the flights undertaken by the air-force. That is true. The times of our meetings (with Renamo) in Pretoria are correct. The times that they indicated I had been present, are correct". He concluded by saying that the violations of the Nkomati Agreement were "technical".

There is yet another way to look at the complicity in breaching the Nkomati Accord. The fact that it reached the very top of the SADF and embraces members of the State Security Council should be noted. More importantly, the fact that most of those indicted in the complicity went on to assume greater heights in the country may reflect the extent of government's involvement. For example, J.J. Geldenhuy later assumed the post of the Chief of Defence Force, despite the fact that he accompanied Louis Nel on his trip to Gorongosa, while A.J. Liebenberg, whose name appeared in several entries in the discovered Renamo diary, later became Chief of Army in November 1985. Robert Davies has postulated three reasons as to why South Africa refused to comply with the terms of the Nkomati Accord. First, is that it was unlikely that Pretoria fully trusted Frelimo, or regarded the measures taken by the Mozambican government as a sufficient retreat from supporting the ANC. Second, Renamo was a major trump card South Africa was not willing to abandon easily. Third, the Nkomati Accord could be just a mere step in an overall effort of forcing the Frelimo government to reach political accommodation with Renamo.

South Africa's relationship with Renamo had a number of intricacies which are not often told. For example, at one stage, it appeared South Africa started seeing the Mozambican civil war in a way different from Renamo, and this divergence of perception soon came into the open. Pretoria made it clear during the tripartite negotiation (with Renamo and Frelimo in September 1984) that it favoured a sort of coalition government in which Renamo would play a subsidiary role to Frelimo. This position arose basically from the belief expressed by many in South Africa that Renamo taking over in Mozambique would not be in South Africa's interest. Robert Davies quoted a top South Africa industrialist who put the position succinctly:

> It is in no one's interest that MNR (Renamo) takes over the government. They have very weak

leadership, no clear ideological direction and absolutely no administration. With them in power and Frelimo in opposition, Mozambique would be in greater chaos that ever before. And we will be the first to feel it.[42]

The slight change of attitude that ensued from this change in perception affected Renamo and the organisation accused Botha of "betrayal" and of "being in league with the Marxists in Maputo".[43]

Another manifestation of fundamental disagreement between some key members of Renamo and South Africa could be seen when, at one stage, some members of the organisation started getting openly critical of deep South African involvement in the affairs of Renamo. Two people — Joas da Silva Ataide and Mateus Lopes — were at the fore of this move. The two of them carried their argument to the Renamo leader, Alfonso Dhalakhama, but their journey ended in death on 30 November 1987. The official explanation was a simple car crash. Some Renamo officials however suspected foul play, and Paulo Oliviera, the former Renamo spokesman who defected in October 1987, argued that South Africa was responsible for the deaths. The mysterious death of Evo Fernandez in April 1988 has also been attributed to South Africa.[44] The rough edges in the Renamo/South African relationship were, however, soon made straight.

With the Nkomati Accord virtually dead, Mozambique was back to where it was before the agreement, with Renamo continuing its activities with more open South African support. This made the Frelimo government embark on extensive reorganisation of the army. A special assault unit of the army — tagged the Red Beret — was trained by the Portuguese. The arrangement made with the British Military Team in Zimbabwe to train the Mozambican forces in Zimbabwe also brought improvements to the performance of the army. For example, in March 1987, the Red Beret commandoes carried out a successful raid on Luabo and Mopela on the north bank of the Zambezi. To reduce the problem created by logistics, the command and control structure of the national army was decentralised, giving increased responsibility to provincial military chiefs within their respective regions. Far-reaching reshuffle also hit the top military posts. The commander credited with much of the success in the Zambezi raid, Air Force Commander General Antonia Hama Thai, was promoted Chief of General Staff, replacing General Sebastino Mabote, who had held the position since independence. All these reorganisations brought improvements to the activities of the army, and they continued until another major development emerged in the Mozambican crisis — the death of President Samora Machel.

Machel died in a plane crash while returning from Kasabe Bay, in northern Zambia, where he had gone for a meeting to discuss the future of Angola. Ordinarily, this may, on the surface, appear unconnected with the civil war in the country, more so when it appeared certain that the plane was not shot down. However, a hidden hand can not, and, in fact, has not been ruled out in the plane crash, and, although not without controversy, the Frelimo government and many people in the region believed that South Africa was involved in the crash. From the account made available by the government, it was alleged that electronic devices from the ground were used to deviate the flight path of the plane — with the pilot still believing that he was on the right course. It was further claimed that the plane the president used for the journey — a Tupolev 134 — was particularly vulnerable to such navigational distortions.[45]

Another story implicating South Africa came from some of the survivors of the crash. Three of them — Daniel Cuma, Fernando Joao, and Almeda Pedro — gave accounts to the effect that South African policemen arrived on the scene few hours after the accident, and instead of helping the victims, went away with documents removed from the crash.[46] South Africa denied any involvement in the crash, putting the blame instead on other technical problems. Foremost in these was the argument that most of the Soviet pilots and crew handling the late President's plane were incompetent, and that the blame of the crash should be put at their feet. More complications arose when South Africa alleged that documents recovered from the crash indicated that the late Mozambican leader and Robert Mugabe of Zimbabwe were planing to overthrow Life President Kamuzu Banda of Malawi. This was denied by both the Mozambican and the Zimbabwean authorities.

The plane crash also claimed the lives of some people who had played major roles in the affairs of the region. One of these was Fernando Honwana, the personal assistant to the President, who played a quiet but important role in the decolonization of Zimbabwe and Namibia and in the relations with South Africa. Another regional political activist who fell victim was Aquino da Braganca, the Director of the Centre for African Studies at the Eduardo Mondlane University in Maputo, a centre that has contributed a lot to the formulation of policies on continental and sub-regional affairs. A total of 37 people died. Joachim Chissano, Machel's Minister for Foreign Affairs, was later elected by the Frelimo Politburo to become the new President, and under him, efforts for peace were renewed.

The Mozambican Civil War in the Cold War Calculation
Unlike Angola, the civil war in Mozambique did not attract much super-power involvement. At independence, Frelimo's declaration that Mozambique had adopted Marxist-Leninist ideology appeared not to have had much impact on the Western world, beyond the security implications the activities that often go in line with such declaration might have on South Africa. The nationalisation of property that followed the declaration had no serious impact on the West — except for individual businessmen (largely Portuguese) who suffered losses. Again, beyond this, the Frelimo government, too, did not attempt to embark on any head-on collision with the West, as the country was more concerned with regional issues.

The first serious strain in the relationship between the Frelimo government and a major western power was in March 1981, when six United States diplomats accused of espionage were expelled from Mozambique.[47] The immediate reaction of the United States to this was to revoke food aid intended for Mozambique.[48] In this case, the Renamo factor was understandably a non-issue, as the organisation was as of that time, hardly known outside the region. But by 1982, Mozambique had started taking initiatives that would ease the tension with the United States. In September 1982, the government appointed an ambassador to the United States. This gesture was however, not reciprocated by Washington, such that late President Machel of Mozambique had to complain about Washington's policy towards Mozambique.[49] The relationship with the West at this time was getting increasingly important to Mozambique, as it was becoming impossible for the Soviet Union and other communist countries to bail the Mozambican economy out of its problems after more than a decade of wars. By the end of 1982, however, it had become certain that the United States had taken interest in the Mozambican civil war, and had influenced the Frelimo government to sign an accord with the South

African government. In fact, it was alleged that the Reagan administration made the increase in American food aid to Mozambique conditional on the reaching of some form of agreement with South Africa.[50] After the Nkomati Accord was signed, some American food aid (largely grains) were given to Mozambique. Again, in April 1984, the US Congressional ban on aid to Mozambique was lifted, and the US Agency for International Aid (USAID) promised initial aid of $500,000.[51]

The Reagan administration rated the civil war in Mozambique extremely low in the priority of tension areas that could attract attention in the cold war thinking. With more contentious issues in the Middle East, Afghanistan and even in Angola, there was apparently little time left for Mozambique. Again, Renamo did not have any credible anti-communist credentials, such that could make it an organisation worth openly supporting by the United States. Thus, all the US was ready to do was to openly disassociate itself from Renamo by condemning its activities, and by giving the type of economic support that would outwardly show positive disposition to the Frelimo government, but at the same time, leaving the handling of the main Renamo problem for South Africa to manage.

Renamo had one initial advantage over Frelimo in the United States. This arose from the fact that an anti-Frelimo upsurge in the US had started even before the creation of Renamo. This was allegedly done by the CIA, through its penetration of the US educated Mozambicans. One of the key people in this regard was Jose Massinga, who would later admit in 1981, to being a CIA agent.[52] Other early defectors who were to become prominent in anti-Frelimo international network were Fanuel Mahliza and Luis Serapio. The latter stayed back in the US, becoming a Professor at Howard University, Washington DC, and for some time, the de facto Renamo representative in the United States.[53] All these people were at the fore of Renamo propaganda in the United States, justifying the "struggle of Renamo against the Marxist Frelimo government". This advantage was exploited by Renamo.

The best evidence perhaps that the United States had the intention of viewing the civil war in Mozambique with cold war spectacles was when in January 1985, the Reagan administration announced the establishment of "a limited military relationship with Mozambique". This agreement involved the supply of about $1 million worth of "non-lethal" military supplies — in the form of uniforms, vehicles and communication equipment to Mozambique.[54] This military assistance was, however, dependent on the Mozambican government agreeing on a substantial reduction in the number of "foreign" military advisers in the country. This, in a number of ways, was the Mozambican version of the linkage theory. On the whole, it was such that, although the United States was not known to have given any direct support to Renamo, nor did it ever openly attribute the problems confronting Mozambique to its association with the Soviet Union or its adherence to socialism, the regulated sympathy given to the country would seem to pre-suppose that Washington — albeit in a subtle way — saw the problem in Mozambique as part of the cold war.

Unlike Angola, the Soviet Union did not make Mozambique an issue of priority. Efforts were made to support Mozambique, but just within what would not heightened the already tense super-power relations in the region. There was a "Treaty of Friendship" between the Soviet Union and Mozambique, under which Moscow was required to intervene whenever there was a threat to Mozambique's security. This was, however, never exercised in a way the Mozambican leadership particularly desired. Although the Soviet Union provided the bulk of the armaments, the material supplied still fell far short of what the Mozambican government needed to cope with Renamo and South African activities. When in 1981 South Africa attacked Mozambique, all the Soviet Union did was to warn — through its ambassador in Maputo — that the Soviet Union would come to the aid of Mozambique if Pretoria ever attacked Mozambique again. Although a Soviet cruiser and three other smaller ships visited Mozambican harbours after the 1981 South African raid on Mozambique, nothing significant was done, and it was not even taken seriously by either South Africa or the United States. It was, in fact, later discovered that the visit was a routine check, and not in response to South African attack. The meeting in May 1982, between the Soviet Defence Minister Ustinov, Marshal Nikolai Ogarkov and Admiral of the Fleet Sergei Gorshkov and the former Mozambican Chief of Staff, General Sebastiao Mabote, in Moscow, and the subsequent visits by Soviet military officers like the one made by General Alexei Yepishev, the head of the main political directorate of the Soviet army, in June 1982, did not result in any significant turn in Mozambique's security plight.

When the Nkomati Accord was signed, the Soviet Union only expressed its displeasure that the US and South Africa were "seeking to draw African countries into their own far-reaching militarist plans".⁵⁵ The signing of the accord in itself signified either Moscow's impotence or its unwillingness to take a more decisive step in solving the Mozambican problem — as such an accord would hardly had taken place if the Soviet Union had been more forthcoming to Mozambique's military needs. In fact, Moscow later gave an implicit endorsement to some form of contact with South Africa over the Renamo issue, when the country negotiated the release of Soviet technicians kidnapped by Renamo with South Africa.

In December 1986, Renamo announced the appointment of Boaventura Lemane as its spokesman in the United States. He worked with right wing pressure groups supporting Renamo in the US. However, it appears that some top members of the Reagan administration actually wanted Renamo to be a beneficiary of direct American support. Among these people were the CIA Director, William Casey, and the White House Communication Director, Patrick Buchanan. Another prominent Renamo supporter was Senator Jesse Helms.

Renamo has an intricate network of support in the United States. Apart from the Heritage Foundation and the Mozambican Research Centre, there is also Freedom Inc., which, apart from serving as a pressure group, also linked the organisation — possibly informally — with key people in US Intelligence. Freedom Inc. was formed in 1987, basically to support anti-communist organisations in Nicaragua, Angola and Mozambique, and by the end of 1988, it had become the most important pro-Renamo organisation in the US.⁵⁶ Among its earliest supporters was Richard Secord, the "mastermind of the Swiss bank-account used in the *Irangate* operation".⁵⁷ Other members include a former US and South African Special Force officer, Robert Mackenzie and Sybil Cline, the daughter of Ray Cline, the former CIA Director of Operations and a leading supporter of George Bush, since the time the latter was the CIA Director.⁵⁸ Freedom Inc. increased pressure on the Bush administration to rate Renamo on the same level as UNITA, as one of the anti-communist forces in Africa. It was actually thought that President Bush would be more sympathetic and give some degree of recognition to appease Freedom Inc., while he abandoned the Nicaraguan Contras. Part of the measures taken by the pressure group was to petition former Secretary of State James Baker, and to increase the publicity for Renamo actions.

The first official contact between Renamo and the United States officials took place on 27 June 1986, when an official of the States Department met a Renamo representative, Luis Serapio. The meeting which was described as "low-keyed" centred largely on "humanitarian" efforts to secure the release by Renamo of a kidnapped American nurse. A second meeting which could not be considered low-keyed took place on 4 November 1986, when Renamo officials and the conservative supporters of the organisation met with Frank Carlucci, President Reagan's National Security Adviser. The details of the meeting were not made public, but White House officials attempted to play down the possible damage it could have on the US policy of not recognising Renamo by saying that it was not aware that any Renamo official was at the meeting.[59]

The western European governments appeared not to have seen the war in Mozambique as an extension of the cold war rivalry, and it is not known that any of them gave official support to Renamo. Britain has been particularly sympathetic to Mozambique's plight, and, perhaps more than any other country in Western Europe, showed the greatest sympathy and consideration for the survival of the Frelimo government. This is largely because of the friendship between the Frelimo leadership and the British government since Mozambique's independence in 1976. There are several manifestations of this friendship. First, Mozambique, at a great cost to itself, closed its border with Rhodesia shortly after its independence to support the British sponsored UN sanctions against Rhodesia. When, eventually, the effort to bring peace to Rhodesia resulted in the Lancaster House Conference, Mozambique again played a mediatory role that was in the larger interest of British intentions in Rhodesia. At the stage when it was apparent that the Patriotic Front delegates — especially Robert Mugabe — opposed certain clauses of the British brokered conference, and wanted to back out, Machel despatched his special envoy, the late Oscar Kambona, to London in order to instruct Mugabe to agree to the terms of the Lancaster House Conference.[60] The decisive role played by Machel's intervention was known and appreciated by the British government. Again, after the successful conference, President Machel sent a special delegate to London to express his appreciation to Mrs Margaret Thatcher and the British government for the resolution of the Zimbabwean problem. In short, all Mozambique did to support the British and the Commonwealth initiative for Rhodesia were such that endeared the country to the heart of the British government.[61] The ideological leaning of the Frelimo government or its cordial relationship with Moscow was not considered relevant in the position taken on the Renamo conflict with the Frelimo government.

The British government also found objectionable the activities of Renamo. With television documentaries bringing home to British public some of Renamo's activities, the British audience and government became more familiar with the plight of the Mozambican government. Renamo's kidnapping of foreign (including British) nationals also affected the organisation's reputation in Britain.

The first practical effort made by the British government in the Mozambican civil war was the acceptance it made to assist in the training of Mozambican army under a British military training programme then going on in Zimbabwe.[62] Mozambican soldiers were sent to Nyanga in Zimbabwe, where they underwent training. Although it was not explicitly started that the training was directed against Renamo, it was glaringly implied. Renamo leader Dhalakhama was to confirm later that the unit of the Mozambican army that has given his movement the greatest problem were those trained by the British army in Zimbabwe. This was why he considered Britain partial. Second, it could be taken that, in another way, the British government had taken part in the war against Renamo with the training it offered the Zimbabwean army fighting alongside the Mozambican army against Renamo. Finally, when Tanzanian forces joined in the coalition against the dissident movements, the British government gave the contingent £800,000. All these point to the fact that the British government did not see any element of cold war politics in the problem Renamo has created for the Frelimo government in Mozambique. Despite all these however, the British government could not accede to the Mozambican request for more British investment in the country. Although the civil war was not given as an excuse, it could be taken as implied, as British companies were not willing to invest in an unstable Mozambique. The few that were willing gave the condition that they could only invest through their South African subsidiaries, which, within the prevailing regional conditions, could be considered as a way of turning down the request.

The relationship between the British government and Renamo changed after the signing of the Rome Peace Accord (to be discussed later). The British ambassador to Maputo (Richard Edis) visited

Dhalakhama in his base, bearing with him a letter from the Overseas Development Minister, Baroness Lynda Chalker, two footballs for recreation and a pile of books on democracy. Whitehall is also said to have offered to train Renamo officers once they join the new national army.[63]

Other countries in Western Europe, too, did not see the Mozambican problem through cold war spectacles. None of them, for example, recognised Renamo, nor gave the organisation the type of implicit understanding they gave UNITA. The only European country with whom the Frelimo government had problems on the issue of Renamo was Portugal. This was, however, more with individual Portuguese than with the authorities in Lisbon. In a way, the problem is understandable, as Renamo had a solid base among disaffected Portuguese businessmen who lost their property during Frelimo nationalisation. However, a protocol was signed in Lisbon in April 1982, which gave the Frelimo government the assurance of Portuguese government support. This provided training for Mozambique military personnel in Portuguese military institutions. A further announcement was made on 4 August 1982, by Lisbon radio to its African listeners that the Portuguese government would institute an inquiry into Renamo activities inside the country.[64]

The efforts for peace in Mozambique
With the death of Machel and the obvious failure of the Nkomati Accord, the Frelimo leadership began considering other alternatives to the Renamo problem. Machel's successor, Joachim Chissano, declared in his inaugural speech, that there would be no compromise, claiming that his government "shall continue with war in order to finish with war".[65] It soon became clear, nevertheless, that this was a statement made more because of the prevailing sad national mood. than one which appreciated the stark realities that confronted the Frelimo government. However, a number of other reasons underlined this stance. The death of Samora Machel attracted considerable sympathy to the plight of the Mozambican leadership. Thus, to sustain the sympathy, any successor had no other reasonable choice than to promise to continue with the cause for which the late president lived and died. This was all the more necessary for Chissano who, though he had considerable international image, suffered some criticism for his lack of military experience.[66] By 1988, some of the grounds for

Frelimo's euphoria had faded, and it became clear that some form of concession to Renamo would appear inevitable.

It may be helpful at this stage to consider what both sides wanted and did not want in any negotiation deal. At the beginning of the negotiation, the Frelimo government wanted peace, but not at any cost. It still wanted to maintain its position as the party in government, and that Renamo should disband and accept the amnesty offer it declared. Frelimo believed that it would not be in the interest of the country to allow Renamo to metamorphose overnight from the "bandits" they believed they were to political leaders. Frelimo's desire to seek peace placed Renamo at an advantage. First, it was certain to the organisation that Frelimo agreed to a dialogue because all avenues open to the government had been exhausted. Second, Renamo appeared to be enjoying the international attention it was getting. The decision to negotiate with it was used as a propaganda that it had become a force to reckon with in Mozambique and southern Africa. The organisation's desire in the entire negotiation was that Frelimo should give room for a "free and fair election". This, on the surface, appeared straightforward, and was such that would have put the Frelimo government in the dock, if it had refused. However, the conditions that would prevail in the country before the election, and how these conditions would be achieved were sources for disagreement for a long time.

The group that first came out with the idea of a dialogue between Renamo and the government was the Catholic Church in Mozambique. In 1984, the church publicly called for open dialogue between the warring sides. The prevailing mood in the Frelimo party at this time was against any dialogue with Renamo, thus the government interpreted the Catholics' call as a way of putting the government and Renamo on equal legitimacy. Another reason why the government objected to the Catholic Church's initiative was because the church condemned all foreign involvement in the conflict, including Tanzania and Zimbabwe who were giving aid to the government.[67] After the government turned down the peace efforts, the Mozambican Christian Council (CCM) — the council that unites all the 17 protestant churches inside Mozambique — came up with another initiative proposing informal contacts with Renamo. The late President Machel gave a tacit endorsement to the request of the CCM leaders to go ahead with low-keyed confidential dialogue with Renamo.[68] The strategy of the government's response at this stage was to investigate first, whether there were hopes of success before effectively giving consent to a more open dialogue. The government also found the CCM's approach more in line with fair play than the position earlier taken by the Catholic church leaders.

When President Chissano assumed office, he gave the CCM the mandate to talk to Renamo, as long as they followed some guidelines. These were: that the church made it clear to Renamo that the talks should not be misconstrued to mean an implicit acceptance of Renamo as a political party; that the purpose should be to persuade Renamo to stop the killing and pillaging they had been doing; and in the case of a future positive development, churches might have to help in the re-integration. These three positions show clearly that the government was not ready to yield any ground to Renamo beyond the amnesty it had already given. It is not known the extent to which the Christian churches believed that this could form any basis of Renamo's acceptance. However, they were sufficiently encouraged to press on. It appears the belief they had at this stage in their desire to mediate was a parallel of the biblical injunction: seek first the government's consent, and all other problems would be solved.

By the end of 1987, the relationship between the government and the Catholic Church had improved considerably, with Chissano's cousin, Joaquim Mabuianga, who was a Catholic priest, facilitating more contacts between the government and the church.[69] This made it possible for the Catholic Church to add its voice to the efforts of the protestants to resolve the conflict. The CCM, which had earlier been careful about being seen as aligning with the Catholic Church, also felt more comfortable, and the Catholic Archbishop for Maputo was incorporated into the CCM delegation to peace talks. The religious leaders made their first contact with Renamo in February 1988 in Washington DC. Not much was achieved from this contact, as those who came to represent Renamo were considered by the mediators as being out of touch with the situation inside Mozambique.

The churches later sought external assistance from the Kenyan government to hold a meeting with Renamo in Nairobi. This was granted and in December 1988, the first meeting was held. A second meeting was held in February 1989, and here, three representatives of Renamo attended. The church leaders expressed their desire to meet Renamo leader Alfonso Dhalakhama, but all efforts in this regard failed. Further efforts to meet him in March, then April, and three dates in July failed, as he was said to have considered it logistically unsafe to attend the meetings. On the whole, these initial efforts failed to achieve much success.

It was in the midst of these that the Frelimo government came up with its 12-principle proposal for peace (see appendices). This proposal detailed the grounds under which the government would negotiate the future of the country. At about the same time, Chissano also announced that his government had contacted Presidents Moi and Mugabe of Kenya and Zimbabwe respectively to act as mediators between the two sides in the conflict. The two presidents met in July 1989 to work out the details of the meeting between Renamo and the church leaders.

Alfonso Dhalakhama personally led the Renamo delegation to the Nairobi meeting with the religious leaders in August 1989. At the meeting, the mediators presented Renamo with the government's proposal, and appealed to the organisation to accept it as the basis for negotiating peace. Renamo reacted by bringing out its own 16-Points proposal (see appendices). It was on this note that the meeting ended, with the religious leaders promising to deliver Renamo's conditions to the government in Maputo.

As would be expected, the two conditions opposed each other in a number of fundamental ways. While it was possible for some form of compromise to be worked out on some of the principles, the government found one of the Renamo points completely unacceptable. This was point 5, which claims that Renamo should be recognised as "an active political force". The government interpreted this to mean a request from Renamo that it should be recognised as a political party. Chissano described the entire Renamo proposal as meaningless. Dhalakhama in turn condemned Chissano's comment, and concluded that the government was not interested in a true peace. In a further mark of defiance, Renamo expanded its conditions by rejecting the "exciting order" it had earlier recognised, and threatened abandoning the peace process. The Kenyan and Zimbabwean governments later took over from the religious leaders. Two unsuccessful meetings were held under their auspices, and the South African authorities were later brought into the negotiation to assist in breaking Renamo intransigence. The Director-General of the South African Foreign Ministry, Neil van Herdeen, represented South Africa. This initiative too failed, and in October 1989, Dhalakhama left Nairobi for Mozambique.

A desperate attempt to save the peace talks was made by the US charge d'affaires in Harare, Ed Fugit, in December 1989. This initiative was contained in a seven-point peace proposal, which was sent simultaneously for the consideration of Presidents Moi and Mugabe. This again failed, as Dhalakhama found unacceptable the clause in the proposal that recognises the legitimacy of the Mozambican government. The failure of this initiative made Moi and Mugabe intensify their efforts to bring peace. This time around, the Presidents suggested that both Renamo and the Frelimo government should engage in direct talks. Dhalakhama accepted this shift in position, as, in his perception, it placed Frelimo and Renamo on the same footing. For Chissano, it was not what was desired but he nevertheless accepted.

Most of 1990 witnessed efforts to bring peace while the war went on. The first major desire for peace in the year came with the visit of President Chissano to the US in March, during which he discussed with President Bush the possibility of "civil protection in the distribution of humanitarian aid".[70] It was during the visit that the US officials made known the efforts made towards reconciliation. It was announced that Renamo accepted most of the proposals put forward by the US for peace, including the recognition of the Chissano government. Renamo, however, issued a statement in Lisbon to the effect that, negotiating under the US proposed terms "would be capitulation", and that its stand that the Frelimo government was "illegitimate" still remained.

By May 1990, it was obvious that the Frelimo government desperately wanted peace, and was ready to grant further concession to Renamo. The first direct talks between Renamo and the government took place in July 1990, in Rome. Renamo was represented by the deputy leader, Raul Domingos, while the Minister of Transportation and Communication, Lieutenant-General Armando Gebuza, represented the government. The meeting was considered successful, and the Italian deputy, Mario Raffaelli, who monitored the talks, too, expressed satisfaction.[71] In fact, so elated were the feelings that fundamental issues like the integration of the two armies were slated for the next round of talks. A second meeting, held in August 1990, also received commendation from both sides, as the communique issued in Rome after the talks described the deliberation as a "fruitful and illuminating exchange of ideas" and that "it deepened the spirit of mutual understanding and respect" established during the first meeting.[72]

The envisaged third meeting had to be postponed, due to technical disagreement over the continuation of war while the peace initiative was on. Shortly before the third meeting was supposed to begin, government troops launched an assault on the Renamo base at Gorongosa. Renamo thus used this as an excuse for backing out from further talks, while the Frelimo government argued that, since Renamo had refused to discuss cease-fire before all other political issues have been resolved, continuation of the war should not be cited as a reason for discontinuing the peace talks. The meeting eventually took place in November, and on 1 December 1990, a partial cease-fire was announced. It was initially restricted to the two vital trade routes — Beira and Maputo corridors — which link Mozambique to hinterland states. Also included in the terms was the restriction of the activities of Zimbabwean troops to 1.8 miles on either sides of the railway lines of the corridors. An International Joint Verification Commission (JVC) was set up to monitor the agreement.

As expected, the partial ceasefire did not work. Although, the Zimbabwean army completed movement to the demarcated location well ahead of deadline, Renamo attacks continued with raids on towns like Chimoio, Motasse and Beira. Attempts were also made to destroy rail links and oil pipelines in Beira.[73] On its part, Renamo disputed the claims that Zimbabwean troops had withdrawn, arguing that many of them stayed on wearing Mozambican army uniforms. The JVC confirmed Frelimo's claim that at least 8 of the 14 allegations of cease-fire violations by Renamo are true. However, the commission claimed that there was no evidence found to support Renamo's allegations that the Zimbabwean army remained in the demarcated region.[74]

Some major conclusions were reached at the eighth round of talks in Rome in October 1991, and "Protocol Number 1 on Fundamental Principle" was signed. This could be described as "a framework for mutual guarantee". Renamo recognised the Frelimo government's legitimacy, and agreed to start operating as a political party. The government was, however, not launched into any feeling of euphoria with the signing of the protocol.[75]

While the Rome peace initiative continues, the SADCC made an attempt to broker a peace meeting between the warring sides. The SADCC chairman, President Mugabe, met with Alfonso Dhalakhama in Gaborone, Botswana, in July 1992. Also present at the meeting were the Botswana President, Sir Ketumule Masire, and Tiny Rowland, chairman of Lonrho multinational, who had promised his shareholders earlier in the year that he would bring peace to Mozambique before the end of 1992.[76] At the meeting, Dhalakhama agreed to a ceasefire, provided the government assured Renamo of amnesty.[77] He also agreed to meet President Chissano personally to discuss the future of the country. Chissano initially refused making his position public, until he had met Mugabe. After the meeting, however, he agreed to meet Dhalakhama,[78] and in August 1992, the two of them met for the first time in Rome.

The process of getting an agreement out of the meeting was particularly difficult, but after three days, "the convergence of self-interest and complex diplomatic pressures" resulted in the signing of an agreement between Dhalakhama and Chissano.[79] At the August meeting, it was envisaged that the peace agreement would be formally signed in October 1992, and that an all-party election would take place in October 1993. Some military issues remained outstanding, especially as regards the composition of the new national army, and the Renamo military chief, Lt. Gen. Herminio Morais, and the head of the Mozambican National Army, Lt. Gen Tobias Thai, were mandated to sort these out. On 15 October 1992, a Peace Agreement was formally signed between Alfonso Dhalakhama of Renamo and the Frelimo President of Mozambique, Joachim Chissano.

The situation in Mozambique appears peaceful but slippery. The peace agreement signed in Rome still appears to be holding, although some of the basic terms of the agreement like the demobilisation of troops as the formation of a new national army are yet to be completed. In December 1992, the United Nation Security Council voted unanimously to establish a UN Peace-Keeping Force — named UNOMOZ — in Mozambique. It is composed of five self-sufficient infantry battalions of 850 men each, as well as an engineer battalion, three logistic companies, a Headquarters Company and air, communications, medical and movement control units. Virtually all the roads and rail links in the country have been opened up, and sub-regional trade with neighbouring countries has started.

The main problem facing the peace process in Mozambique, and one which could derail the entire process, is the availability of funds to carry out the peace-keeping initiative. The entire operation has proved particularly expensive, as what has to be achieved is not only an immediate peace, but also minimum socio-economic infrastructures to ensure that the country does not revert to war after the departure of

UNOMOZ. Considering the fact that 17 years of civil war has destroyed virtually all the infrastructure of the country, the financial implications of this could be imagined. Although there have been impressive pledges, a significant percentage of them has not been received. This has resulted in a situation where the Mozambican election has been postponed from October 1993 to October 1994. This in itself means additional expenses, but it was considered inevitable against the background of the slow and difficult process of bringing peace to Mozambique.

4 Anti-Government Forces in Zimbabwe: ZIPRA Dissidents and Muzorewa Auxiliaries

The groups that emerged as the dissident forces in Zimbabwe differ from UNITA and Renamo in a number of ways. First, unlike these other organisations, the Zimbabwe dissidents never had an identifiable leadership nor any publicised plans (no matter how incoherent) for a post-crisis Zimbabwe. In fact, they never declared any intention of wanting to replace the Mugabe administration. Second, no parity or near parity existed between them and the government forces — either in terms of weapons or men under arms. Third, and possibly because of their numerical inferiority, the dissidents neither challenged the government forces in an open military operation nor did they have any geographical portion of the country they could call their zone of control. Although there were areas where, for a number of reasons, they enjoyed support, this was nothing near what could be described as a liberated zone. All these ultimately made the Zimbabwean dissidents more a security than a military threat to the Mugabe government. Beyond these, however, the anti-government forces in Zimbabwe did display some of the activities that gave particular coloration to dissident operations in Angola and Mozambique.

The anti-government forces in Zimbabwe may be divided into two major groups. These were the former members of the Zimbabwe People's Revolutionary Army (ZIPRA), the armed wing of Joshua Nkomo's Zimbabwe African People's Union (ZAPU); and the Auxiliary force — the force created to sustain the short-lived

Muzorewa administration in power, but disbanded immediately after independence by the Mugabe government. For different, and in some cases conflicting, reasons, these two groups found causes to challenge the Mugabe administration in a dissident operation between 1982 and 1987. Like in Angola and Mozambique, the Zimbabwean dissident crisis, too, had its roots in the country's history, as the reasons exploited by the dissident forces and the prevailing circumstances that created and sustained the unrest were largely legacies of the country's war of liberation.

It is difficult to get at all the reasons why ex-ZIPRA soldiers took up arms against their ZANLA comrades, with whom they had fought the liberation war and formed the first government of the country. But it is possible to identify some of the factors which underlay this decision. The first, which could be considered as the root cause, dated back to the period of the liberation war, during which both ZANU and ZAPU saw each other more as rivals, than as comrades dedicated to the termination of the white minority regime in their country. This rivalry and tension which extended to the military wings of both parties could not be effectively resolved throughout the period of the liberation war, and they served as the foundation of post-independence problems.

Developments after the Lancaster House Agreement (where the cease-fire and the subsequent constitution that gave birth to Zimbabwe were agreed) inflamed the ZANU/ZAPU tension. Since 1976, ZANU and ZAPU had, under pressure from the OAU and the Frontline States, formed the Patriotic Front alliance. The alliance presented a joint front at the 1977 Geneva talks on Rhodesia and at the Lancaster House Conference in 1979, although, underneath, deep divisions still existed between the two parties. The presentation of a united front at these two talks was interpreted by ZAPU, as well as many of the people in Matabeleland, to mean that the two parties would fight the independence election together.[1] This is now considered curious because the alliance was accomplished with considerable difficulties in the first instance, and even during the conferences in Geneva and London, there were no sufficient indications that the differences between both sides had been overcome to the extent of contesting an election on a single ticket. What, perhaps, appeared more curious was the belief some Ndebele people had that Mugabe would serve as Nkomo's deputy under the joint ticket. Shortly after the Lancaster House Agreement, however, ZANU announced its intention to fight the election separately, to the obvious dislike of many ZAPU members.[2]

The immediate post-independence situation in Zimbabwe brought to the fore a number of contentious issues, whose handling inevitably inflamed the tension. First, the Mugabe government was confronted with the task of integrating the three armed units that fought in the war of liberation (ZANLA, ZIPRA, and the Rhodesian army) into a new national army.[3] This was one of the terms of the Lancaster House Agreement. Perhaps more than any other single factor, ZIPRA's objection to some of the steps the government took during the formation of the new national army, as well as the developments that took place in the army after its creation, contributed most to the decision of some of the guerrillas to embark on dissident activities.

ZIPRA's first objection arose from the belief that some of its units were not considered for integration into the new national armed forces. These wings, according to ZIPRA, were the intelligence wing and the air force. ZIPRA (and almost implicitly, ZAPU) believed that ZANU used its power as the party in government to punish ZAPU and its armed wing on the issue of the creation of the new Zimbabwean National Army (ZNA).[4] The ZIPRA elements who eventually got into the army further alleged that ZANU and its ZANLA found it more convenient to move closer to the former Rhodesian army than with ZIPRA.[5] This marked the beginning of tension which was later to underline the dissident crisis.

Another development which gave ZIPRA members cause for concern was the way the initial promotion exercise in the army was handled by the government. ZIPRA's belief during the liberation war was that its training was largely geared along conventional lines, and that they were better conventional soldiers than their ZANLA counterparts. All these gave ZIPRA the impression that, in any conversion from guerrilla to conventional soldiery, they, irrespective of political considerations, should at least be given equal treatment in the command and control structure of the new army. Many even argued that, if political considerations should be used at all in the allocation of command positions in the army, it should not be so glaring as to make non-ZANLA members of the army feel irrelevant.[6] In short, ZIPRA believed that political consideration played a greater role than professionalism in the creation of the ZNA.

The statistical facts of the case seem to support ZIPRA's allegation that the officer cadre of the ZNA was not evenly distributed. Although the British Military Advisory and Training Team (BMATT) handled the integration exercise, the appointment of the first crop of officers was largely influenced by the government. Of the 29 officers commissioned in April 1981 to mark the beginning of the "Zimbabweanisation" of the officer cadre, ZANLA's dominance was glaring. Although, there was a sort of parity at the apex — with the former ZANLA and ZIPRA commanders, Rex Nhongo (later to become Solomon Mujuru) and the late Lookout Masuku, becoming lieutenant generals, and their deputies, Josiah Tungamirai and Javan Maseko, being made major generals — the set of new brigadiers and colonels were in favour of ZANLA, as it had five of the eight brigadiers and 11 of the 17 new colonels.[7] A closely related complaint was the partiality ZIPRA alleged was taking place in favour of ZANLA over the issue of foreign training. Some of them alleged, for example, that more ZANLA officers were sent abroad for training, while there were again allegations that officers selected for training in the country's new Army Staff College were mostly from the ZANLA ranks. For example, some of them alleged that when some ZIPRA officers "failed" an examination for selection into the Zimbabwe Army Staff College, they were replaced by ex-ZANLA officers.[8]

The government's decision to create a special brigade of the army (known as the 5th Brigade) introduced yet another complication. This brigade, which was composed almost exclusively of former ZANLA guerrillas, was trained by the North Koreans, and it received preferential treatment from the government. There were some reasons why the ex-ZIPRAs in the army felt uncomfortable with the creation of the 5th Brigade. First was the exclusivity of the membership. Second, North Korea, which trained the brigade, had supported ZANU during the liberation war. Thus, it was easy to predict the possible use of the brigade. Third, the prevailing political conditions in the country at the time of the creation were such that predicted anti-ZAPU assignment for the new brigade, more so when President Mugabe made it clear that the brigade was created — among other reasons — to deal with politicians who, having lost the election, were resorting to banditry.[9] All these gave former ZIPRA combatants the belief that there must be something ominous about the 5th Brigade, a belief which was further heightened by the local name of the brigade, *Gukurahundi*.[10] ZIPRA's final complaint was on the demobilization exercise carried out at the end of the military integration, which they argued was biased in favour of

ZANLA.[11] True, while statistics may support more ZANLA compulsorily demobilised, proportional representation gives a different picture.

It was thus obvious that, during the first year of independence, ZIPRA guerrillas in the national army had complaints against the government. The ethno-political set-up in the country was such that many Ndebele people, too, shared this belief, as they argued that Prime Minister Mugabe did not do for the Ndebeles as much as he did to achieve reconciliation with the whites. True, it was actually the case that Mugabe did far more to mend fences with the whites than with the Ndebeles, but this would appear more an effort to woo the whites who still controlled the economy and to assure them of their continued safety under the new dispensation, than to treat the Ndebeles marginally.

The differences between ZANU and ZAPU started to appear not long after independence. For example, in a speech to parliament on 26 June 1980, Prime Minister Mugabe accused ZIPRA (and almost implicitly, ZAPU) of undermining his government. This charge was officially denied by Nkomo, who, in turn, accused the ZANU government of being responsible for "atrocities worse than any committed by the [Smith] regime".[12] Nkomo made another attack on 12 August 1980, when he alleged that a complete train-load of ZANLA arms brought in from Mozambique disappeared overnight after arriving in Zimbabwe. This was later denied by the government. Although, nothing came out of these accusations and counter accusations, they point to the fact that, as early as June 1980, relations between the two parties in the coalition government had gone sour, and that an open manifestation of this disagreement was just a matter of time.

The ZANLA/ZIPRA tension reached its first peak in November 1980, when an armed clash occurred between the two wings. In some ways, this may be taken as the first major crack that was to lead to the dissident activities. More clashes were to occur later, such that, during the first year of independence, there were at least five such occurrences, resulting in the death of about 500 people and more than 1000 injured.[13] The last of these clashes, which took place in February 1981, in Entumbanne, has major relevance to the dissident operation that started the following year. This makes a brief story of this clash worth recording here. By the end of 1980, only about 15,000 of the estimated 65,000 guerrillas had been trained, while the rest remained in the assembly points with their arms. The Joint High Command (JHC) that was responsible for the integration exercise then decided to transfer the untrained guerrillas from their cramped camps to low-cost housing schemes near Harare and Bulawayo. Conflict, however, broke out among the ranks of the guerrillas taken to Bulawayo. When the clash became serious, ZIPRA forces in Essexvalle (later to be renamed Esigodini) moved out of their camps to offer assistance to their colleagues who were in revolt in Bulawayo. Armed Personnel Carriers and other heavy equipment were used in this march to Bulawayo. The Prime Minister then had to use white-led troops to quell the riots, and in the process, some of the ZIPRA armoured vehicles were destroyed and about 200 people were killed.[14] While not supporting the use of white-led forces, many ZAPU and ZIPRA leaders, especially Nkomo, Lookout Masuku (the former ZIPRA Commander) and Dumiso Dabengwa (the former ZIPRA Head of Security) all used their influence to pacify the rioting ZIPRA combatants.

All the armed clashes that occurred had two major connections with the dissident operation that later engulfed Zimbabwe. First, it led to the first major ZIPRA desertion from the national army. Although these people did not immediately resort to dissident activities, they remained deeply opposed to the developments in the army and in the country. The second impact was on those who stayed on in the army after the unrest. To this group of people, the forceful suppression of the revolt by the government showed them the extent to which the government was ready to go in suppressing rebellion in the army. Having thus realised the dangers and consequences inherent in protest, some incensed ex-ZIPRAs stayed on in the national army, waiting perhaps for an opportunity to get out of the army and demonstrate the anti-government sentiments that were bottled up in them.[15]

Apart from ex-ZIPRA combatants, the other group of people that took part in Zimbabwe's dissident crisis were members of the Security Force Auxiliaries, disbanded by the Mugabe administration shortly after independence. It would appear that the basic reason why this group took up arms was because of the government's decision not to consider them for integration into the new national army. Thus, these people, most of whom still retained their arms, waited for ways in which they could be relevant to those who did not wish the Mugabe administration well. Some of them got employment with the South African Defence Force (SADF), where they took part in activities against the

Zimbabwean government, while others stayed until the outbreak of the dissident operation when they took to the bush.

Any attempt to understand the causes and course of the dissident activities in Zimbabwe must consider the prevailing social and economic situation in the country on the eve of the outbreak of the dissident operation. Although, the liberation war had ended, some of the issues the war was fought to redress were still in place. Foremost among these was the land issue. The Lancaster House Agreement had stipulated that pre-independence land distribution should remain as it was for a period of time. This left many Zimbabweans disappointed, a feeling that was particularly pronounced in the Matabele province, where the pre-independence racial distribution of land was more disproportionate.[16] There were other cases where the expectations of independence appeared unfulfilled, as many blacks expected rapid "Zimbabweanisation" of all the facets of life, without considering the fact that the system the government inherited had been the basis for running the government for almost a century, and as such, called for gradual and tactful removal. This economic situation was particularly significant, as some of those who took part in the dissident operation did so largely for economic reasons.

In short, it could be seen that there were many groups of disenchanted people in Zimbabwe who would not hesitate to use any opportunity available to them to express their objection to some of the political and military policies of the Mugabe administration. Apart from the ex-ZIPRA combatants and Muzorewa Auxiliaries, there were also common criminals to whom the new order was anathema, either because they expected too much from independence and thus believed that the government was not doing enough, or because their social attitude motivated such negative tendencies. All that these groups of people were thus waiting for was an opportunity to express their pent-up emotion. This came with the arms cache controversy.

The Countdown: The arms cache controversy and the outbreak of violence

The ultimate catalyst for the dissident operation in Zimbabwe came with the controversy that surrounded the discovery of arms in some areas of the Matabele province of the country. This discovery and the reactions that followed it brought together all the pent-up emotions discussed earlier, and later triggered off dissident activities in

ZIMBABWE

Zimbabwe. The government announced the discovery of the caches in February 1982, although it is possible that the actual discovery was made much earlier.[17] The bulk of the arms was discovered on two sites — Ascot farm, near Bulawayo, and Hampton ranch, in the midlands, not far from Gweru.[18] Both sites were owned by a private firm called Nitram, which ZAPU had set up shortly after independence. Many ZIPRA guerrillas who were demobilised from the army had invested their gratuities into these projects, while many of them took up employment in these and other ZAPU-sponsored projects after independence.

Government's reaction to the announcement of the alleged discovery was swift. Nkomo and some ZAPU ministers — Josiah Chinamano, Joseph Msika, and Jim Mtuta — were removed from their posts and dismissed from the government.[19] Two weeks after this clampdown, two former ZIPRA leaders, Lt.-General Lookout Masuku, (who was then the deputy commander of the ZNA) and Dumiso Dabengwa, were arrested and detained, while all the properties owned by ZAPU were also confiscated, irrespective of whether arms were found on them or not.[20] The government alleged that ZAPU was planning a coup, and that Nkomo and Peter Walls (the former commander of the Rhodesian army then living in South Africa after his expulsion from Zimbabwe) were making joint contacts with South Africa to overthrow Mugabe.[21] It was further alleged that the arrested ZIPRA leaders had been recruiting guerrillas for secret training in South Africa and had also been in contact with the KGB of the Soviet Union to plan action against the Mugabe government. It should be mentioned that, at this time, the relationship between the Soviet Union and the Mugabe government was not particularly cordial, due largely to the role Moscow played in the Zimbabwean liberation war.[22]

In its reaction to the government's allegations, the ZAPU Central Committee declared that it was "dismayed" by the government's attempt to "build a case" against the party. The Committee claimed that the administration of the army and the responsibility for the former combatants and their weapons lay with the Joint High Command which the government had set up, and not with any political party. ZAPU also claimed that the sites on which the arms were found were not owned by the party perse, but by a co-operative union established after independence by the former combatants of the party.[23]

Neither Nkomo nor ZAPU actually denied that arms might have

been found on some of the sites. However, the party argued that both ZIPRA and ZANLA cached arms after independence.[24] Nkomo personally denied having any knowledge of the sites ZIPRA used for its caches, but argued that, if the two major sites (Ascot and Hampton) were parts of the sites used, then the government, or (as some ex-ZIPRA believed) members of the former Rhodesian Intelligence, had transported more arms to the caches in order to present a misleading impression that ZAPU was planning a large scale war. To prove the case for freeing the arrested ZIPRA commanders, the former ZIPRA Liaison Officer, Brigadier Charles Grey, argued in court that ZIPRA soldiers sometimes disobey orders, thus, it was possible that they took the law into their hands by caching the arms.[25] In the end, the two men were ordered to be released for lack of evidence, but they were immediately re-detained under the emergency powers laws.[26]

The government specifically held Dumiso Dabengwa responsible for being the coordinator of the caching process. Mugabe accused him of having connived with the Zambian government to ensure that the ZIPRA arms being transferred from the country to Zimbabwe were handed over to ZAPU, instead of to the government which then controlled the national security.[27] It was for this reason that the government decided to hold on to Dabengwa, despite the court's instruction that he should be free. The government claimed that it had withheld certain information from the court for "security reasons", and that it was on the basis of this that Dabengwa was re-detained.[28] In an interview with me, Dumiso Dabengwa denied emphatically the allegation of any complicity in the arms cache. The government did not give any reason for the continued detention of Lookout Masuku. It is thus possible that he was a victim of the Zimbabwean equivalent of the then prevailing "common purpose" syndrome.

The ex-ZIPRA guerrillas had only one interpretation for all the government's reactions to the arms cache controversy: that they were designed to make ZAPU scapegoats and avenge old disagreements on them, all with the grand design of consolidating ZANU power in the country. The decision to confiscate ZAPU properties and freeze its accounts was particularly difficult for ZAPU members to accept, as it meant a loss of investment (for those who had shares in the companies) or loss of jobs (for those working on the farms). Many argued that the confiscation of these properties across the board was unjustified, especially as arms were discovered on only two of them. All this accumulated disenchantment resulted in mass desertion from the army. This was considered as the only viable option left, as the Entumbanne experience had shown them the dangers inherent in protesting from within the army. A dissident option became all the more attractive since the dismissal and detention that followed the discovery of the arms caches had provided a disenchanted operational base. This disenchanted base was also exploited by the Muzorewa auxiliary force and other groups who believed they had an axe to grind with the Mugabe government. The Zimbabwe dissident operation had taken off.

The dissidents' actions and the government's reactions
The dissident activities started in the early months of 1982,[29] and were concentrated largely on Matabeleland, as well as some areas of Zimbabwe midlands. The dissidents embarked on an extensive campaign of murder, mutilation, rape, and other acts of terrorism. The initial targets were ZANU party leaders in Matabeleland, and between September 1983 and May 1984, 32 top ZANU officials in Matabeleland were killed.[30] However, as time went on, and as participants in the dissidence became more diversified, they became less discriminatory in their selection.

It is ironical, however, that beyond their anti-government activities, the various groups that took part in the Zimbabwean dissident activities lacked common aims. The ZIPRA deserters had the main aim of forcing the government to comply with some demands. These demands were basically three: (a) the return of ZAPU property confiscated in the wake of the arms cache controversy; (b) the release of Dumiso Dabengwa and Lookout Masuku from detention and (c) the reinstatement of Nkomo and others dismissed from government. These were the advertised demands, but it is likely that some of them would also want a situation where ZANLA's influence in the new national army would be reduced. The Muzorewa Auxiliaries (who for some unknown reason were called Super-ZAPU) had no declared aim. It is possible that, beyond embarrassing the government, some of them would prefer a situation where they would be incorporated into the army. The third category of dissidents — the common criminals — had no known objective beyond tormenting the people and possibly getting the next meal.

This lack of common purpose affected the relationship between the dissidents — especially the ZIPRA dissidents and the former

Auxiliaries — so much so that they were occasionally engulfed in skirmishes when they met in the bush. For example, the ex-ZIPRA dissidents claimed that they objected to the auxiliaries flirting with South Africa — a country they considered as the enemy of the Zimbabwean state. It is not clear whether this was a pretext for giving their own activities an ideological focus or a genuine intention of not having anything to do with South Africa. However, some of them claimed that the weapons they used for their dissident activities were actually seized from the Auxiliary branch of dissidents.[31] There were allegations that members of the national army took part in the dissident activities.[32] The alleged aim of the security forces, in this regard, was to tarnish the image of ZAPU, and thus justify the repressive response of the army in quelling the unrest. It is however fair to add that all the senior army officers with whom I talked denied this allegation.

The sources of the weapons used by the dissidents depended on the group to which they belonged. The largest group (the disaffected ZIPRA) got their weapons mainly from undiscovered caches as well as weapons seized from the armoury after the dissident operation took off. They also made use of arms captured from the Super-ZAPU, who, in turn, used un-surrendered arms and those obtained from South Africa. The third group — common criminals — used the arms they kept back after the war and other easily available weapons like machetes, knives,[33] etc. The members of the security forces (if indeed they took part) could have easily used their official arms.

The action of the dissidents which brought them to international attention was the kidnapping, in July 1982, of ten foreign tourists in Bulawayo province. The victims were touring the Victoria Falls with a London Safari group called Encounter Overland, when the dissidents waved them to a stop at a road block in Nyamandlove, about 80 kilometres from Bulawayo. They were herded at gun point into the bush. The tour leader was later released, with a ransom note signed by "ZIPRA forces", demanding, in return for the tourists' safety, the reinstatement of ZAPU property and the release of the detained ZIPRA leaders. The three women in the group, too, were later released, but the dissidents held on to the remaining six — two each from Britain, America and Australia. A combined army and police search was mounted a few hours after the ambush with reconnaissance planes, helicopters, ground-troopers to scour the dense forest. A reward of Z$10,000 (later raised to Z$20,000) was offered to any one who could give any information leading to the location and safe release of the hostages. Taped messages appealing to the dissidents to release the tourists were aired on all the channels of the Zimbabwean Broadcasting Corporation in the Shona, Sindebele and English languages. The government refused to negotiate any deal with the dissidents, and the tourists were consequently killed.[34]

Similarly, in August 1982, three British tourists were killed in Nyanga — another holiday resort in Zimbabwe. As in the case of the six tourists, the ZIPRA dissidents claimed responsibility for the incident. However, the most bizarre activity of the dissidents was the Esigodoni massacre in which 16 white missionaries were killed. This was the most brutal anti-white violence in Zimbabwe. The murder was attributed to a man called Morgan, but widely known as Gayigusu.[35] Another major case of white murder during the dissident activities was that of a Republican Front Senator, Paul Savage, his daughter Colleen, and a family visitor from Britain, Sandra Bennett. Mrs Savage was seriously wounded, when about 20 armed dissidents attacked their house on 4 April 1984.[36]

These cases of white murder may lead one to a wrong assumption that part of the dissidents' intention was to avenge pre-independence wrongs by the white minority in the country. However, there seems to be no concrete evidence to support this assumption. The anti-white sentiments expressed during the dissident activities should be seen more as the manifestation of general insecurity in the country than of retaliation for old wounds. This position becomes all the more plausible when one considers the fact that some of the whites killed were visitors, some possibly visiting Zimbabwe for the first time. The few white victims attacked by the dissidents were chosen largely with intent to blackmail the government. The dissidents saw the whites as the Achilles heel which could be exploited to make the government comply with their demands. They realised the importance which the Mugabe government gave (for economic and public relations purposes) to the security of the whites. Thus, blackmailing the government along that direction was considered expedient, more so as it put the government in a no-win situation: the government could either agree to their demands and their victims would be spared, or their victims would be killed to show the world that, contrary to the impression the government might want to create, all was not well with Zimbabwe.

Between 1 February 1982 and 13 March 1986, police reports gave stunning figures of 7,313 acts of vandalism. Of these, 1,136 were reported in the months of March and August 1982.[37] But still, these figures could be wide of the mark, as many people would prefer the long prison sentence (the punishment for refusing to give information about the whereabouts of the dissidents) to being marked down for retribution by the dissidents.[38]

The military operation during the unrest was a replay of the military tactics of the liberation war, but this time with roles reversed. In one of the bitter ironies of Zimbabwean politics, it became the turn of the new Zimbabwean army to adopt the military strategies of their erstwhile enemies (the Rhodesian army) against former comrades; while the dissidents went back to the tactics they had adopted against the Rhodesian army during the liberation war. The first strategy adopted by the dissidents was to blend into areas where they found themselves accepted. In fact, most of them went back to the areas where they had operated during the liberation war and exploited the prevailing disillusionment to forge a fairly coherent political opposition. Another military operation which brought back memories of the liberation war was the timing of the dissidents' offensives, which were mostly carried out during the rainy season. This was akin to the guerrilla strategy during the liberation war when they took the advantage of the green vegetation to launch attacks. Thus, as the Rhodesian army had to contend with increased guerrilla attacks during the period, the Zimbabwean National Army had to cope with increased dissident operations.

All these made the government forces resort to some of the old strategies of the Rhodesian army. For instance, the idea of placing an entire area under curfew for alleged support for the dissidents was an exact replay of the Rhodesian army's punitive measure for supporting the guerrilla cause. Also, the government troops reactivated what, during the liberation war was called "Pseudo Operation". Under this practice, the Rhodesian army impersonated the guerrillas and begged for food and assistance from the local populace. If these were granted, the soldiers would come back few hours later to punish the people for assisting the guerrilla cause. Thus, the army which came to contain the dissident operations in Matabeleland used this method to find out those supporting the dissidents.

It is difficult to differentiate the activities of the "Super-ZAPU" (ex-Muzorewa Auxiliaries) from those of the ZIPRA dissidents. In fact, beyond the difference in name, it made no difference either to the government or the force that was sent to contain the unrest. The Matabele people also found it difficult to distinguish between the two groups, even though the style of operation made it possible for the civilians to separate the two groups from the common criminals, whose only motive was to rob in order to obtain food and money for daily survival.[39]

The government saw the entire dissident activities through one prism, and this was that they were sponsored by Nkomo and other ZAPU members who felt aggrieved by the government's reaction to the arms cache episode. This position could be seen in virtually all the statements made by the Prime Minister in parliament during the period of the dissident operation.[40] This introduced the first question into the Matabeleland crisis: to what extent was the ZAPU leadership responsible for the activities of the dissidents? The government believed that ZAPU and ZIPRA leaders, especially Nkomo and Dabengwa, had some form of authority and control over most of the dissidents, and the government's attitude to these people, especially Dabengwa, was guided by this belief. It is worth noting, however, that the government had no reliable evidence to link either of the two men to the dissident operation.[41] Even now, the degree of the exact influence of Nkomo and/or Dabengwa on the dissidents can not be proven. There is a thinking which might lead one into a quick belief that such influence existed. This is that the dissident activities started soon after the ZAPU leaders were punished over the arms cache and ended when they were re-integrated into national politics. However, this argument misses the point, as it trivialises the multiplicity of factors that triggered the crisis. Before the dismissal of the ZAPU leaders, there were pent-up emotions, and the arms cache only provided a pretext and a disenchanted operational base for the expression of these emotions. The fact that the activities ended after Nkomo and others were reintegrated into national politics could also be attributed to one or two possibilities: either the incorporation pacified the noted disenchantment the dissidents had exploited among the Ndebeles, or the dissidents were genuinely impressed by the Unity Agreement and wanted to give peace a chance in the country.

Another belief the government held throughout the dissident activities was that the Ndebele people gave the dissidents succour and assistance in their actions against the government. This belief was based on the argument that the dissidence could not have taken place in a vacuum. This is somewhat controversial. It is possible that many people in Matabeleland assisted the dissidents. For ethnic reasons and possibly because of the belief in their cause, many Ndebele people could have supported the dissidents' cause. This, however, does not translate to a support for their methods. Besides, it was, indeed, the case that many of the dissidents obtained food and other materials for survival from the local people, but more often than not, most of these were obtained by force.[42] This is voluntary and coerced domestic support apart, the Zimbabwean dissidents were also beneficiaries of South African support.

The Pretoria Connection

In Zimbabwe, the two anti-government forces (Muzorewa auxiliaries and ex-ZIPRA guerrillas) received South African support, though in varying degrees. The link between South Africa and the Muzorewa auxiliary force is a fairly long one, as Pretoria had supported Ian Smith's initiative that resulted in the "transfer" of power to Muzorewa as the Prime Minister of Zimbabwe-Rhodesia. When the initiative collapsed, and the Lancaster House Agreement ordered a fresh election, South Africa gave Bishop Muzorewa financial support for his campaign. After independence, many members of the auxiliary force, possibly out of fear for their security, fled to South Africa. The exact number is not known, as Western sources put it at 1,500,[43] although President Mugabe said they were up to 5,000.[44] These people stayed on in South Africa until the time was ripe to be used against Zimbabwe.

For a long time, the possibility of South Africa's involvement in the arms cache controversy that eventually ignited the dissident crisis was not considered. It has, however, been suggested in Paul Moorcraft's recent study that South African agents then working in the Zimbabwean Criminal Investigation Organisation (CIO), might have encouraged the cache in 1980, only to tip off the government later to precipitate a civil war.[45] Dumiso Dabengwa, who was allegedly in the centre of this crisis also mentioned that the CIO performed a most discreditable role in the arms cache controversy.[46]

David Martin and Phyllis Johnson have provided detailed accounts of how South Africa exploited the dissident problem to destabilise Zimbabwe.[47] The South African support was through the provision of financial and military support for the dissidents. The military assistance was provided in camps in North Transvaal. Further indisputable proof came from captured dissidents who confirmed that they received military training from Mandumbo and Gumbo along the Limpopo river. Like Charles van Nierkerk in Mozambique, Malcolm (Mat) Calloway became a recurring name in South African links with the Zimbabwean dissidents. Calloway was a former member of the Rhodesian Police Special Branch, who, while with the Rhodesian CIO, worked at Dett, where he was responsible for organising assembly points for ZIPRA guerrillas returning from the bush as part of the Lancaster House Agreement. The close contact formed during this period was allegedly employed to recruit dissidents. When his double dealing was discovered, he escaped to South Africa, where he was placed in charge of recruiting disaffected ex-ZIPRA guerrillas for the South African destabilization of Zimbabwe.[48] The Pretoria regime was later forced (by the depth of information at the disposal of the Zimbabwean government) to acknowledge association with Calloway.

There was also Kevin Woods, who, like Calloway, stayed behind after independence to work for the Zimbabwean CIO as a Senior Administrative Officer in Matabeleland. His main duty here was to prepare intelligence reports on the threats posed by the dissidents for the Prime Minister. He started spying for South Africa in 1983 but was caught in 1988.[49] Again, as in Mozambique, South Africa was alleged to have organised a radio station transmitting anti-government propaganda into Zimbabwe.

Unlike in Mozambique, it appeared South Africa did not attempt to exploit Zimbabwe's economic dependence to assist the dissident cause. True, South Africa threatened Zimbabwe with the withdrawal of locomotives on loan and the abrogation of the preferential trade arrangements between the two countries, but these threats were before the outbreak of the dissident activities in Matabeleland and they were not carried out in full force. It would, perhaps, have been more difficult for Zimbabwe to handle the dissident problems if Pretoria had compounded it with the exploitation of Zimbabwe's economic dependence on South Africa. Armed with all these perceptions of the crisis, the government reacted to the dissident activities. The reaction took different forms — army sweeps, curfews, and detention. All these resulted in enormous human rights violations and, more than any issue in post-independence Zimbabwe, brought the government to the tribunal of international opinion.

The fighting elephants and the suffering grass: Matabele people in the cross-fire

> We were like a beast between two carnivores. One carnivore was the army, and they ate us from the front. The other carnivore was the dissidents and they ate us from the back. We had nothing left but our bones. (A peasant farmer at Matopo Mission of Matabeleland, as quoted by Terence Ranger).[50]

The main part of the government's military activities against the dissidents was carried out by the 5th Brigade of the National Army. This brigade, as noted earlier, was dominated by former ZANLA combatants.[51] It has now been alleged, with some justification, that the 5th Brigade carried out their operation in Matabeleland with such remarkable ruthlessness that it bordered on genocide. It would appear that the brigade considered everybody in Matabeleland as dissidents, or supporters of dissidents, as there were many allegations of grave atrocities levelled against members of the brigade. These include rape, flogging, and murder. The typical sequence of operations of the brigade upon arrival in any village begins with bringing out the list of army deserters — described by the Ndebele people as the "death list". The refusal or inability of the people to provide satisfactory details as to the whereabouts of these people attracted punishment from the brigade, and many people were believed to have been killed in the process.[52] Many also argued that, apart from the brutality, the brigade members used their actions as a cover to promote party political support, as the soldiers were said to have demanded to see ZANU membership cards, and those who could provide them were left untouched. This was, however, denied by the former members of the 5th Brigade.[53]

The government on its part argued that sending the 5th Brigade was the most effective way of handling the crisis, as the use of other brigades could result in ex-ZIPRAs from these brigades having to fight against their colleagues who had deserted the army. Another action that caused considerable hardship for the civilians was the curfew imposed by the government. This was enforced in such a way that shops were not opened and ill people could not receive medical attention. Many people were also believed to have lost their lives as a result of this policy.

The extent to which the government supported the activities of the 5th Brigade is not clear. The former Minister of National Security, Sydney Sekeremayi, did not rule out the possibility of some soldiers getting overzealous, and as a result, maltreating civilians. Implicit in this, however, is that such people were not carrying out the government's instructions. The former President, Canaan Banana, while also not ruling out maltreatment, added that neither he (as the President and the Commander-in-Chief of the Armed Forces), nor Prime Minister Mugabe, who was also the Defence Minister, ordered that civilians should be maltreated.[54] He also told me that the repressive activities were carried out without their knowledge, and that when such came to their notice, they were immediately rectified.[55]

Despite these official denials, many people believed that, while the government may not have given the brigade direct instructions to carry out their activities, it did not do much to discourage them either. Those who held this belief pointed to some of the remarks made by some ZANU party officials during the unrest — remarks which, they argued, could encourage overzealous members of the armed forces towards extremism. For example, a ZANU parliamentarian, Mr Nyazika, suggested that soldiers operating in Matabeleland should be given an extra "bush allowance".[56] Another name that figured prominently in this allegation of instigatory pronouncements was Enos Nkala, the then Minister of State for Defence and the most prominent Ndebele man in ZANU.[57]

As would be expected, parliament became the venue for the exchange of heated arguments, often bordering on verbal abuse between ZANU and ZAPU members, with the white members taking sides with ZAPU. While ZANU accused ZAPU of encouraging the dissidents and serving as their public relations platform, ZAPU, in turn, berated ZANU for unleashing the 5th Brigade and creating a reign of terror in Matabeleland. Nkomo was at the forefront of the effort to give publicity to the activities of the brigade, and he did this with some relentlessness before he had to flee the country.[58] In this attempt, however, he blundered on one occasion. In a press conference, he announced that soldiers from the 5th Brigade operating in Matabeleland had killed Mr Gumede, the former President of Zimbabwe-Rhodesia.

However, a few days later, Gumede came out safe and sound. This became the evidence used by the government to argue that some of the allegations levelled against the 5th Brigade excesses were inflated and untrue.

The handling of the Matabeleland unrest also attracted the attention of white parliamentarians, not the least of whom was Ian Smith, the former Prime Minister. This reaction went along a predictable line, with Ian Smith in particular, accusing the government of wrong handling of the crisis. He questioned the effectiveness — nay wisdom — of the military option the government adopted to what he saw largely as a political problem, and warned that the government was "making the mistake [he] made — solving a political problem with military means".[59] Another white parliamentarian who made comments that turned out to be most prophetic was Senator Oatt. In his speech to parliament on 15 March 1983, he suggested the withdrawal of the 5th Brigade from Matabeleland; the re-incorporation of ZAPU into government; and the granting of amnesty to the dissidents.[60] His words were quite prophetic: "strong arm tactics by the fifth brigade will only serve to exacerbate rather than cure the situation". All these suggestions which were berated at the time they were made were to be adopted by the government four years later.

Just as the unrest and the government's handling of it were getting critical reactions from home, observers outside Zimbabwe, too, became more concerned in the affairs of the country. In this regard, the Association of Catholic Bishops blazed the trail of criticism of the government's action with its international press conference. The bishops condemned the human rights violations that went along with the activities of the 5th Brigade and other clampdown measures adopted by the government in Matabeleland. The then Minister for Information, Nathan Shamuyariya, reacted by calling the press conference "irresponsible and propagandistic".[61] Prime Minister Mugabe called it a false allegation by a "sanctimonious prelate", while the journalists who gave it publicity were called "reactionary foreign journalists and a band of Jeremiahs".[62] There was domestic opposition as well. Senator Garfield Todd, a former Prime Minister and a respected voice of reason in Zimbabwe, gave a clear indictment of the activities of the soldiers in Matabeleland, when he said the way the government went about the Matabeleland problem had done no good to the country's image.[63] Nobody, not even the ZANU hardliners in the Senate, challenged him.[64] All these — especially the criticism from the bishops — had their impact on the government, as a few days after the comments, the 5th Brigade was withdrawn from Matabeleland, and its members were sent for re-training. This marked the beginning of efforts towards finding solution to the dissident problem.

The Unity Accord and the end of discord
It may be inaccurate to see the Unity Agreement signed between ZANU and ZAPU in December 1987 entirely against the background of the dissident activities that bedevilled the country in the preceding five years, as there had been some attempts (though not backed up with serious efforts) to unite the two parties shortly after independence. However, there can again be no doubt that the extent of the dissident activities served as a catalyst that speeded up the efforts to unite the two parties.

Concerted efforts to unite ZANU and ZAPU started around mid-1985, with both parties having different motives for this renewed attempt at mutual accommodation. The ruling ZANU party was getting concerned at the negative international image that the dissident problem was giving the country, and against the background of its belief that ZAPU had contacts with the dissidents, some form of unity with the party was considered desirable. Secondly, and on a wider consideration, ZANU might have wanted to start informal contact towards the eventual creation of a one-party state in the country. ZAPU, too, had some reasons for responding to the establishment of some form of unity with ZANU. First, was the activities of the army sent to Matabeleland. By 1985, it was clear to the Matabele people that the government was determined to keep the 5th Brigade in the region until the dissident operation stopped, and due to the hardship that had been their lot since the arrival of the brigade, the Matabele people were willing — quite easily — to find other solutions to the problem. A second reason was the desire of Nkomo and other ZAPU leaders to wash off the government's propaganda that they were anti-democratic, and that despite occasional denunciation of the dissident activities, they were actually seeking power through them.[65] Thus, ZANU and ZAPU went into the rounds of negotiations that ultimately resulted in the signing of the accord. A major role in bringing both sides together was played by Canaan Banana, the then President of the country.

The series of meetings that culminated in the signing of the Unity

Agreement started in September 1985. This inaugural meeting was chaired by President Canaan Banana, and it was attended by Simeon Muzenda and Maurice Nyagumbo for ZANU, and Joshua Nkomo, Joseph Msika, and Naison Ndolvu for ZAPU. The meeting agreed in principle that the two parties would unite, but even then a number of difficult issues were actually identified. To handle all the problems, a committee comprising equal number of members from both parties was set up. ZANU was represented by Maurice Nyagumbo, Emmerson Munangagwa, and Eddison Zvobgo,[66] while ZAPU was represented by Joshua Nkomo, Joseph Msika, and Naison Ndolvu.

This new committee again faced problems. The first was on the name the proposed merger party would adopt. Obviously, each of the parties wanted to ensure that its identity was not lost in the new name of the party, more so when this would be the quickest and most glaring way through which the people would know which of the parties had conceded more in the accord. ZANU wanted its name retained, on the grounds that it was the larger of the two parties, and that those who voted for it in the 1980 and 1985 elections would be unhappy at any change. While ZAPU never suggested that its name be adopted, it nevertheless, argued that the name ZAPU had historical significance as the original party from where ZANU broke off. Thus, any name the merger party would take should acknowledge this historical significance and have ZAPU incorporated into it. Equally linked to the issue of name was that of the party's emblem, which both sides wanted to ensure did not clearly show or presuppose the total domination of one over the other. After a most protracted debate, the two sides settled for the name "ZANU(PF)".[67] Perhaps not surprisingly, the issue of leadership was not contentious, as both agreed that Robert Mugabe should continue as the party leader.

The issue of the dissident activities expectedly came up for discussion during the unity negotiations. ZAPU had included in its proposal for unity the granting of amnesty for all the dissidents. This evoked reaction from some ZANU members. The late Maurice Nyagumbo, obviously one of the ZANU hardliners, interpreted this as implicit alliance between ZAPU and the dissidents,[68] while Simeon Muzenda felt that the entire dissident problem would be a major issue to be addressed after the Unity Agreement. ZAPU argued that its inclusion of the amnesty call into its proposals was not "as a pre-condition for unity, but as a catalyst towards the reduction of political

ZIMBABWE

tension in the country".[69]

There could be no doubt that ZAPU negotiated from the position of weakness, and that ZANU was not ready to make much concession. It would also appear that Nkomo himself recognised this, as could be seen in the way he preempted those who might want to criticise the party's (ZAPU) leadership of conceding too much to ZANU. At the signing of the accord, he said:

> I want to stress here for people who will look at this document and start analysing it to see who has gained and who has not gained. Let me say that what is contained here is the true feelings of both of these political parties. The document may appear incomplete — all agreements are that way. But the important thing is the spirit behind the document and not the document behind the spirit.[70]

The Agreement was an 11-point accord, the core of which united both parties. Point number eight of the Agreement specifically addressed the dissident activities in Matabeleland:

> That the present leadership of PF ZAPU shall take immediate and vigorous steps to help eliminate and end the insecurity and violence prevalent in Matabeleland.

Implicit in the wording of this particular point is the fact that, either the PF ZAPU had control over the dissidents operating in Matabeleland, or that the party had not been cooperating with ZANU in the latter's bid to rid the territory of dissident operations.

Beyond technicalities, however, concerted efforts started to implement policies that might lead to the ending of the dissident problem. First, an amnesty was promulgated by the government on 19 April 1987, and signed on 28 April 1988. Those who could claim the amnesty were "dissidents, dissidents' collaborators, and ZAPU political refugees". Agents of foreign states and those who acted in the interest of foreign states were excluded. Those qualified for amnesty were, however, to give themselves up within a stipulated period. It was initially uncertain whether the dissidents would trust the government enough to come out. In fact, within hours after the announcement, some dissidents killed a Catholic missionary at Empadeni mission, near Plumtree. This however, did not deter the government, and ZAPU too added its voice to impress it on the dissidents to come out of hiding. These calls were heeded, and it in fact, got to a stage when some of the dissidents who surrendered warned their colleagues still in the bush that if they did not heed the amnesty call, they (those who accepted the amnesty conditions) would come to the bush and bring them out by force.

At the end of the amnesty period, 135 dissidents gave themselves up, and it was astonishing to discover that it was only this number that had brought untold hardship to the country for more than five years. Another source of surprise was the relative degree of organised command and control structure among the dissidents. Although, they came out in batches, there were evidences of "formal" organisation in the behaviour. In fact, one of them who claimed to be a "Commander", Editor Nkomo (no relation of Joshua Nkomo), confirmed their degree of cooperation when he explained that it had taken them some time to respond to the amnesty call because they were "discussing the best way of surrendering in disciplined groups rather than individuals".[71] This was a far cry from the disorganised bunch of bandits the government and many people actually expected. Again, as part of the amnesty deal, Mugabe (who had then become the President) freed 75 members of the security force then serving jail terms for murder in Matabeleland. The dissidents who killed the missionaries in Esigodoni were also unconditionally freed. As of this time, some of them had been arrested, but they had not been formally charged. The release of these people however raised some criticism, as many felt that they needed psychiatric treatment before they could be released back into society.

Some of the dissidents who surrendered misconstrued the government's gesture by drawing up a list of conditions that could guarantee peace. These included the return of all confiscated ZAPU property; the total re-integration of the former dissidents into society; release of all political detainees; release of all the dissidents captured before the amnesty, and the withdrawal of Zimbabwean troops then fighting in Mozambique against Renamo. These demands were read out by the dissidents' "political commissar", Lancet Mkwananzi.[72] The last of these conditions — withdrawal of troops from Mozambique — raises a fundamental question of the possibility of a link between

Renamo and the dissidents in Zimbabwe. However, nowhere has any such link been found. Thus, it is possible that the Zimbabwean dissidents included this condition to attract the sympathy of the group of people who, at that time, had started getting somewhat critical of the government's military presence in Mozambique. The government was magnanimous in the way it handled the initial excesses of the returning dissidents. This was greatly assisted by ZAPU. For example, Nkomo came in when some ex-ZIPRA members raised the issue of the return of the confiscated ZAPU property. He said the government had taken over the property, and since ZAPU was then an integral part of the government, there was no issue of returning to the party what already belonged to it.[73] Initially, it was thought that the re-integration of the former dissidents into society would be a difficult problem, as many of their victims might want to retaliate. This, however, turned out to be an unnecessary fear, as their re-entrance was relatively hitch-free. In fact, by 1990, some of them had started representing their constituencies in the newly merged ZANU(PF) National People's Organisation.[74]

Post-Unity accord Zimbabwe
Although, the Unity Agreement united ZANU and ZAPU and also brought an end to the dissident activities that had fed on ZAPU/Ndebele disaffection, it is also possible to argue that some members of ZAPU objected to certain clauses of the Unity Accord. First, many ZAPU members objected to the new name, which they argued never cared to hide the obvious second fiddle position of ZAPU. Closely related to this was the objection many ZAPU members had to the continued use of the ZANU party slogan *"Pamberi ne ZANU"* (Forward with ZANU), for the new party.[75] Second, many of them thought that it would have been better to vote to elect a new leader, instead of having him appointed. In short, these people did not see the Agreement as a case of merger, but of ZANU swallowing ZAPU. It must be mentioned, nevertheless, that these people did not consider any military or dissident action to redress what they saw as a structural imbalance in the new political order.

The promises of the Unity Accord brought developments which went further to test the durability and efficacy of the arrangement. As Welshman Ncumbe rightly pointed out:

> Various sections of the population of Zimbabwe felt

> released from the constraints of party political rivalry which had inhibited virtually all domestic expressions about national problems. People were able to direct their attention to real issues and could air their views without being mistaken as supporters of ZAPU or dissidents, hence being labelled as enemies of government.[76]

The first manifestation of this desire to express feelings without inhibition came from the students of the University of Zimbabwe and the Harare Polytechnic, who accused government officials of corruption. This was later supported by the Bulawayo-based newspaper, *The Chronicle*. The paper published allegations that top government officials used their privileged positions to get vehicles directly from the Willowgate Motor industries, only to sell them at prices far above the controlled prices. The President was forced to investigate the allegation, and a judicial commission of inquiry, headed by Justice Wilson Sandura, was set up. At the end of its investigation, the Commission concluded that some ministers, parliamentarians, and a governor had either abused their powers, or sold vehicles at prices above the controlled price.[77]

The anti-corruption crusade brought to the fore a crisis that had all along been brewing inside the ZANU party. This had to do with Edgar Tekere, the former Secretary-General of the party and the country's first Minister of Manpower Development. Tekere had always been a controversial member of the party, a factor which resulted in his expulsion in 1988 for anti-party activities.[78] He formed his own party, — Zimbabwe Unity Movement (ZUM) — and the party won most of its initial supporters from youths as well as radical lecturers from the University of Zimbabwe. It, however, got nothing but contempt from the ruling party. President Mugabe dismissed the formation as nothing more than an entertainment value, and forecasted that ZUM will "zoom itself into doom".[79]

The formation of ZUM shortly before the 1990 general elections in Zimbabwe gave the party the opportunity to test its popularity at the poll. At the presidential election, Tekere contested against the incumbent Mugabe. Although the party was only able to win three parliamentary seats, Tekere won about 16% of the votes cast for the presidential election. This was a major cause of concern for the ruling party's desire to create a one-party state. A particular cause of concern for the ruling party was the poor turn-out for the election. Only 54% of the registered voters voted at the election, and many people — especially those known to have opposition to the ruling party — claimed that the apathy towards the voting was an objection to the government's policies. They claimed that many people voted by abstaining. Whether this was true or not is a matter of opinion.

The political situation in Zimbabwe since 1990 has been somewhat stable — though admittedly not without hiccups. Such include opposition from the students of the University of Zimbabwe over some government policies they consider to be inimical to academic freedom in the country. This reached a peak when attempts were made to disrupt the proceedings of the November 1991 Commonwealth Conference in Harare. On the larger national politics, the opposition is still trying to make its position credible, with the ruling ZANU party, too, trying to cope with minor intra-party conflict, serious famine and economic problems. It soon became clear that Edgar Tekere could not provide the effective leadership for the opposition, and the search for a credible opposition now seems to centre on the Forum for Democratic Reform Trust. Among the names now being suggested for leadership are the Revd Ndabaningi Sithole, the former ZANU leader who returned to Zimbabwe in 1992 after years of exile in the United States, and Enock Dumbutshena, the former Chief Justice of the country. Also involved are many former members of ZUM, including Alois Masepe, Douglas Mwonzora, and Masipula Sithole.

ZANU, meanwhile, has had to cope with the loss of some of its members, if not to the opposition, at least to the more critical section of the community. Foremost among these is Enos Nkala who, despite his role in the alleged atrocities of the 5th Brigade in Matabeleland resigned from ZANU and has since been critical of the Mugabe administration. Allegations of improper handling of the economy have further made the government unpopular. These however, do not appear to have as much effect as the dissident activities of the 1982-87 had on national unity.

5 Ethnicity and Anti-Government Activities in Southern Africa

Very few concepts in politics, especially those of plural societies, have been taken as being as important as ethnicity. In the same vein, very few have been treated with such extent of emotion as the same concept. Although this chapter does not go into the profound questions of epistemology, use and/or misuse of ethnicity in the general terms, some of the background considerations of the concept that are relevant to this book are identified and discussed. While the study of most of the ramifications of ethnicity is considerably old, the gradual development of the sociological and anthropological theory on ethnic phenomenon is relatively recent — dating back only to the late 1960s and the early 1970s.[1] This was when the experience of multi-ethnic states pointed out the flaws in nation-building. Since then, however, it has had an appreciable literature, made now more profound by the end of the cold war and the attendant upsurge of ethnic issues in Yugoslavia and other former communist societies in Eastern Europe.

In this chapter, an ethnic group is defined as "a group of people who define themselves as distinct from other groups because of its cultural difference".[2] Somewhat implied in this definition is the uniformity of culture and descent. Thus, the ethnic group is in itself, a form of social organisation, "in which the participants make use of certain cultural traits from their past".[3] Against the background of the cultural and historical similarities, it has often been the case that ethnic groups do perceive threats or see fundamental issues like economy, politics and religion in a similar, if not, in fact, the same way. This tendency makes ethnicity susceptible to all kinds of manipulation. More often than not, many have been led to consider ethnicity as primordial, and as a legacy that must be defended by force. Where there are political leaders that can exploit this situation for personal and/or group interest, it has often resulted in wars with other groups perceived as taking steps inimical to the interest of the ethnic group. Again, as Nancie Gonzales has noted, some ethnic groups have long historical roots that maintain latent conflict and intermittently produce violence, but in other cases, ethnicity has been invented or reawakened as a reaction to outside force.[4]

To the large part, the root of ethnic problems in post-independence Africa is easily traceable to the haphazard nature of the colonial division of the continent. Virtually all African countries have inside them many different ethnic groups, brought together only for the convenience of colonial administration. These groups were held together with a combination of force and persuasion during the colonial administration. But with the end of colonialism and the attainment of independence of these states, the inadequacies of the colonial creation became obvious.

Ethnic problems in Africa have manifested in a number of ways. First is a situation where different ethnic groups were lumped together within a nation state. In this situation, intergroup relations have often resulted in conflict, with some groups, especially minorities, fearing and/or believing that they are being badly treated. This tendency largely, to the large part, accounted for the Nigerian civil war, where the Ibos in the eastern part of the country attempted to secede from the federation. There is again what Stephen Ryan described as "ethnic overhanging".[5] This is a situation where an ethnic group is spread over more than one state. Examples of this abound, although it has resulted in fewer conflicts than in places where ethnic minorities within the national frontiers go to war to fight or forestall oppression. At independence, most African countries realised the need to take steps to recognise the ethnic composition of their respective states. Fundamental issues like sharing of political offices, allocation of revenue and location of amenities are all done with due cognisance of ethnic difference. Conscious attempts were also made to bring people together in institutions and in youth associations.[6]

Although the impact of ethnicity on African politics has been the subject of several studies,[7] its role in explaining dissident activities in southern Africa has always been taken for granted. Of course virtually every student of southern African political and military affairs knows that the war in Angola is between the Ovimbumdu-dominated UNITA and the largely Mbundu MPLA; or that ZANU and ZAPU were dominated by Shonas and Ndebele respectively. However, beyond this, not much is known. Little is known, for example, about the extent to which the issue of ethnicity was used by individuals who clad personal ambitions with ethnic interest, or the extent to which the governments in these two countries considered ethnic balancing in their reactions to the conflict. This chapter addresses some of these issues. The intention in the chapter is not to hold ethnicity as an infallible tool of explaining the dissident activities in southern Africa. Ethnicity is not considered here as the only factor that explains the dissident phenomenon. Rather, the intention is to consider how the issue has been exploited in the dissident activities, and as one which may offer some explanation to some of the actions and inactions of the major participants in the anti-government activities in southern Africa.

In both Angola and Zimbabwe, there can be very little doubt that ethnic politics played an important role in explaining the take-off of anti-government activities. While not removing the obvious role played by other factors like economic and social discontent, ethnic politics in these regions brought together all these factors, and the dissident activities in these countries thus manifested, at least at first, as tension between two ethnic groups, with one in the government, and the other alleging victimisation.

Mozambique's case appears somewhat different. Due largely to the way Renamo emerged, ethnic considerations did not play a particularly significant role in the affairs of the organisation. Unlike both the UNITA rebels and ZIPRA dissidents, both armed wings of political parties before turning, to armed opposition, Renamo took off as a rebel movement. Thus, the issue of ethnicity that has often permeated the creation and development of political parties could not influence Renamo. However, two other factors accounted for the low influence ethnic politics have on the war in Mozambique. First, is the fact that the war of liberation in Mozambique — unlike the cases of Angola and Zimbabwe — was fought with the minimum infiltration of ethnic politics. There was thus no foundation upon which ethnicity could base an involvement in the subsequent civil war. Second, the fact that Renamo was externally created denied it any strong root in local politics. The external creator had exploited the most viable source of discontent in the country, which, as of then, was not ethnicity but division within the Frelimo cadre.

In both Angola and Zimbabwe, the roots of ethnic involvement in the post-independence civil conflicts are traceable to the period before independence. This, as mentioned earlier, was the result of geography and artificial boundaries, as much as the policies advanced by erstwhile colonial masters. In Zimbabwe, the Shona-Ndebele rivalry which has often been used (even if simplistically) to explain the dissident activities had existed before the advent of colonial rule. However, the antipathy between the two groups, which was used to justify the imposition of colonialism, did not prevent them from coming together to fight the advent of foreign rule. It may, perhaps, be helpful to provide some basic information about the two major groups in the country. The Shonas had, for centuries before colonialism, occupied the portion of present-day Zimbabwe in which they presently live. The Ndebeles, on the other hand, migrated to their present abode as a result of the *Mfecane*.[8] They defeated the Shona people inhabiting the portion of present-day Zimbabwe which they (Ndebeles) now occupy. These Shona elements are called the Kalangas. Over the years, the Kalangas were assimilated into the Ndebele community, and they are now seen by others (as they too see themselves) as Ndebeles. In fact, Joshua Nkomo, who later rose to become an almost undisputed leader of the Ndebeles, is, in actual origin, of Kalanga stock.

In any attempt to consider the impact of ethnicity in the affairs of post-independence Zimbabwe, it should be pointed out that the Shonas are not the monolithic ethnic group they are often portrayed to be. They are, in fact, more of a conglomerate of ethnic groups like the Karangas, from the Masvingo province; the Manicas from Eastern Highlands; Zezurus, from around Harare, etc. It is often usual for these units to come quickly together when vital national politics require a measure of solidarity. However, it must also be mentioned that, this does not always happen, as members of these units do occasionally find it expedient to break with others on issues of vital political significance. Even in post-independence Zimbabwe, conscious efforts to balance forces between members of these Shona sub-units became an important aspect of national politics.

In Zimbabwe, like in most other African states, personalities came to play significant roles in personifying ethnic groups. This was clearer in the case of the Ndebele people, where Nkomo was taken, rightly or wrongly, as the spokesman in whom the Ndebeles put their trust. Since the time he entered politics, he had taken most of the Ndebele ethnic group with him. When ZAPU broke up in 1963, and some of its members formed ZANU, the political situation in the country later assumed an ethnic dimension, and it was this time that many Ndebele people became strong in their support for ZAPU and for Nkomo.

The Shonas, as of this time, had no leader that wielded the type of control Nkomo had over the Ndebeles. This was as much the product of the segmentation of the ethnic group as was the growth of ZANU as a political party. Mugabe, who (at least by the virtue of his leadership of the party) could be considered to be the leader of the Shona people contained therein, fought a series of battles with a number of leading figures from the other Shona groups before assuming the leadership of the party and the country. The Shona leaders who, at one time or the other contested against Mugabe include Revd Ndabaningi Sithole and Bishop Abel Muzorewa, both of whom belong to different sub-ethnic units of Shona from Mugabe. In short, while at independence, Mugabe's leadership of the country was not in dispute, the same could not exactly be said as regards his leadership of the Shona people. Once the country became independent, Mugabe preferred assuming national, rather than ethnic leadership. Ndabaningi Sithole soon left the country for the United States, and after his election defeat, appeared to have had diminished interest in ethnic and national politics. Bishop Muzorewa, too, had by independence, become a spent force, whose reputation had been irreparably dented because of his alliance with Ian Smith. Thus, when eventually the dissident problem emerged, there was no individual that could technically be called the Shona leader.

At independence, Zimbabwe was confronted with a number of contentious issues which touched on the chord of ethnic emotions, the handling of which obviously required some ethnic balancing. The first of these, and one which was to play a major link with the dissident operation, was the issue of the integration of the former guerrillas into the new national army. Everywhere in Africa, the military has come to be associated with power, control over which politicians always want to monopolise. With the pattern the war of liberation took, it was certain that the government had a potentially explosive problem at hand, as the Ndebele-dominated ZIPRA needed to be convinced that their interest would always be protected under a ZANU government. There were also the members of the former Rhodesian army who were

ETHNICITY

also unsure of what the future looked like in the new dispensation.

Also important was the land issue, which has always been a controversial one in the country. Although the colonial distribution of land was unfair to all the blacks in the country, the Ndebele people believed they were more affected. The expectation many black Zimbabweans had during the liberation war — a belief they were led to have by the freedom fighters — was that, with independence, there would automatically come land re-allocation. Thus, land re-distribution was at the core of ethnic and political issues at independence. Finally, there was the issue of office allocation. After ZANU had contested the election separately from ZAPU and had won, the latter had waited anxiously to see the extent to which ZANU's advertised magnanimity of inviting ZAPU to government would reflect on the issue of office allocation.

Within a year in office, many ZAPU members — and almost implicitly Ndebele people — believed that ZANU had failed in the handling of these three sensitive issues. As mentioned in Chapter Four, many of them believed that the military integration exercise was not fairly handled. The land issue too, was, in their belief not handled with the type of dispatch they believed it deserved. The allocation of office — especially at the ministerial level — was also considered disproportionate. Nkomo and three other ZAPU members were allocated full ministerial portfolios.[9] This was in a 16 man cabinet. Also, of the 13 deputy ministers, only two were from ZAPU. Thus, only six Ndebele people from ZAPU were in the cabinet of about thirty members. The other Ndebele member of the cabinet was Enos Nkala, who was a strong member of ZANU. In fact, many people believed that he was only Ndebele in origin, as his actions and policies did not go along with that of most people in the ethnic group.

Still on the issue of office allocation, many Ndebele people believed that offices allocated to ZAPU Ndebele members were relatively insignificant ones. The only ZAPU member given an office of some significance was Nkomo in the Home Affairs Ministry, but even in this case, sensitive branches of the ministry were removed and taken to other ministries. For example, control of tribal trust territories and that of Police Special Branch, which were in the Home Affairs ministry, were transferred to the Ministry of Local Government and Housing and the Prime Minister's office respectively. These were offices controlled by Shona members of the ruling party. Nkomo was later transferred from the Home Affairs to another ministry before ending up as a Minister without Portfolio. The transfer to a Minister without Portfolio was considered by many as a demotion, which many ZAPU members considered as insulting to a politician of Nkomo's standing in the country. This feeling, according to some Ndebele-speaking people, was made worse by the jest they alleged the Shona people made of them, that their leader was a "Minister without Job".[10] This was the situation when the arms cache controversy emerged.

The alleged discovery of the cached arms further inflamed ethnic tension. After the government announced the discovery, many Zimbabweans, allegedly Shonas, carried placards that brought the leaders of ZAPU, especially Nkomo into shame. Such placards include "Check Nkomo's stomach for more arms", etc. The Ndebeles were not impressed at the alleged discovery. Many of them believed that both ZANLA and ZIPRA had cached arms, and that the government's claim that only ZIPRA's caches were "discovered" was a clear pretext for getting rid of Nkomo. Many of them went further to argue that, despite the discovery, the real onus rested on the government to prove that there was actually a plot to overthrow Mugabe.[11]

When Nkomo and other ZAPU members were dismissed from the government, many Ndebele people interpreted it as a clear indication that they were being schemed out of government. Although Mugabe still retained some Ndebele ZAPU members, and even went further to promote some of them, it really made no impact on the people of Matabeleland, most of whom saw in the expelled leader their real political representative. The detention of Lookout Masuku and Dumiso Dabengwa seemed to confirm the fear of most Ndebele people that ZANU was determined to wipe out ZAPU. The expulsion of Nkomo, Chinamano, Msika and Mtuta was seen as a move to deprive them of their proper representation in the government while the detention of Masuku robbed them of their main voice in the military.

Against all this background, it was certain that when the dissident operation started, there was an almost neat ethnic framework within which it could fit in and manifest. The dissidents did not need to divert energy into convincing the people of Matabeleland that there was need for some form of unconventional protest against what was seen as largely ZANU dominated government. While all these may not translate into the Ndebele people starting dissident action, it was, at least the case that many of them saw the need to do something against what they

ETHNICITY

perceived as suppression by the majority Shona. However, it is not known to what extent the Matabele people actually supported the means employed by these dissidents to express the common objection. What later proved certain was that the dissidents obviously exploited the prevailing ethnic mood to pursue their operation.

The extent to which the government interpreted the problem as an ethnic issue is equally large. Although always portrayed as a security problem (which it obviously was) the government still did not lose sight of the ethnic dimension. In a way, the government was not expecting an ethnic problem on the scale of the Matabeleland unrest. What the government feared most at independence was racial, and not ethnic conflict. Against the background of this expectation, more efforts were devoted to racial issues. Thus, when the Matabeleland unrest emerged, the government had to devise a way of addressing it. This accounted for some of the initial policy errors that could be seen in the handling of the Matabeleland crisis.

Initially, the government attempted to separate the ZAPU leadership from both the rank and file of the party and the general Ndebele people. This could be seen, for example, in Mugabe's attempt to blame the arms cache exclusively on the ZAPU leadership. To prove that he was neither against the entire ZAPU party or the Ndebele people, Mugabe extended some gestures. For example, an Ndebele man in the cabinet, John Nkomo (no relation of Joshua Nkomo) was promoted from a deputy minister to full ministerial appointment. Also in his utterances, the Prime Minister refrained from accusing the Ndebele people, either of conniving in the arms cache or even in the dissident outbreak. It was after no success attended the efforts to separate the Ndebele people from the dismissed ZAPU leaders and detained ZIPRA commanders that Mugabe started taking policies that affected the Ndebeles as a group. The government, at that stage, believed that, perhaps, a more across the board policy had to be taken that might affect all the people in the Matabele province. This resulted in the dispatching of the 5th Brigade to Matabeleland and the dusk to dawn curfew that brought untold hardship to the people in the province. In fact, it was confirmed by a top ZANU member that the reason why the 5th Brigade was sent was basically to ensure effectiveness, as they would not be sympathetic to the dissidents who were largely from the former ZIPRA ranks.[12]

The activities of the army that was sent to quell the riot in

Matabeleland did a lot to evoke ethnic passion. As the 5th Brigade was specifically sent largely because of its ethnic cum military exclusivity, it was alleged that they carried out their pacification mission with a measure of brutality. While it is only fair to note that this has always been denied by the 5th Brigade, it should be noted also that the allegations persist, and many of those who claimed to be victims of the brigade's activities maintain that the unpleasant memories will remain with them for a long time to come. It was, in fact, alleged that the commander of the 5th Brigade at the time it first entered Matabeleland, Perence Shiri, came from Prime Minister Mugabe's sub-unit of the Shona ethnic group.[13] Many people living in the Matabele region during this period believed that the brigade was specifically sent to treat all the inhabitants of the region either as dissidents or as supporters of dissidents. Many wondered whether the government would have sent in the army to quell any similar riot that might occur in a non-Ndebele speaking area with the massive employment of force such that was used by the 5th Brigade in Matabeleland. The activities of the 5th Brigade did a lot to worsen inter-group relations between the Shonas and the Ndebeles, as it convinced the latter that the Shonas were actually determined to eliminate them. While this may not necessarily be the case, it was certain that most of the members of the brigade that operated in Matabeleland had within their minds an ethnic and political perception of their assignment.

There were some individuals who, though they were Ndebele-speaking, held important offices in ZANU. Two most important in this respect were Canaan Banana, the state President, and Enos Nkala, a minister and member of the ruling ZANU Central Committee. These two people played important — if, at least in one case, controversial — roles in the politics of the dissident activities. Enos Nkala was regarded by ZANU as a most valued member during the entire period, and he was employed on a number of political fronts to counter Nkomo's leadership of the Ndebeles. This was a role Nkala discharged with much enthusiasm. In fact, he was, at one stage, made the Minister of Home Affairs, where he was in control of most of the police activities in Matabeleland. In Nkala's perception, the Matabele people deserved whatever punishment they suffered due to what he saw their blind adherence to Nkomo, whom he held in contempt. Nkala never had any objection to the involvement of the 5th Brigade in Matabeleland. In fact, some of his utterances during the crisis could have encouraged over-zealous members of the armed forces towards extremism. Many Ndebele people continue to hold Nkala in much hatred and contempt for his role in the Matabeleland unrest. Thus, when, in 1988, he was found guilty of corruption by the Sandura Commission of Inquiry, many of the Ndebele people wondered why "his master" (apparently referring to President Robert Mugabe) whom he served religiously "against his own people" could not save him from the clutches of Justice Sandura over the Willowgate scandal.[14] He was to fall out with Mugabe a few years later.

Canaan Banana was in a different category from Nkala. Although an Ndebele in ZANU, he was not as hated as Nkala by the Ndebeles. First, he was a far less temperamental person, and throughout the crisis period, he avoided making statements which could aggravate the already heightened tension in the country. It was also possible that his position as the state ceremonial president called for neutrality (within what was possible) in the ZANU/ZAPU disagreement over the dissident crisis. However, it appears that the Ndebele people respected him. Even if they believed that he might (because of his position in the government) owe allegiance to ZANU, he could still be considered amenable to fair play and justice. For example, he was never mentioned specifically as being associated with any of the controversial policy decisions of the period. It is possibly against this background that he was accepted by both sides to play the mediatory role he subsequently played in bringing both ZANU and ZAPU to the negotiation table — a factor which eventually resulted in the end of the dissident operation. It was immediately after he performed this important role that he resigned to pave the way for Mugabe's ascendancy into executive presidency.

There emerged during the unrest, an informal alliance between the whites and the Ndebele people, and nowhere was this better manifested than in the parliament, where the members of the Rhodesian Front and ZAPU were always in accord to oppose the ruling ZANU party. The white members of the parliament maintained a consistent position that the government's approach to the Matabeleland dissident crisis was not only wrong but also counter-productive. Many argued that the average Ndebele man in the bush was there for a cause, and for lasting peace to come to the country, the cause(s) that drove them to the bush should be addressed. They considered the Matabeleland unrest as a political problem to which the government was employing a military solution.

As would be expected, this was exactly in line with the ZAPU position. Thus, both parties (ZAPU and the Rhodesian Front) were in an informal accord over all issues — especially security related ones. However, this was a marriage of convenience that had very little or no impact on ZANU in the parliament, as the party's large majority was sufficient to see any of the party's bills through.

In Angola, the ethnic undertone of the civil war also came out clearly. The fact that the war lasted much longer than that of Zimbabwe made the impact of ethnicity more pronounced. However, what appears to have accounted more for the prominent position of ethnicity in the conflict is the fact that the two ethnic groups that dominated the parties in conflict both have populations that are fairly substantial. Unlike Zimbabwe, where the Shonas outnumbered the Ndebeles by about seven to one, the Ovimbundus and the Mbundus both have percentages of the country's population that are individually substantial, and as such, neither found it easy to defeat the other.

The origin of the post-independence ethnic problem in Angola could also be traced to the facts of history, geography and style of colonial administration. The Portuguese colonial masters had grouped together these units of different ethnic and cultural traits for convenient administration. They further planted in them mutual hatred and suspicion for each other. The first full impact of this manifested when the liberation war started. Apart from the fact that parties were formed along ethnic lines, it was actually the case that each of the parties had different geographical zones from where it operated during the war. For example, the MPLA operated at different times from a number of fronts, but it was the case that they never actually got down to entering the Ovimbundu heartland. As this was where Jonas Savimbi comes from, it was relatively easy for UNITA to hold sway over this area for most of the period of the liberation war, especially provinces around Huambo, Bie, Cuando Cubango and Cunene.[15] The FNLA, too, operated from the north among the Bakongos. Thus, it could be seen that, right from independence, Angolans had fixed events in the country into an ethnic framework — with a zero-sum concept of political events.

Between the collapse of the Portuguese regime and the outbreak of civil war there were massive population shifts, as most people considered it unsafe for the outbreak of a civil war to find them in a region outside their own. Many Ovimbumdu people moved en-masse to their central highland roots. The same applied to the Bakongos and the Mbundus, who moved back to the northern and Luanda regions respectively. When eventually the MPLA proclaimed independence, violent disagreements along ethnic lines were clearly visible. Since there was an ethnic framework within which they could operate, both UNITA and FNLA refused to accept the MPLA's declaration, and they went ahead with their own declarations of independence. Thus, it was the case that, as of the time the civil war started, the ethnic lines had been distinctly drawn.

The role of ethnicity soon assumed a more significant dimension when the civil war started in full swing. The MPLA, having won the war and formed government (even if unacceptable nationally), started a process of getting non-Mbundu people into the party. Apart from wanting to present an image of a "National Party", this move was also to break the UNITA control of the Ovimbundu people, and the FNLA over the Bakongos. Among the Bakongos, the MPLA was able to make some inroads. Although not particularly much, initially, it soon increased over time, as the FNLA soon faded out as a strong national party in the country. However, not much success attended the MPLA's effort to get Ovimbundu people into the party. Even by 1982, when the MPLA membership had increased considerably, the Ovimbumdu representation was still very low. In fact, the only Ovimbundu in any major position in the party was the Transport Minister, Faustino Muteka.[16] It was possibly against this background that the MPLA Central Committee decided to embark on a campaign to increase the party's membership considerably. This, however, did not achieve the desired result of attracting the Ovimbundus into the party.

UNITA exploited the ethnic advantage enormously, although at a later stage it found the allegation that it is an ethnic party "unfair". As the party was militarily very weak initially, the most important internal factor that accounted for its early development was its successful appeal to ethnic emotion. The party was able to convince most of the Ovimbundu people that the MPLA government could not be trusted, and that their safety could only come if and when they rose and fought against what the UNITA successfully painted as the hard time ahead. After the organisation had taken off militarily, it started to attempt warding off the "exclusively Ovimbundu" image it had. Part of this method was to get the non-Ovimbumdu members of the party to occupy positions of importance. Thus, it became easier for pro-UNITA writers to point to non-Ovimbumdu members of the UNITA executives (even though these members were few and might occupy offices that were, in reality, relatively insignificant), as a justification that the party is not an ethnic party.[17]

In both Angola and Zimbabwe, the deep involvement of ethnicity in the civil war raises the fundamental question of the extent to which an average citizen of these countries was a tool in the hands of political leaders who might want to satisfy personal interest; or whether they felt genuinely aggrieved or threatened enough to embark on some of what they did during the unrest in the countries. Secondly, it raises the question of the extent to which those that emerged as leaders in these circumstances had hidden expectations of personal advantages in the leadership they offered during the crisis. Certainly, all these may be difficult, if not impossible to determine. However, it is possible to differentiate between the cases in the two countries.

In Zimbabwe, the percentage of the two ethnic groups could make the minority legitimately fear extermination. As the Ndebeles represent just about 20 per cent of the population, against the Shona's 70 per cent, there could be the tendency for the former to fear domination and possible extermination in case of war. Thus, it may be the case that, genuinely and willingly, they believed there was the need to do something about what they perceived as the Shona attempt to steamrole them. This may not be taken as the case with the Ovimbundus in Angola. With a population that exceeds all the other groups, the fear of extermination can not be convincingly argued. It appears probable, in fact, that if there was any fear at all in their decision to take up arms against the government, it was largely that of loss of face.

Again, and closely related to the above, was the fact that, as of the time dissident operation started in Zimbabwe, the average Ndebele citizen could easily refer to examples of what the ruling party had done that he considered to be antithetical to the Ndebeles' larger interest (rightly or wrongly depends on perception). Not the same could be said easily about Angola, as the MPLA government had, in fact, not settled down in office before the civil war started. Thus, while in the case of Zimbabwe, it may be taken as a case of "alleged" persecution, in Angola, it was mainly that of "feared" persecution. Taking all these factors on board, it becomes easier to imagine that the emergence of opposition from the Ndebeles in Zimbabwe had more genuine appeal among the populace than was the case in Angola.

While recognising that circumstances do create leaders, it must be noted that it was not the post-independence exigencies that created Nkomo as the leader the Ndebele people looked up to during the dissident crisis in Zimbabwe. He had been accepted, at least to a great extent, as the leader of the Ndebeles for several years before the dissident unrest started, and this arguably reduced the extent to which he wanted to manipulate the dissident unrest to satisfy personal ambition. This position becomes all the more reasonable with the way he handled the crisis. As shown in Chapter Four, never for once did he accept the leadership of the group, and he even declared on a number of occasions that he never wanted their support. The compromise he accepted by the Unity Accord shows further the extent to which he was ready to place group interest ahead of his personal motives. All these may not be taken to be the case with Savimbi in Angola, whose emergence and activities show that, while he may have wanted to serve the Ovimbundus, he obviously did not hide his personal ambition to seek power through them. The extent of his personal ambition could also be seen in the way he suppressed internal opposition to his rule in UNITA, and how he allegedly ruled over the UNITA held territory.

Although the Mozambican civil war did not take off as an ethnic issue, it should be noted that, more by accident than design, most of those initially recruited into Renamo were from the Ndau ethnic group. This, as Alex Vines has noted, was largely as a result of geographical convenience rather than calculated plans, as the Ndau people live along the border with Rhodesia.[18] This location made them useful in the sort of espionage and counter-insurgence the Rhodesian minority regime wanted the organisation (Renamo) to play. This factor eventually made the Ndaus prominent in the Renamo leadership during the early years. In fact, Alfonso Dhalakhama is said to be the son of a prominent Ndau chief.[19]

A second factor exploited in this regard was the propaganda that the Frelimo leadership was dominated by the southerners from the Gaza province of Mozambique. All the three presidents the Frelimo party has had so far — Mondlane, Machel and Chissano — came from the Gaza province. The propaganda further worked because most of the Ndau people were relatively unaffected by the Frelimo activities during the liberation war. Despite all this, it must be stressed that, while ethnicity may have accounted for some of the initial activities of Renamo, the organisation is certainly not an ethnic dominated party like UNITA.

Although the leadership of the party was dominated by the Ndau people, the same could not be said for the rank and file of the organisation who came from all over the country.[20] The Ndau prominence in Renamo has not affected the members of the ethnic group that stayed on in the Mozambican national army, neither is there any evidence that members of the ethnic group who have not joined the organisation suffer any retribution for the activities of other members of their group that have chosen to join the dissident movement. It appears that both the government and the people of the country did not read any serious ethnic undertone into the dissident activities.

However, the handling of the Renamo crisis by the Zimbabwean government has evoked considerable ethnic politics inside Zimbabwe. This has arisen out of politics and geography. The portion of the Zimbabwean territory most affected by the Renamo activities across the border has been one of the most militarised in the sub-region — having been at the frontline of the liberation war and later of the Renamo activities. These people thus wanted peace after several years of wars, and most of them opposed the determination of the Zimbabwean government not to undertake a dialogue on the Renamo issue.

There are other local ethnic politics that have come to affect the impact of Renamo activities on Zimbabwe. This is the fact that the Ndau people living in the eastern part of Zimbabwe (the area most affected by Renamo activities) have a fairly long history of strained relations with the leadership of the ruling ZANU party. The root of this antipathy could be traced, at least to an extent, to the history of the ZANU conflict after its breakaway from ZAPU in 1963. The leader of the ZANU party, at the time it broke away, Revd Ndabaningi Sithole, is from this sub-unit of the Shona ethnic group. Thus, when eventually he was removed from the leadership and was replaced by Mugabe, many people from this section of the country either stayed uncomfortably inside ZANU or, in fact, left the party with him. Thus, when he formed his own political party (ZANU Ndonga), many people from this part of the country formed the greatest part of the membership. When eventually the Renamo crisis started having impact on the people in this part of the country, many of them believed that the central government in Harare chose the option it took because the portion of the country affected is one in which it has little support, and as such it should not dissipate much energy. In all the elections held in the country since 1985, the ruling party has always suffered defeat in this region. In the 1985 general election, the defeat was by the ZANU Ndonga party of Ndabaningi Sithole, while in the 1990 election, Edgar Tekere's ZUM defeated the ruling party. In short, the portion of the country worst affected by Renamo activities is again one from which the ruling party does not enjoy much affection.

Renamo has always exploited this situation as part of its wider desire to destabilise Zimbabwe. Apart from physical attacks, Renamo often embarks on propaganda against the Mugabe administration. For example, after attacking the Zimbabwean territories, propaganda leaflets are often distributed to the local inhabitants, instigating them to turn against the Mugabe administration. Information included in such are particularly incisive.[21] This has worked, but not to the extent Renamo would have wanted. All it has done so far is to make people more critical of the government's handling of the Renamo unrest, but it never moved near the emergence of any unrest such that Renamo would have wanted. Another factor that has made the people more critical of the government is the concentration of security activities in the region. For some years, there have been units of Zimbabwean army stationed in this area to forestall Renamo attacks. Although the Ndau people do not regard the army as one of occupation, the concentration of security attention with the inevitable restriction of activities that goes along with it is something they do not enjoy either. In a situation where politicians of the opposite party need support, all these issues have been linked with ethnicity and have all come to affect politics in a sensitized nation like Zimbabwe.

There is yet another dimension to the involvement of ethnic politics in the Renamo link with Zimbabwe. This is the fact that the dissidents that surrendered during the 1987 amnesty in Zimbabwe, made withdrawal of Zimbabwean troops from Mozambique one of the conditions for the resolution of the Zimbabwean dissident problem. Although it is almost certain that no working relationship existed between the ZIPRA dissidents and the Renamo rebels, this demand by ZIPRA dissidents that the Zimbabwean National Army fighting against Renamo should be withdrawn, shows an important, but often unconsidered factor. This is the fact that there had always been some form of cordial relationship between the Ndebele people and the Ndau-speaking portion of the Shona ethnic group. It is thus possible that, apart from wanting to exploit the prevailing mood of the period which was against the deployment of Zimbabwe troops in Mozambique, this

ZIPRA dissident request could be a manifestation of this Ndebele/Ndau understanding.

6 Counting the Economic Cost

Any attempt to assess the economic cost of dissidence and anti-government activities in southern Africa immediately runs into difficulty, as many of the ramifications of the operations cannot be reduced to raw statistics. True, figures are available in some cases where the actions are quantifiable, but expectedly, such cases are few, and the majority of the activities remain difficult, if not impossible to quantify. For example, how does one assess the implications for the Angolan economy of a farmer in Cuito Cuanavale who could not attend to his farm because of the civil war in the country; or the impact for the Mozambican economy of the commercial shops in the country's Sofala region which are either looted or could not open for fear of Renamo attack; or worse still, the petty stealing of a solo dissident operating in the Matabele or the Midland province of Zimbabwe? This is one of the numerous difficulties associated with the attempt to put figures on the economic implications of dissident activities in southern Africa. However, countries in the region are in no doubt that these implications would run into billions of dollars between 1980 and 1990.

Virtually all the studies that have considered the conflicts in southern Africa have directly or indirectly discussed their links with economics. Most of these have grouped the subject under the wider topic of South Africa's destabilization of the countries in the region. This again confirms the extent to which South Africa had taken an active role in the conduct of the civil conflicts in these countries. However, it has to be conceded that the concept "economic destabilization" is perhaps more loaded than the economic costs of dissident activities being considered in this chapter. This is basically because the former concept takes in other forms of economic hardships South Africa brought to bear on these countries, and not necessarily those that manifested in the support given to the anti-government activities. In short, economic costs of anti-government activities — as it is being conceived in this chapter — is an integral part of the wider concept of destabilization.

There is a consistent and mutually reinforcing link between South Africa, the colonial economy inherited by the southern African states, and the economic implications of the activities of anti-government forces in the region. The history of southern Africa is such that it has developed enormous inter-state economic relations. The relative economic wealth of South Africa, coupled with the racial and ideological similarities between the successive South African governments and the colonial regimes in the southern African states, made some forms of formal and informal contacts inevitable for the governments that eventually took over in these countries after independence. This puts South Africa at a considerable advantage to exploit a number of dependencies. For example, the issue of migrant labour and its dependence on South African transport routes developed largely during the colonial administration, but it was used to assist the cause of the anti-government activities in most of these countries in later years.

Perhaps a helpful way of measuring the economic implications of anti-government activities in southern Africa is to divide the activities into two sections — regional and internal, with the regional focusing on how dissident activities in each of the countries have affected the entire regional economy, and the internal concentrating on the implications for the individual countries. Of course this division is somewhat confusing, as there are cases where the dividing lines between the internal and the sub-region overlap. However, this method should help to uncover some of the ramifications through which the factor has manifested.

Joseph Hanlon has identified the disruption of ports and railways as the area where dissident activities most affected the sub-regional economic life.[1] This is basically because the disruption of the routes inevitably places the countries at the mercy of South Africa which virtually holds the monopoly of the ports and rail lines (should others be disrupted). So much is this weapon considered by South Africa that academics and policy makers in South Africa have always rated it as a primary weapon against the neighbouring countries.[2] It is thus not surprising that it has been in this area that the anti-government forces in southern Africa (with South African support) disrupted the regional economy.

The activities of Renamo in Mozambique have been particularly significant in this respect. These have arisen from two inter-related factors, the first of which is the strategic location of Mozambique vis-a-vis other countries in the region (especially the landlocked ones), while the second is the role of South Africa which seems to have identified Renamo as the organisation that could be used to frustrate the efforts of the countries in the region in their desire to be free of South Africa's economic control. UNITA in Angola, again largely because of Angola's location as one of the "entrances" into the southern African hinterland and the extent of South African support, have equally had some negative impact on the economic situation in the sub-region. The anti-government forces in Zimbabwe had little or no impact outside the country, as Zimbabwe's location as a landlocked country coupled with the extent of the unrest in the country and its relatively short duration, did not make it possible for the ZAPU dissidents and the Muzorewa auxiliaries to penetrate the sub-regional social and economic life.

As mentioned in Chapter Three, Renamo devoted most of its activities towards the trade routes that are the fulcrum of regional economy. At this stage, the significance of the trade routes for the regional economy may be considered. The first of Renamo's targets was Beira. This is a Mozambican port town which links most of the landlocked southern African states to the sea. Zambia and Zimbabwe are notable in this regard. It has 290 kilometres of road network, railway and oil pipeline which connect it to Zimbabwe. In the colonial period, the route accounted for nearly all trade transactions of white Rhodesia. It was closed against Ian Smith in 1975, when Mozambique became independent, but was later reopened when the minority regime in Rhodesia collapsed. For landlocked Zimbabwe, Beira is the nearest and the most convenient access to the sea. Again, oil pipelines run from Beira to Mutare in eastern Zimbabwe, and most of Zimbabwe's refined oil passes through Beira. For many years also, Beira served Zambia as its main port of exit for copper.[3]

The port of Beira is also important to the SADCC's aspiration of eliminating dependence on South Africa, especially in the area of transportation. During the 1992 drought, the corridor was an essential route for import of maize.[4] This apart, the route is faster and cheaper than South African routes. For example, while it is 698 kilometres to Harare in Zimbabwe, South Africa's nearest port to Harare (Durban) is 2,077 kilometres away. Against this background, the SADCC arranged a £200 million rehabilitation programme for the corridor. If Renamo had allowed this to go on well, the dependence of the nine SADCC countries on South African railways and harbours would have reduced from 68 per cent to 40 per cent after the first phase, which would have increased the cargo handling capacity of the port twofold, while in the next two years (by which time the rehabilitation would have been completed) the dependence would have been completely eliminated.

Renamo's second target was the Maputo route. This is often called the Limpopo corridor. The corridor runs 524 kilometres from the port of Maputo to the Zimbabwean border town of Chikualakuala, and is regarded as one of the most important trade corridors for Zimbabwe and Swaziland. Malawi and Botswana benefit equally from the route. It was built in 1957 to facilitate direct export to Maputo, and it has the capacity to carry 3 million tonnes of goods per year. With its specialised handling facilities for bulk goods like sugar, coal, citrus, ferrochrome and containerised items, the port of Maputo is capable of handling all of Zimbabwe's and Botswana bulk mineral exports. Although Beira is nearer, the Limpopo line is considered more viable, as the tracks are straighter and more level than those to the port of Beira.

The third was the main route linking Malawi to the Indian Ocean port of Nakala in Mozambique. This route is called the Nakala corridor. It was constructed through an agreement between Kamuzu Banda of Malawi and the Portuguese authority in Mozambique, through which a rail line would be constructed between Mpimbe in Malawi to Nova Freixo in Mozambique, from where it would link up with the existing line from the port of Nakala.[5] Banda expected three major long term benefits from the construction. First, he expected an extensive integrated transport network through the region, with Malawi occupying a major position in this network. Second, he eyed the increase in foreign exchange that could come as a result of tourism, while the third is the assurance of market which was considered close at hand, especially for the large pulpwood plantation in the Vipya Plateau in the northern region, and the expectation of the bauxite deposit on the Mlanje Plateau.[6] The Nakala corridor now serves as Malawi's main access to the sea. The port also caters for some Zambian goods.

Equally relevant in South African support for Renamo is the Cabora

ECONOMIC COST

Bassa project. The place of the dam in the South African, Mozambique and Renamo axis deserves some mention because of the apparent contradiction it might presuppose in South Africa's relationship with Renamo. The entire project has always been shrouded in controversy.[7] In 1969, the Portuguese colonial authorities started a dam on the Zambezi river in Tete province of Mozambique. The controversy that has always surrounded the project centred on the extent to which the dam would be in the interest of the Mozambicans, on whose territory it was constructed, as the bulk of the electricity it produces goes to South Africa. Perhaps the only benefit Mozambique had from the project was that South Africa was to pay the country convertible currency for the electricity obtained from the dam.[8] Renamo has always attacked Cabora Bassa and has always disrupted the electricity supply from the dam, which ironically serves South Africa with 8 per cent of its electricity and in which South Africa has financial investment.

The implications of Renamo attacks on these routes to the regional economy could be viewed in three ways. First, money spent to reconstruct the damaged oil and rail pipelines; second, the expenses incurred in the efforts of the countries in the region to police these routes; and three, the excess costs incurred in the use of the longer and more expensive South African routes. Exact figures for these are not easily available for all the countries in the region, but it is reckoned that between 1984 and 1988, Zimbabwe incurred US$2.5 million in Renamo sabotage of pipelines,[9] and between 1980 and 1989 there was a difference of Z$1.5 billion in the use of South African routes (instead of Mozambique's).[10] Finally, the country is believed to be spending over Z$100,000 daily to maintain the troops guarding the trade routes that links Zimbabwe with Mozambique.[11]

For Mozambique, the economic implications of the disruption of these lines are twofold. First, money that could have accrued to the country from the use (by other countries) of the ports could not come. Attendant on this is also the fact that the country itself could not export the little commodities it produces to other countries. This thus virtually closed one of the few sources of foreign exchange for the country. Secondly, repairing the damaged tracks has always been the responsibility of both Mozambique and the affected country. Thus, at least theoretically, both Zimbabwe and Mozambique would repair any damage done to the route between Beira and Mutare in Zimbabwe.

Another major trade route that has suffered considerable attack — such that affected adversely sub-regional economy — has been the Benguela rail line in Angola. The rail was created by the colonial Portuguese. The idea of the route was conceived in 1902, with the main aim of transporting copper to the sea, and in the following year, the construction company — *Companhia do Caminho de Benguela* — was formed by the Tanganyika Concession. This company was owed by Sir Robert William, who initially conceived the idea of the rail line. Under the contract agreement, the Tanganyika Concessions took 90 per cent of the share capital, while Portugal took 10 per cent. This was to remain valid for 99 years, whereafter the state (now the Angolan government) would automatically own the railway with all its property, both stationary and circulating. The actual construction began in 1903, and by 1906 the line had linked Lobito to Benguela. It was officially opened in June 1929, and by July 1931 a further extension linking Katanga and Central Zaire to Lobito had been completed. While it was operational, the railroad was helpful for the transportation of copper from Zambia and Zaire, and it was envisaged that it would be helpful in linking Zambia and Zimbabwe to the sea.

For most of the liberation war between Portugal and the liberation movements, the Benguela rail line remained unaffected. However, after independence, when the civil war began, control over Benguela became the target of all the contestants. For most of the period of the civil war, therefore, the line was under considerable attack such that it could not serve the original intention of its construction. On a number of occasions, it had to be closed down either for repairs or because of attacks. The disruption of the Benguela rail line has been a major economic disaster for Angola and a number of the countries in the region that depends on the line, especially Zambia and Zaire. Although Tazara railway (a Tanzania-Zambia railway) had been open since 1975, the Benguela rail route was still needed to enable Zambia export some of its mineral resources independent of South Africa.

Another major problem that has affected the sub-regional economy in this regard arises from the refugee problems created by the wars in these countries. This implication is grievous, both for the countries from which the refugees migrated, and to their new hosts. For the former, the mass exodus of people who could have contributed to the growth of national economy would be lost, while their hosts, too, would have to share with the refugees economic resources that are hardly sufficient initially. Again, the Renamo activities in Mozambique have created the greatest problem in this regard. The civil war in Angola created lesser refugee problems, while, due largely to its duration and extent, the dissident activities in Zimbabwe did not result in a refugee problem serious enough to have significant impact on the regional economy.

Mozambique's refugees are scattered in Malawi, Tanzania, Zambia and Zimbabwe. Although the UNHCR and a number of voluntary agencies have often assisted these countries in taking care of Mozambican refugees, it is often the case that the aid has not been enough to address the needs of the refugees who increase daily. Again, not all of the refugees report at the UNHCR camps. This thus made them inevitably rely exclusively on the host country's economic resources. As would be expected, it is practically impossible to get actual figures of the economic implications in this regard; however, the problem transcends the issue of the host countries having to share food. Also involved is the enormous ecological degradation in the host countries. For example, recent UNHCR figures estimated that roughly 11 million trees were cut for shelter needs during the initial period of refugee influxes in Africa in 1989. This figures represents the desertification of over 12,000 hectares of land. A further four million tons of wood fuel were consumed in the continent.[12] Although these are figures for the entire continent, they do point to the economic and ecological implications of hosting large scale refugees as is the case in some southern African countries.

The economic implications of the anti-government activities on individual countries could be brought under five headings.[13] These would be: direct physical damage; manpower loses; extra military expenditure; environmental implications; and the loss of foreign investments and assistance. Direct physical destruction is always the most prominent manifestation of war, and the civil wars in southern Africa have enormous evidences of these. Oil pipelines, railways, hospitals, schools, farmlands etc. suffered regular destruction. These are again more prominent in the cases of Mozambique and Angola. In Angola, the destruction of physical structures has been estimated at more than $10 billion.[14] Mozambique's figures would come closer to about $17 billion. What may also be considered as a direct physical damage to the Angolan economy has been the cost the war has had on the exploitation of the country's oil and diamonds — the two main export materials. With the constant disruption by the war, the oil in the Cabinda field has not been fully exploited for national economy. In the same way, the war has also resulted in a situation where the country's diamond productivity has fallen from 2 million carats a year in the early 1970s to 714,000 carats in 1985 and by 1987 it was operating at a loss. The dissident activities in Zimbabwe created far less destruction of properties and infrastructure. Although there were a few cases of destruction of property in the Matabele province and some parts of the Zimbabwean midlands, these were comparatively negligible and they were, in fact, far more of exception, than convention.

The economic impact of this direct damage of infrastructure could be divided into two. The first arises from the fact that these infrastructures could not provide the amenities they were created to perform. These could be seen in the cases of hospitals and schools which could not operate. Again figures of these are not available for all the countries, but for Mozambique figures provided by the Health Ministry in 1987 noted that Renamo attacks on health facilities have deprived about two million of health care.[15] Between 1982 and 1986, Renamo was alleged to have destroyed 211 health posts and clinics and have looted or forced the closure of another 374.[16] The Mozambican Minister of Justice, Ossumane Ali Danto, said more than 350,000 children are prevented from going to school every year due to the destruction of educational infrastructure and the acts of banditry. Between 1980 and December 1987, fighting rendered inoperative 1,800 primary schools, 720 health units, 900 shops and 1,300 trucks, buses and tractors.[17] All these have implications that extend into the future. For example, a school destroyed could prevent students from getting education for months. The other economic implication of the direct physical damage raises the issue of post-war reconstruction. This again would fully manifest when the war ends and the cost of reconstruction is calculated.

Both Renamo and UNITA have again attacked installations that affect the economies of Mozambique and Angola. For example, Renamo, for a long time, closed the roads leading to the rich Gurue district — which contains Mozambique's major tea plantation. The organisation, in fact, dealt a series of major blows to the Mozambican tea industries, especially those in the central provinces of Zambezia. In February 1987, Renamo destroyed two of the main producing areas of the state owned tea company, Emocha.[18] UNITA, in Angola, also

ECONOMIC COST

attacked the economic projects the government had mapped out for rehabilitation. For example, in a statement it issued on 16 January 1988, the organisation said that structures like the Lomaum Dam, the timber project in Cabinda, the coffee plantation in northern Angola and diamond production in Luanda province would be its military targets.[19]

A second way through which the wars in these countries affected the economy of individual countries comes from the loss of man-power that could have contributed to the economic development of their respective countries. This has come in three different forms. First is the manpower lost directly to war — either dead or so physically disabled that they can no longer contribute to the economic development of their countries. Second are those who have had to take to the military, either voluntarily or through conscription, but who could have otherwise been more productively employed in another segment of the society, if the country had not been at war; while the third man-power loss came through hours and days lost by the people who could not go to work because of the fear for their personal safety.

All these are not easily quantifiable, but they exist in all these countries in varying degrees. Mozambique is the worst affected in this regard. With close to a million dead or physically disabled, the loss of man-power to the country's economy can be imagined. More manpower has been lost in the percentage of the population that had to be mobilised. Although there has not been any conscription in the country, a significant percentage of the population has had to be in the national army. The fact that Renamo, too, has recruited and, in fact, conscripted further reflects the depth of the man-power shortage that has come through mobilisation. Mozambique now has a shortage of able bodied men to handle many important segments of the society. This again is an issue whose impact may take some time to manifest fully. As most Renamo recruits are under-aged, it is possible that at the end of the war, they may find that they have neither the education nor the skill to be relevant to the development of the country's economy. It is not possible to count the hours or days lost as a result of the people who could not go to work because of the civil war in the country. However, as virtually all the provinces of Mozambique have some form of Renamo presence or the other, and as life could not operate fully in this circumstance, it may be taken that there is enormous disruption of economic life in this respect.

Angola, too, has suffered considerably in this regard. A significant percentage of the country's middle-aged population has been lost in the war, such that the average age of the population in the country now is about 19 years, with 42 per cent less than 15 years of age. Again, the country has one of the highest incidence of loss of limbs largely through war and land mines explosion. As of 1986, the estimated population of such people was more than 40,000. The population of those with other forms of physical disability is equally significantly high. This has had enormous impact on the national economy as it robbed it of skilled man-power that would have contributed to the building of the national economy.

Zimbabwe did not suffer much in this regard. Although the activities of the dissidents and the members of the national army sent to address the unrest resulted in loss of lives, it was not as much as those of Angola and Mozambique. The curfew imposed by the government in the dissident affected area of the country resulted in financial losses, as shops could not open for several days, and people could not go to work; some economic losses must have arisen from this.

The third economic implication emanates from the increase in the consideration given to defence. Since their independence, defence has taken a significant percentage of the national budgets of these countries. Although this had been to address South Africa's destabilization in general, the civil conflicts in these countries have reinforced the need to spend on defence a percentage of the economy that far outstrips what would otherwise have been necessary. Perhaps the most direct impact of this on the national economy is the fact that resources that could have been diverted towards other projects have had to go inevitably into defence.

The economic implication arising from the adverse effect of the war on the environment constitute the fourth point. This factor, like others hitherto discussed, comes in a number of forms, and most are unquantifiable. The environmental and ecological implications of hosting refugees have already been discussed. Other forms of environmental degradation come with the systematic decimation of the forest. Angola is a major victim in this regard, as UNITA was accused of decimating the Angolan forest to get timber which was subsequently exported to South Africa to pay for the country's assistance in the war. Allegations of large scale poaching have also been levelled against UNITA. Elephants and rhinos are killed and the ivories obtained from them are again exported to South Africa. Similar allegations have been levelled against Renamo. The *Windhoek Advertiser* quoted a former Renamo rebel that the organisation smuggles ivory into South Africa and Malawi in exchange for food and other items like sugar, rice, soap etc.[20] The Mozambican government estimated that Renamo has reduced the country's elephant population by 70 per cent.[21]

The second set of environmental degradation comes from the adverse implications caused on farmlands. The environmental pollution caused by oil spillage, burning and destruction of farmlands, planting of mines etc, has been enormous, and could have contributed to the serious drought that faced the sub-region in the early 1990s. As always, Mozambique and Angola have been the worst affected in this situation, and like most of the implications earlier discussed, this is again one where it will take several years before the manifestation would have full impact. Zimbabwe was least affected in this regard, as the dissident operation is not known to have resulted in enormous environmental problems.

Finally, economic problems have come through the gross reduction in foreign investment and foreign interest in these countries during the period of the civil conflict. Even Zimbabwe, which escaped most of the economic implications of the dissident activities, got a considerable share of adverse implications in this regard. The dissident activities in the country occurred at a time when the government was trying to convince western investors to come and invest in the country. The relatively peaceful transition to majority rule and the immediate post-independence reconciliation policies of the Mugabe government seemed to be attracting investors to the country. Mugabe had even gone as far as to assure western investors that the Marxist position he maintained during the liberation war was for propaganda purposes, and that it should not discourage them from investing in the country. This was the situation when the dissident operation started, and it set prospective investors back considerably. Many such investors felt that the long anticipated political instability had come, and that it would be unwise to invest in a country that was not stable. Zimbabwe also lost considerable amounts of money in tourism during the dissident operation in the country. As tourism accounts for a significant percentage of the country's income, the implications of this for the national economy were profound. After the six tourists were killed during their proposed trip to the Victoria Falls, a number of Western governments advised their nationals to avoid travelling to Zimbabwe on holiday until the security situation in the country improved. The loss of revenue in this respect is believed to be significant.[22] The Renamo activities against Zimbabwe also forced the country to close some of the holiday resorts in the eastern border towns of the country, with some significant amount of money lost in the process.

The activities of UNITA also created adverse implications for foreign economic investment and cooperation with Angola. As it was part of UNITA strategy to hold foreigners hostage, investing or having technical arrangements to assist in reconstructing the country have become an unpopular enterprise for western companies and governments.

The situation in Mozambique was such that it was practically impossible for any foreign investor to take an interest in the country. Some foreign countries have also warned voluntary workers intending to work in Mozambique that such is being done at enormous personal risk. Although a number of western governments sympathised with the plight of the Mozambican leadership, this was not made to translate into investment in the country. For example, after Machel's visit to western capitals in 1984, all he got was a little financial assistance, and not real investment needed to revamp the nation's economy. Renamo too has, on a number of occasions, held foreigners hostage, with the attendant consequence of undermining the confidence in the country as a safe place to visit and/or invest. It is, therefore, not surprising that very few (if any) new investors actually came to the country after 1980. Only those with roots dating back to the period before independence like Lonrho and some Portuguese and South African multinationals have remained in the country, and the extent of their productivity is equally reduced considerably.

The ultimate result of all these is that, by the middle of the 1980s, all the countries have incurred significant economic problems and have been forced to go to the World Bank and the IMF for financial assistance. As of now, Mozambique is one of the world's poorest and most dependent nations, with a debt estimate of $4.7 billion.[23] The payment of the interest on this debt alone costs the country a quarter of its export earning every year. Although the present economic situation of Mozambique could not be attributed only to Renamo, as other factors — like the absence of skilled man-power at independence and the wrong applications of socialist policies — also played their own part in the economic problem, it is also the case that the percentage of the role played by these other factors is remarkably low, and that the war with Renamo accounts for the greatest percentage of the reasons for the present economic predicament of the country.

7 Conclusion

This concluding chapter has two main objectives. First is to analyse some of what appear to be the features of the dissident and rebel activities in the three countries discussed in this book; while the other is to use the on-going events in the countries and the prevailing global/sub-regional developments to consider the future of anti-government activities in southern Africa.

It can be seen from the preceding chapters that both Angola and Mozambique were more affected by the rebel activities than Zimbabwe. This could be seen in the fact that the armed rebellion against the Zimbabwean government was resolved with relative ease. A number of reasons accounted for this, the most important being the rather organised process of power transfer in the country at the end of the liberation war. This made it possible for the county to escape some of the problems that confronted both Mozambique and Angola, and it further gave the government the legitimacy and the international sympathy to tackle the problems that eventually emerged. Thus, despite what could be considered the imperfections of the Lancaster House Conference, it assisted the government that took over in Zimbabwe in preventing some of the problems that could have occurred in post-independence Zimbabwe.

In all the three countries discussed, the manifestation of opposition to the central government showed some consistent features — especially in the military operation and in the pattern of external support. In all cases, the military activities took off at the time the dissident forces were weaker than the forces loyal to the central government. The only place where there was near parity was in Angola, but still UNITA, at the time it took to rebellion, was militarily weaker than the MPLA government. However, this numerical inferiority may be said to have served the cause of the dissidents in all these countries. Conscious of it, they avoided direct attacks on the government, opting

CONCLUSION 139

instead for guerrilla tactics. In almost all cases, this put the government troops at considerable disadvantage. It is rather an irony that the government troops that had used guerrilla tactics against colonial and minority regimes in their respective countries had to find themselves at a disadvantage in the use of the same tactics. It needs to be conceded, however, that in future years — due to massive external support — UNITA, and to an extent Renamo, engaged the government forces in open combat.

Another consideration that threads through is the support the dissident forces received from South Africa. As the country was then ideologically opposed to the governments in Angola, Mozambique and Zimbabwe, it was convenient to assist those movements that took up arms in these countries. One factor, however, needs to be mentioned here. Although South Africa has been linked (in one form or another) with anti-government activities in Angola, Mozambique and Zimbabwe, in no case did Pretoria create any of these organisations. All, the dissident forces were created by circumstances independent of South Africa. It is possible that, among other reasons, South Africa did not bother to create any force in these countries because of the technical difficulties this process would entail. Forming a rebel movement in another country has a string of difficult stages that should be followed. In what appears to be a descending order of difficulties, these include: (a) identification of an exploitable situation; (b) identification of those who could best utilise the exploitable situation; (c) the actual formation of the movement; and (d) sponsorship and maintenance. As the first three stages had been completed in the cases of Angola, Mozambique and Zimbabwe, all Pretoria had to do was to sustain the movements already created, and to fine-tune them to serve South Africa's purpose.

A number of factors guided the extent of South Africa's support for these rebel movements. The two most important of these were the extent to which these movements were established, and that to which they fitted into South Africa's destabilization strategy. In this calculation, UNITA was the best favoured. Apart from being well established, with a strong ethnic base, UNITA proved relevant to Pretoria's grand design in Namibia. Renamo, though not organised enough to the level of UNITA, was equally favoured because of its numerical strength and because of the role it could play in South Africa's desire to disrupt major economic routes in the region.

In Mozambique, South Africa's policy was less outwardly

manifested than in Angola. While there was no doubt in the mind of the South African leadership of the need to destabilize Mozambique, they had no clear idea of how to go about it until Rhodesia brought Renamo on a platter of gold. Before 1980, all South Africa did against Mozambique was to cause economic hardship for the country by cutting down the number of its migrant labourers. Even the first military attack did not come until May 1981, six years after independence. Thus, the handing over of Renamo was, for the hawks in the South African military establishment, a welcome opportunity.

South Africa's support for Zimbabwe's dissident forces was slightly different from in Mozambique and Angola, as it was neither open nor extensive. There seems to be a number of reasons for this. First, as mentioned in Chapter One, Zimbabwe occupies a somewhat special place in South Africa's consideration, as the two countries had, in the past, established a special relationship which would appear to have developed into a bond between them. A number of considerations reinforced the soft gloves with which South Africa handled Zimbabwe in the immediate post-independence era. First was the special goodwill that attended the birth of Zimbabwe, and the remarkable magnanimity with which Mugabe, considered an avowed Marxist, sought accommodation with the Rhodesian whites; second was Mugabe's stand that Zimbabwe would not accommodate South African liberation fighters; while the third was the organised transition Zimbabwe enjoyed. Thus, when eventually the dissident problem started, Pretoria found it difficult to penetrate effectively. Another opportunity that came with the timing of the emergence of dissident activities in Zimbabwe is the fact that, at the time, Pretoria was already deeply committed on several fronts — Angola, Mozambique, Namibia and the containment of internal opposition to apartheid. South Africa thus had little time left for Zimbabwe, more so when the dissident forces that emerged were not properly coordinated.

The ascendance of F.W de Klerk in South Africa brought such fundamental changes to sub-regional events such that many writers are now anxious to draw similarities between him and the former Soviet leader, Mikhail Gorbachev.[1] The basic similarity between the two leaders, and one which goes on to explain other less significant parallels in some of their actions, is that both of them, at a certain stage, realised that the old order, to which they owed their pupillage as politicians and statesmen, could not withstand the stress and strain

CONCLUSION

future years would place on it. Thus, both saw the need for some form of reform that would placate the in-coming force, while at the same time, salvage what was possible from the old order that was destined to crumble. However, the major difference between the two leaders is that the South African President did not concede enough to "reform" himself out of office prematurely.

The history of regional destabilization, at the time President de Klerk assumed office, showed that the degree of success that attended it, compared with the cost, had made it not worth of continuation. In Angola, it had not succeeded in getting the MPLA government out of office, and had only hardened the country's resolve, with backing and sympathy from the Soviet Union and Cuba, to stand up to South Africa. The battle of Cuito Cuanavale had again shown the leadership in Pretoria that the tide in Angola was getting serious, and that another way could as well be sought to address the conflict. In Mozambique, although South African involvement was less costly than in Angola, the hapless situation in which South Africa's destabilization had placed the country, had portrayed Pretoria as the bully of the weak. The evidences discovered to prove Pretoria's discreditable violation of the Nkomati Accord further dented the reputation of the republic. There was again the economic dimension. The extensive regional destabilization and the internal suppression of anti-apartheid movements had resulted in enormous defence spending which could no longer be sustained because of reversals in South Africa's economic situation. Thus, by 1989, a fundamental re-thinking of destabilization was already being considered by some sections of the white community inside South Africa.

Shortly after de Klerk assumed office, it was thought that the days of sub-regional destabilization were numbered, and that the numbers were few. The intertwining of events in South Africa makes it such that de Klerk's internal reforms had wider regional implications. His efforts to eliminate apartheid, which resulted in the un-banning of the ANC and other movements, for example, had enormous sub-regional implications, as it subsequently precipitated the decision of the organisation to drop its armed struggle. With these two developments, (the un-banning of the ANC and the latter's stoppage of armed struggle) the main reasons that underlined the tension between South Africa and the neighbouring countries, i.e. support for the "banned ANC" in its "armed struggle", were removed. Other internal reforms subsequently reinforced the new found rapport between South Africa and the countries hitherto accused of sponsoring "terrorism" against Pretoria.

F.W. de Klerk's initial policy towards the dissident movements, especially in Angola and Mozambique, was somewhat blurred. The euphoria of his domestic reforms has often made people to assume that a similar "sympathetic" approach was immediately extended towards the countries in the region. The truth, however, is that not much changed initially in the relationship between South Africa and the rebel forces operating against the governments of Angola and Mozambique. What immediately underwent a significant change was the direct military raids often carried out by members of the SADF, during the Botha years, but not the "behind the scenes" military assistance often given to Renamo and UNITA.

De Klerk's initial policy in Angola needs to be placed in proper context. Even the Botha regime, despite its commitment to supporting UNITA, had since the Cuito Cuanavale battle been co-sponsoring peace talks between UNITA and the MPLA government, alongside the United States and the Soviet Union. Thus, all de Klerk did in this respect was to continue the initiative already begun by the Botha administration. Another development which speeded the Angolan peace talks was the independence of Namibia in March 1990. This again was an initiative that started under Botha. The Namibian independence removed a major obstacle in the Angola dialogue.

There are, however, reasons to believe that some form of South African sympathy for UNITA again started after UNITA refused to accept the outcome of the October 1992 elections in the country. It is not certain whether this new sympathy has, as yet, manifested in the supply of military assistance to UNITA. What is however certain is that, although "Pik" Botha attempted playing the role of a peace-maker after the elections, he actually supported openly Jonas Savimbi's position that the election in Angola was not fair. While "Pik" Botha reserves the right to make public any observation he might have concerning the elections, it is equally possible that this position was made public to justify the possible clandestine assistance some quarters in South Africa might, in future, give to UNITA. This apart, the Angolan Foreign Minister, Pedro de Castro van Dunem, accused the South African government of supplying UNITA with 15 aircraft and logistical support after the elections. He further accused Pretoria of

CONCLUSION

infiltrating the "Buffalo Battalion" into northern Angola to support UNITA armed operations.[2]

Dissident activities in southern Africa emerged at a period when the cold war was at its peak, and, in its own way, it contributed — at least in the case of Angola — to the tension that characterised the relationship between the United States and the former Soviet Union. It could be seen that it was only in the case of Angola that the issue of anti-government activities in southern Africa manifested in the characteristic east/west, capitalist/communist divide. In Mozambique and Zimbabwe, super-power involvement in the rebel activities was reduced to the barest minimum. In fact, in the case of Zimbabwe, it was virtually non-existent. A number of factors account for the low in the tempo of the cold war interference in both Mozambique and Zimbabwe. First, the birth of the two countries did not evoke the type of international involvement the Angolan independence struggle evoked. Thus, there was no need for the super-powers to extend their rivalries to the two countries. Second, the anti-government activities in these countries (when they eventually emerged) were not ideologically focused, and again, they presented the western world (which would have supported them against "Marxist" governments in these countries) with an unpalatable option. This was because the West was confronted with the option of having to choose between "socialist" governments and organisations which, though they make anti-socialist proclamations, have such human rights records with which the West found it difficult to associate themselves. However, when the east/west ideological tension that underlined this support ended, the crisis became easier to handle.

Zimbabwe still remains the most stable of the three countries discussed in this book. Since the Unity Accord solved the dissident problem there has not been any form of armed opposition to the government. There are, however, two considerations that should give some concern for the future. The first is the accusation levelled against the government that death squads were sent to assassinate leaders of the Ndebele people who are working to expose the activities of the 5th Brigade in Matabeleland during the dissident activities. Among those listed in the death list were George Moyo, Dr Jonathan Moyo and Professor Welshman Ncumbe.[3] While no concrete evidence was cited to support this, it needs to be noted that any attempt to harm these people would create security problems in the country. The second issue of concern is the recent rumours that Renamo is organising a dissident force against the central government in Harare.[4] Although this movement has not taken off, the Zimbabwean government has confirmed its awareness of the rumours, and has promised to address the situation in all ways it deems fit.

Now to consider the future of dissident activities in southern Africa. Peace is still as far from Angola as it was before the peace accord. Savimbi's call for another election is not likely to have any sympathy, more so when the UN that could conduct such election is now engaged in several other fronts in Mozambique, Somalia and former Yugoslavia. The fact that the organisation believed that the election UNITA rejected was free and fair may not make the UN interested in conducting another election in Angola, as it might again not be accepted by UNITA if it lost. All these point to the fact that Angola may still be in conflict for some time to come.

Three external factors must be considered in discussing the future of the war in Angola. First is the recognition of the MPLA government by the Clinton administration. Although this may not translate into direct military support for the MPLA government against UNITA, it is a major morale boaster for the Angolan government and a diplomatic blow for UNITA. Second is the assumption of black majority rule in South Africa. Although the Mandela administration will spend some time formulating its foreign policy course, it is almost certain that the pre-majority rule South African support for UNITA has gone for good. Third is the independence of Namibia. Despite all these factors, which imply diplomatic and military setbacks for UNITA, the organisation has continued its war in Angola. The main reason for this is that UNITA still has considerable military and financial strength to continue the war despite the absence of military and financial support from Washington and Pretoria. This has again been reinforced by the organisation's control of the oil and diamond rich provinces of Angola. The sale of these could obviously bring money that could be used to buy arms from foreign markets.

A likely situation in the near future (if UNITA continues its intransigence) is the imposition of sanctions against the organisation. Already, the UN Security Council has delayed the imposition of stronger sanction in the hope that the peace negotiation between the parties will bring positive result. If in the end the UN Security Council decides to impose such sanction, it would have an easy passage.

CONCLUSION

However, the failure of the previous initiatives in Rhodesia (during the UDI) and South Africa, should not give the MPLA government the euphoria that such a sanction, if imposed, would work.

In the event that UNITA and the MPLA agree to solve their differences, then the country would have the opportunity to begin afresh. This, in a way, would put Angola in the position Zimbabwe was at independence, the basic difference, however, being the fact that Angola now has to recover from a civil war, and not from the liberation war that was Zimbabwe's lot a little over a decade earlier. However, the issues that would need to be addressed in this possibility would be similar to those which Zimbabwe addressed at independence. Obviously, this is the best option for the country, but it is also one whose handling could bring out a number of other problems.

First, the MPLA government would have to face the difficult task of looking for an appropriate office to give to Savimbi. While UNITA may insist on a sensitive post — possibly having to do with national security — it is not likely that this would be granted by the MPLA government. It is also possible that divisions may emerge within the MPLA over the extent to which the party should accommodate UNITA. All these, however, are issues that could be resolved at the leadership levels of both parties. Even after the issue of office allocation has been resolved, other explosive issues abound. These include the integration of the army and the police force, and efforts at reconstruction, rehabilitation and reconciliation.

The experiences from the military integration exercise carried out in post-independence Zimbabwe shows how difficult such an exercise could be. It is, in fact, likely to be more difficult in the case of Angola, as the UNITA and the MPLA forces have actually fought as enemies, whereas in the case of Zimbabwe, at least two of the three armed units that were integrated had, even if uncomfortably, fought as allies. After the integration exercise had been completed, major issues like the division of the Command and Control structure, appointment and promotion in the army are likely to remain contentious issues in the years ahead. All these, again, could easily be handled with the support and goodwill of all the warring sides. Extensive reconciliation would also have to be extended to other aspects of life, and this is likely to be achieved — if over time. It is certain that most Angolans who are already weary of war would support a new found peace in the country. It would only remain for the government to harness these feelings together and start a new life in the country.

Angola would have to face task of post-war reconstruction amidst a very tight budget. This appears to be one of the most difficult tasks that would face the country in the future. The years of war and the global recession have depleted the country's economy, and this could make effective reconstruction difficult for many years to come. The country's balance of payments is in deep red, with an external arrears of over US$2,000 million.[5] The future again has not given sufficient indication of positive returns. The country which, in the 1970s, was the world's fourth largest coffee producer, now produces less than 5 per cent of the average production of the period. Diamonds, which again used to be a major source of revenue, have suffered considerably. While it is possible that the country would get some sympathetic consideration from Western donors, it is not likely that this would be sufficient to address all the reconstruction that the country would have to attend to. The implicit danger in this is the fact that many people who would not be able to cope with the economic problems in the country may resort to individual or group banditry.

The problem of the FLEC's attempt at secession would also remain, even if UNITA agrees to join the MPLA. It is, however, possible that the issue would be easier to resolve. The MPLA promised during the election to give the people of Cabinda a better deal. This was refused by FLEC, which insisted that nothing short of secession is acceptable. It is certain that the MPLA government would not accede to secession of Cabinda, as the province accounts for more than 80 per cent of the Angolan oil. With more money needed now more than ever before, secession of Cabinda would be unimaginable for the MPLA government.

Although justifiable argument could be made that the former cold war contestants that inflamed the Angolan war should ensure that the war is brought to an end, it is also realistic to accept the fact that only Angolans could end their war. With Russia facing internal political and economic problems, and the United States still absorbing the lessons from Somalia, it is almost certain that neither of these countries would embark on any adventurous foreign policy in Angola. All that could be expected from them is the support for UN resolutions on the conflict in Angola.

The establishment of durable peace in Mozambique still has a number of major obstacles to cross, and it may take few years before

CONCLUSION

it can be known whether or not the country has left behind its dissident problem. The first problem has to do with the transformation of Renamo into a political party. A lot of money is urgently needed to ensure this transformation, otherwise it could be an excuse to be used by Renamo, in case it loses the election (presently slated for October 1994) to Frelimo. With a number of the promises made in this respect still unfulfilled, the return to civil unrest in Mozambique may have unwittingly begun. Closely related to this is the enormous amount of money needed by UNOMOZ to conduct elections. Although the UN is overstretched financially and in human resources, more money would have to be diverted to Mozambique before any meaningful election could be conducted.

The aftermath of the election in Angola has raised the fear that Renamo, too, may take up arms again if it loses the election. Although the Renamo leader, Alfonso Dhalakhama, has assured sceptics that he would not go the Savimbi way if he loses the election, the fears in this regard still remain valid, as many people in the organisation may not accept defeat easily. Already some form of division has been suspected in the Renamo leadership, with Vincente Ululu — appointed by Dhalakhama in late 1992, as the new Secretary-General — and Raul Domingos — deputy leader and the Head of Organisation — increasingly holding divergent views on the issue of accommodation with the Frelimo government. The same thing could be said of Frelimo, which, though confident it would win the election, should also prepare the minds of its supporters to accept unlikely eventualities. In short, both sides would have to accept the outcome of the election before there could be peace in the country. Perhaps the only way to solve this possible crisis is for both sides, after the election, to come together and form a government of national unity.

Back to the promised election. It is almost certain that there is still a long way to go, and speculations have started that the election may again, be postponed until sometime in 1995. It is, however, not known whether the ceasefire would hold till then. A number of factors still pose threats to the conduct of the election. These include: the presence of some 2.5 million land mines scattered all over the country; the refusal of some refugees to return home; lack of transportation and the absence of basic services in the country.

After an acceptable election has taken place in Mozambique, major issues like the rehabilitation of refugees, re-constitution of the new national army and general reconciliation could then advance in top gear. Already all these have started, but the real implication of their demands would be realised after the election. The process of constituting a new national army, for example, is such that it would stretch the patience and magnanimity of both Frelimo and Renamo. For example, the agreement signed by the two sides calls for a drastic reduction in the number of the members of the armed forces. This would obviously result in the demobilization of several thousands of members of both sides. It cannot be determined, as yet, how these people would take their forced demobilization, but it is possible that many of them who prefer being in the army could become security risks if forcibly demobilised. This tendency becomes all the more likely, as Mozambique is presently too poor to provide incentives that could make demobilization an attractive option. The second problem that could emerge with the creation of the army is that of office allocation. Renamo would obviously want some senior positions in the army, navy and air force. While the Frelimo government would definitely have to make some concessions in this regard, it is not known whether it would be able to satisfy Renamo in this respect, as there may be some positions which the government would not want to concede. This could either be because of the security nature of such positions or because the government might feel that Renamo members would not have sufficient experience to discharge the requested duties effectively.

The process of reconciliation is likely to be a bit more difficult than it was in the post-dissidence Zimbabwe. This is mainly because of the extent of the civil war in the country. Although the euphoria of a peace agreement has covered this for now, the durability of the entire process will be tested in future years. The cost of reconstruction, too, is enormous. Presently, Mozambique is the world's poorest, hungriest and most aid dependent nation, with a debt of about $4.7 billion.[6] Just paying the interest of the debt costs the country a quarter of its export earnings every year. The drought ravaging southern Africa has made recovery all the more difficult for Mozambique. 75 per cent of the country's population suffer from malnutrition, while one-third could be wiped out by drought if relief materials do not get to the people urgently.

There are two somewhat conflicting views on the economic future of Mozambique. Some people believe that the descending peace on the

CONCLUSION

country is coming rather late, as most Mozambicans have only their life left to lose.[7] An observer, Tambayi Nyika, noted that Mozambique would need up to 50 years of massive injection of funds, and that it could take "a full generation to heal the scar inflicted on civilians, particularly women and children".[8] It was further noted that a whole generation of children between 4 and 19, has been totally wasted, as they have known nothing but violence, raping and looting.[9] As the inability of the government to provide food and other socio-economic facilities for the people in the past has accounted for some of the dissident activities, the deepening economic hardship in the country may further increase the propensity for violence.

The second, however, paints a more positive picture. This optimism was outlined by the Centre for the Development of Industry (CDI). The Centre opines that Mozambique "offers interesting prospects for investment and technical and commercial partnership for European countries".[10] Seven key areas of the country's economic sector have been identified. These include agri-foodstuff; fishing and fish processing; building materials; textiles and garments; wood and furniture; metal working; and engineering and chemicals. The CDI report believes that various European firms are now showing interest in developing some of these potentials. Whichever of these, what is needed immediately is a lasting peace in Mozambique.

The UN has taken an active role in the efforts to bring peace to Angola and Mozambique, organising, in both cases, cease-fire that brought warring parties in both conflicts together. The UN effort in this regard has been facilitated by the end of the cold war. In the management of the Angolan crisis, however, the organisation made a number of initial mistakes. This is not altogether unexpected, as the conflict in the country has made a pendulum switch from the cold war battle-ground to that which is of little consequence to the countries that previously contested its future.

Some of the errors made in the UN management of the September 1992 election in Angola have been enumerated by the former UN Secretary General's Special Representative in the country, Margaret Atlee. She complained that she was confronted with a hopelessly inadequate mandate from the outset. Apart from having just a fraction of the staff and resources she needed, she said she could only advise, but could not act.[11] In short, the UN could only monitor the election, but could not supervise it. Against the background, the UN mission in

Angola became irrelevant, when war broke out after the election. It seems the organisation has learnt a lesson from the Angolan experience, as there is now greater tact in the handling of the Mozambican election.

There is a wider sub-regional factor that may influence the future stability of Mozambique. This has to do with the future role of the Inkatha Freedom Party (IFP) of South Africa. As the relationship between the IFP and the ANC gets worse over a catalogue of national issues inside South Africa, the possibility of some form of alliance between the IFP and any other regional movement that opposes governments known to have any support for the ANC cannot be ruled out. Although the relationship between the ANC and the Mozambican government became sour after the Nkomati Accord, things have improved over the years — especially since the release of Nelson Mandela — such that, in the clearly demarcated lines of sub-regional alliances of friendship, the Frelimo government leans more on the side of the ANC, and shares the beliefs of other members of the Frontline States that the Inkatha is not the instrument of change the region wants. It is thus possible that, at some stage in the future, some form of alliance could develop between the IFP and Renamo, or any other group that intends creating problems for the central government in Maputo. It is only against Mozambique that the Inkatha could play such a role effectively. The independence of Namibia makes it impossible for any South African movement to influence the events in Angola without consulting the SWAPO government, and as SWAPO would almost certainly not support any anti-MPLA activity, it is difficult for the Inkatha to influence the events in Angola.

It is not likely that there would be any serious conflict of the magnitude of the Matabeleland unrest in the years ahead, as it appears that that phase of the country's development has gone for good. This, however, does not mean that the government in the country would not come under considerable pressure in the years ahead. Whether this would result in violent tension depends on the way it is managed. The impact of the Economic Structural Adjustment Programme (SAP) seems to have compounded the problem for the government. Although this is not likely to result in serious conflict, it could be exploited in future years if efforts are not made to alleviate the problems of the people. A factor that could have further compounded this problem was the recent drought in the country. However, this, instead of affecting the government of President Mugabe, seems to have strengthened it. It

CONCLUSION

is believed that many Zimbabweans, especially those living outside the capital cities, were particularly impressed by the way the Mugabe administration handled the drought problem.

The pressure of democratic reform may create its own problems again in the future, but as of now, the Zimbabwean opposition are still deeply divided, and as yet, it appears they have not been able to present their stance in a coherent way. What perhaps would have to be the first problem the opposition party would have to address is how to make itself a credible alternative. This, however, may not be long in coming. If and when this happens, both the government and the opposition would have to test their popularity in elections.

On the whole, it appears that by the end of 1993, a new set of legacies that would determine the future of Southern Africa had clearly emerged. The legacies of the 1970s and 1980s that were characterised by wars of liberation, South Africa's destabilization policies and the cold war rivalries had, by this time, given way to a new set of legacies that offer opportunities and challenges to the countries in the region. All the dependent countries in the region had obtained independence, while South Africa itself was undergoing changes which promise a future majority rule. The cold war too has ended. However, apart from the issues raised earlier in this conclusion, three issues are likely to determine the wider sub-regional security for the remaining part of the decade. The first is the present unstable nature of the transition process in South Africa, which would almost certainly create implications with wider sub-regional ramifications. The second is the difficult economic situation of most of the countries in the region, now further compounded by the drought that has devastated most of the countries; while the third is the wind of democratic changes now spreading across the continent like a cosmic hurricane. The reaction of the incumbent governments of these states to these changes will go a long way to determine sub-regional stability.

NOTES

1. Introduction

1   For more on the impact of colonial domination of Zimbabwe, see Michael Macara, "The Political Sociology of Racial Domination, Rhodesia 1860-1965", Unpublished PhD Thesis, University of Rhodesia, 1974. On Mozambique, see Eduardo Mondlane, *The Struggle for Mozambique* (Harmondsworth: Penguin,1978). For Angola, see Gerald Bender, *Angola Under the Portuguese* (Heinemann, London, 1978).
2   Books on the Angolan liberation war include: Fred Bridgland, *Jonas Savimbi: A Key to Africa* (Mainstream Publishing Co., Edinburgh, 1986); William Minter, *Operation Timber: Pages From The Savimbi Dossier* (African World Press, Trenton, 1988); Keith Somerville, *Angola: Politics, Economics and Society* (Frances Pinter, London, 1986). On the Mozambican War of Liberation, Eduardo Mondlane's *The Struggle for Mozambique* is one of the few detailed ones. One noticeable feature of the works on the Angolan war of liberation is that most were written by foreigners. It is hoped that when durable peace comes to the country Angolans will come together to write a more detailed and balanced history of their war of liberation. Published works on the Zimbabwean liberation war include David Martin and Phyllis Johnson, *The Struggle for Zimbabwe: The Chimurenga War* (Faber and Faber, London, 1987); Robert Mugabe, Our War Of Liberation (Mambo Press, Gweru, 1983).
3   For more on this, see Fola Soremekun, *Angola: The Road to*

Independence (University of Ife Press, Ile-Ife, 1984).
4   These figures are from the 1970 census, as quoted from Donald Morrison, Robert Mitchell and John Paden, *Black Africa: A Comparative Handbook* (Macmillan, London, 1989), p. 358. The political situation in the country has made the conduct of any meaningful census impossible.
5   For more on this, see John Stockwell, *In Search of Enemies* (Andre Deutsch, London, 1978).
6   These include *Uniao Democratica Nacional de Mocambique* (EDENAMO); Mozambique African Nationalist Union (MANU); and the *Uniao Africans do Mocambique Independente (UNAMI)*.
7   For some of these reactions, see, Kenneth Young, *Rhodesia and Independence: A Study in British Colonial Policy* (Eyre & Spottiswood, London, 1967).
8   There were a number of nationalist movements before the ANC. In fact, the genesis of effective movements could be dated back to 1934, when the Southern Rhodesia African National Union was formed. Another movement which predated the ANC was the City Youth League, formed in 1955. The ANC, however, was the movement from which most of the post-independence issues took their antecedents.
9   Several books have given accounts of the split up of ZAPU in 1962. However, two of these may be considered together, Joshua Nkomo, *The Story of My Life* (Methuen, London, 1984), p.109—119, and Nathan Shamuyariya, *Crisis in Rhodesia,* (Andre-Deutsch, London, 1965), p. 173—193.
10 For a narrative account of how Mugabe rose to become the ZANU leader, see David Martin and Phyllis Johnson, *op. cit.,* p. 191—214.
11 Books in this regard have focused mainly on South Africa's destabilization of the region. These include: David Martin and Phyllis Johnson (ed), *Destructive Engagement: Southern Africa at War* (Zimbabwe Publishing House, Harare, 1980, Ben Turok (ed), *Witness From The Frontline: Aggression and Resistance in Southern Africa* (Institute of African Alternative, London, 198); and Thomas Callaghy, *South Africa in Southern Africa: The Intensifying Vortex of Violence* (Praeger, New York, 1983).
12 As quoted from A.E. Ekoko, "South African Defence Strategy in Africa, 1932-66: A Study in Dream of Empire". Unpublished paper.
13 *ibid.*
14 Sam Nolutshungu, *South Africa in Southern Africa: A Study in Ideology and Foreign Policy"* (Manchester University Press, Manchester, 1975), p. 162.
15 It needs to be noted that, at this time, independent African states had started taking critical views of the apartheid policy. Some of them had, in

fact, contributed to the process that saw South Africa out of the Commonwealth.
16 *Cabora Bassa: The Struggle for Southern Africa,* World Council of Churches Publication.
17 MPLA Communique 4/70 28-3-70.
18. Mondlane, *op. cit.,* p. 162.
19 Quoted from *Cabora Bassa: The Struggle for South Africa.*
20 As of the time of the coup, the death toll in the colonial conflict for Portugal had reached 11,000 dead and 30,000 wounded. Many hundreds of Portuguese had also left the country to avoid conscription, while trade deficit had reached $400 million per annum with inflation at around 23 per cent. See Keith Somerville, *op. cit.,* p. 40.
21 The Portuguese African colonies were Guinea Bissau, Mozambique, Cape Verde Island, Sao Tome and Principe and Angola. These got independence on 10 September 1974, 25 June 1975, 5 July 1975, 12 July 1975 and 11 November 1975 respectively.
22 Apart from an historical linkage dating back to the beginning of the century, Rhodesia had always been considered as an extension the of South African republic. Again, unlike Portugal, which could leave its colonies in the region if the going got tough, Rhodesian whites were considered by Pretoria as having a greater stake in southern Africa — a stake similar in nature to the one white South Africans had.
23 Prime Minister Verwoerd of South Africa considered Ian Smith's action as being rash. After the UDI, Verwoerd was quoted to have secretly opined that he had "offered advice to three Rhodesian Prime Ministers, the first two were wise enough to take it". See Robert Good, *UDI: The International Crisis of the Rhodesian Rebellion* (Faber and Faber, London, 1973), p. 21.
24 For example, Pretoria ignored the U.N. imposed sanctions on Rhodesia, and many South African companies injected investment into the Rhodesian economy.
25 Richard Leonard, *South Africa at War: White Power and the Crisis in Southern Africa* (A.D. Donker, London, 1983), pp. 82—85.
26 J.E. Spence "South Africa's Military Relations With Its Neighbours", in Simon Baynham (ed), *Military Power and Politics in Black Africa* (Croom Helm, London, 1986), p. 297.
27 The problem of Rhodesia had since the early 1970s attracted the attention of many African members of the Commonwealth. Shortly before the Lancaster House Conference, the Federal Military Government in Nigeria nationalised British Petroleum (BP), to express dissatisfaction with the British handling of southern African problems. For more on the Commonwealth involvement on the southern African affairs, see Olusola

NOTES

Akinrinade, "African and the Commonwealth: The Impact of an International Organisation in Foreign Policy making". Unpublished PhD thesis, University of London, 1988.
28 See "The Price of Solidarity" *Africa* (May 1980), p. 21.
29 *Southern Africa*, Vol. XII, No. 3 (March 1980), p.4—20.
30 The English translation is Mozambican National Resistance Movement (MNR). The organisation has, however, adopted the Portuguese acronym.
31 *"Facts on File"* (March 1980), p.161.

2. Angola

1 Black Carlota was a worker at the Triunvirato Sugar Mill in Matanzas province. With only machete as her weapon, she led her fellow blacks in revolt.
2 Wilfred Burchett, *Southern Africa Stands Up: The Revolutions in Angola, Mozambique, Rhodesia, Namibia and South Africa* (Urizen Books, New York, 1978), p. 91.
3 *ibid.*
4 Fred Bridgland, Jonas *Savimbi: A Key to Africa* (Mainstream Publishing Co., Edinburgh, 1986), p. 135.
5 *ibid*, p. 132.
6 *ibid*, p. 135.
7 *ibid.*
8 *Star International*, South Africa, July 1977.
9 Nigeria, which had earlier supported a government of national unity for Angola later changed stance to support the MPLA. This was based on the argument that UNITA's close association with South Africa disqualified it as a worthy member of any government of national unity. For more on this, see, Joseph Garba, *Diplomatic Soldiering*, (Spectrum, Ibadan, 1987), p. 17-39.
10 For example, UNITA claimed in August 1977 that between May and July 1977, "237 MPLA, Cuban, Russian, and Nigerian troops were killed". *African Confidential*, 19 August 1977.
11 Assis Malaquias, "Angola in the 1990s: Prospect For Peace" in Larry

Swatuk and Timothy Shaw, *Prospect For Peace and Development in Southern Africa in the 1990s* (University Press of America, Lanharm, 1991), p. 54.
12. Hermoed-Romer Heirtman, *War in Angola: The Final South African Phase* (Ashanti Publishing Limited, Gilbraltar, 1990), p. 10.
13. Kenneth Maxwell, "The Legacy of Decolonization", in R. Bloomsfield (ed), *Regional Conflicts and US Policy: Angola and Mozambique* (World Peace Foundation, Algonac, 1988), p. 19.
14. Roberto was an in-law to the Zairian President Mobutu, and the Bakongo ethnic group from where he came shares a border with Zaire. All these qualified Roberto and the FNLA to receive some form of assistance from Zaire.
15. Michael Wolfer and Jane Bergerol, *Angola In the Frontline* (Zed Press, London, 1983), p. 220.
16. Gerald Bender, "Angola, the Cubans and American Anxieties", Foreign Policy, No. 31 (Summer 1978), p. 29.
17. Jake Miller, "America and the Angolan Civil War", *Transafrica Forum*, Vol. 8, No. 4, Winter 1991—92.
18. Victoria Brittain, *Hidden Lives, Hidden Death: South Africa's Crippling of a Continent* (Faber and Faber, London, 1988), p, 50
19. "Jimmy Carter on Africa", *African Report*, Vol.21, No.3, May—June 1976.20 Cyrus Vance, *Hard Choice: Critical Years in American Foreign Policy*, (Simon & Schuster, New York, 1983), p. 103.
21. Kenneth Maxwell, "The Legacy of Decolonization", in R. Bloomsfield (ed), *Regional Conflict and US Policy: Angola and Mozambique* (World Peace Foundation, Algonac, 1988), p. 13.
22. *ibid.*
23. Colin Legum, "The Soviet Union, China and the West in Southern Africa", *Foreign Affairs*, July 1976, p. 749.
24. Arkady Shevchenko, *Breaking With Moscow* (Ballantine Books, New York, 1985) p. 365.
25. Gerald Bender, "Washington's Quest For Enemies", in R. Bloomsfield (ed), *op. cit.*, p. 189.
26. *ibid*, p. 187.
27. *ibid.*
28. Brittain, *op. cit.*, p.52.
29. *ibid.*
30. Bridgland, *op. cit.*, p. 257.
31. *ibid.*
32. *ibid.*
33. Bridgland, *op. cit.*, p. 293.
34. The "capture" of Cuangau, which Bridgland gave considerable mention in

NOTES

his book was perhaps the first major victory of UNITA. To imply as he did that there had been significant accomplishments before this is not correct.
35 *Guardian* (London), 3 August 1977.
36 Brittain, *op. cit.* p. 117.
37 Gordon Winter, *Inside Boss* (Allen Lane, London, 1982), p.540.
38 Anne Seidman, *The Roots of Crisis in Southern Africa* (African World Press, Trenton, 1984), p. 126.
39 *ibid.*, p. 127.
40 *ibid.*, p. 209.
41 Morgan Norval, *Death in the Desert: The Namibian Tragedy* (Selous Foundation Press, Washington, 1987), p. 125.
42 *ibid.* p. 171.
43 *ibid.* p.183.
44 Paul Moorcraft, *African Nemesis: War and Revolution in Southern Africa, 1945—2010* (Brassey, London, 1990), p. 194.
45 *West Africa*, 3 June 1985.
46 *ibid.*, p. 68
47 Brittain, *op. cit.*, p. 65.
48 Two well known writers on Southern African affairs, David Martin and Phyllis Johnson, tagged it as "Destructive Engagement". See their book, *Destructive Engagement: South Africa at War* (Zimbabwean Publishing House, Harare, 1986). A foremost Professor of International Relations in Africa, the late Professor Olajide Aluko, dubbed it "Obstructive Engagement" (personal discussion); while President Mugabe of Zimbabwe called it "Constructive Instigation". See Brittain, *op. cit.*, p. 67.
49 Seidman, *op. cit.*, p.92.
50 *ibid.*
51 Quoted by Seidman, *ibid.*, p. 7.
52 Jake C. Miller, "America and the Angolan Civil War", *Transafrica Forum*, Vol.8, No. 4, Winter 1991-92, p. 57.
53 Victoria Brittain, *op. cit.*, p. 160.
54 *ibid.*
55 *Herald Tribune*, 14 June 1987.
56 *Guardian*, 9 July 1987.
57 For more on the role of the Soviet Union in the liberation politics in Southern Africa, see Jack Spence, *The Soviet Union, the Third World and Southern Africa,* South African Institute of International Affairs, Bradlow Series, No. 5, 1988; and Daniel Kempton, *Soviet Strategy Towards Southern Africa: The Liberation Movements* (Praeger, New York, 1989).
58 Assis Malaquias, *op. cit.*, p. 55.
59 *West Africa*, 6—12 April 1992, p. 602.
60 See Lisa Alfred, "US Foreign Policy and the Angolan Peace", Africa Today

61 *Southscan,* 25 May 1988.
62 Guy Arnold, *South Africa: Crossing the Rubicon* (St Martins Press, New York, 1992), p. 19.
63 There was an earlier attempt in 1985 to capture Mavinga, but this failed. With the purchase of $4 billion worth of sophisticated Soviet military equipment and the possession of MIG 23s, the Angolans made a second trial.
64 Donald Rotchild, "Conflict Management in Angola", *Transfrica Forum,* Vol.8, No.1, Spring 1991, p. 92.
65 *ibid.*
66 *ibid.*
67 See *African Confidential,* 15 July 1888.
68 *Jane's Defence Weekly,* 30 April 1988.
69 Karl Maier, "Stalingrad Waits in the African Bush", *Christian Science Monitor, 14* March 1988.
70 Raph Nwechue, *Africa Today* (Africa Books Ltd, London, 1991), p. 510.
71 *ibid.*
72 It would appear that President dos Santos was initially unaware that Savimbi was also invited to Zaire at the same time with him. It was said that when he got to know of this he wanted to cancel the journey, but was persuaded by other Frontline Presidents.
73 He was a veteran of the liberation struggle who had recently formed the "Progressive Group" — not a political party.
74 Raph Nwechue, *op. cit.,* p. 514.
75 *Keesing's Record of World Events,* September 1991, p. 38423
76 *ibid.*
77 Before the election campaign started, Daniel Chipenda was the chief election organiser for the MPLA.
78 Horace Campbell, "Angola: Peace, Democracy and Elections", *Africa World Review,* Nov. 92/April 93, p. 34.
79 "Angola: Ballot in place of Bullet", *Newswatch,* 14 September 1992, p. 44.
80 *ibid.*
81 For more on this, see *African Confidential,* Vol. 33, No. 20, October 1992, p. 2.
82 *Africa Analysis,* No. 168, 19 March 1993, p. 26.
83 *Africa Analysis,* No 174, 11 June 1993, p.1.
84 See Colin Simpson, "Angola: Another Year of Bloody War", *African Topics* (Nov—Dec 1993), p. 16.

3. Mozambique

1. Gordon Winter, in his celebrated book *Inside BOSS*, claimed that the South African Intelligence was responsible for the creation of Renamo. See *Inside BOSS* (Penguin, Harmondsworth, 1981). This does not appear to be correct, although his claim that he was one of its earliest propagandists could be true.
2. For more on Ken Flower's account of the formation of Renamo, see *Serving Secretly: Intelligence Officer on Record, Rhodesia to Zimbabwe, 1964—1980* (John Murray, London, 1987).
3. See Paul Moorcraft, *African Nemesis: War and Revolution in Southern African 1945—2040* (Brassey, London, 1990), p. 261.
4. Ken Flower *op. cit.*, p 302.
5. One of the organisation's first training camps was at Rusape in Rhodesia, where one Peter Brunt, a former Rhodesian CIO officer, assisted in the training. The propaganda assistance came in two Fronts. First, the creation, in June 1976, of a radio station called *A Voz da Africa Livre* (The Voice of Free Africa). The station transmitted anti-Frelimo propaganda to Mozambique from Gwelo, Fort Victoria and Umtalli, all inside Rhodesia. Fake interviews claiming support for Renamo from inside Mozambique were conducted and broadcast. A second propaganda strategy was to carry out military operation in the name of Renamo. This was meant to inflate the reputation of the organisation as a viable insurgent force.
6. Ken Flower, *op. cit.*, p. 262.
7. David Martin and Phyllis Johnson (ed), *Destructive Engagement* (Zimbabwean Publishing House, London, 1986), p. 19.
8. Paul Moorcraft has a fairly detailed account of the January 1981 raid. See Moorcraft, *op. cit.*, p. 265—6.
9. Colin Legum, *The Battlefront of Southern Africa* (Africana Publishing Company, New York, 1988), p. 246.
10. Alex Vines, *Renamo: Terrorism in Mozambique* (James Currey, London, 1991).
11. William Minter, "Correspondence In Southern Africa", *New York Review of Books*, June—July 1989.
12. Virtually all works on Renamo agree that the organisation depends largely on conscription.
13. He was mysteriously killed in April 1983. For more about the activities of Orlando Martin, see "Mozambique: Havoc in the Bush, *African*

Confidential, Vol. 23, No. 15, 21 July 1982, pp 1—5.
14   See "Secret Airlift to Machel's Foe", *Observer* (London), 2 December 1983.
15   Allen Issacman, "The Escalating Conflict in Southern Africa: The Case of Mozambique", Unpublished Manuscript, p. 19.
16   Moorcraft, *op. cit.*, p. 267.
17   Allen Issacman, *op. cit.*
18   Why exactly Banda withdrew his support is not known. Some writers — especially those with sympathy for the Mozambican government — argued that Banda repented because of the threat carried to him by the Presidents of the Frontline States that military action would be taken against him. However, another school of thought — albeit a one-man school — believes that Banda co-operated with the Frontline States because Renamo no longer needed the Malawian base. This is the position of Moorcraft in *African Nemesis*.
19   *Herald* (Harare), 31 March 1989.
20   The atrocities of Renamo have been the subject of several studies. One of the most comprehensive in this regard is the "Summary of Mozambican Refugee Account of Principally Conflict Related Experience in Mozambique" April 1988. This Report is often called "The Gersony Report".
21   *African Confidential* recorded the story of one Manuel Antonio, leader of a peasant militia called *Naparama* who later fought on the side of Renamo. He laid claim to mystical power and later became famous through his tours of the countryside. He created a brotherhood and inoculated his followers with a special vaccine *Barama* which would make them invulnerable to bullets. He was however killed in combat in December 1991. See, *African Confidential*, Vol. 33, No. 1, 10 January 1992, p. 5.
22   Figures supplied by the UNHCR in Harare.
23   Alex Vines, *op. cit.*, p. 162.
24   Vines, *op. cit.*, p. 62.
25   Colin Legum, *op. cit., p. 249*
26   Mohammed Mawani, "Nkomati Fable Dawn", *New Africa*, October 1984, p.15.
27   F.O. Akinbinu, "Mozambique—South Africa Relations". Unpublished M.Sc. Dissertation, University of Ife, 1987, p. 69.
28   Paul Fauvet, "The MNR Changes its Colour", *MOTO*, March 1985, p. 15.
29   After the signing of the Nkomati Accord, crowds stood at every station on the route between Maputo and Nkomatiport, cheering and waving placards proclaiming "Forward With The Socialist Policy Of Peace".
30   Moorcraft, *op. cit.* p. 261.

NOTES

31 Quoted from J.O Nana, "The Political and Strategic Implications of the Nkomati Accord on the Frontline States". Unpublished M.Sc. Dissertation, University of Ife, 1985.
32 Julie Frederikse, "The Long-Awaited Peace Still Seems Far Away", *MOTO*, March 1985, p.5.
33 Keith Somerville, *Angola: Politics, Economic and Society*, (Pinter, London, 1986), p. 67.
34 Stephen Chan, *Kaunda and Southern Africa: Image and Reality in Foreign Policy* (British Academic Press, London, 1992) p. 54.
35 Robert Jaster, *South Africa and Its Neighbours*, Adelphi Papers, 1986, p. 28.
36 *ibid.*
37 Julie Frederikse, *op. cit.*
38 *Times* (London), 18 January 1985.
39 *Observer* (London), 10 June 1984, p.31.
40 *Times* (London), 11 February, 1985, p.7.
41 *The Star* (Johannesburg), 7 October 1885.
42 Robert Davis, *op. cit.*, p.19.
43 *ibid.*
44 Karl Maier, "Between Washington and Pretoria", *African Report*, November—December 1988.
45 *Samora : Why He Died*, A Mozambican Ministry of Information Publication.
46 *ibid.*
47 *Keesing's Contemporary Archives*, 1982, p. 31329.
48 Seidman, *op. cit.*, p. 128.
49 *Keesing's Contemporary Archives*, 1983, p. 32540.
50 *ibid.*, p. 129
51 *International Herald Tribune*, 13 June 1984.
52 Brittain, *op. cit.*, p. 109.
53 *ibid.*, p. 109—10
54 *Keesing's Contemporary Archives*, January 1986, p. 34086.
55 Robert Jaster, *op. cit.*, p. 28.
56 See, "USA/Mozambique: Politics and Money in Freedom Inc", *African Confidential*, Vol. 30, No. 3, February 1989.
57 *ibid.*
58 Robert Mackenzie and Sybil Cline were to get married in 1990.
59 *Keesing's Contemporary Archives*, February 1988, p. 35686.
60 David Smith and Colin Simpson, *Mugabe* (Pioneer Head, Salisbury, 1981), p.151.
61 For more on this, see, Olusola Akinrinade, "Mozambique and the Commonwealth: The Anatomy of a Relationship", *The Australian Journal*

of Politics and History, Vol. 38, No. 1, 1992, pp. 62—82.
62 This is the British Military Advisory and Training Team (BMATT). The team was sent primarily to assist in the integration and the subsequent conversion of the Zimbabwean guerrillas to conventional soldiery.
63 *African Confidential*, Vol. 33, No. 23, 20 Nov. 1992, p. 8.
64 *Keesing's Contemporary Archives*, 1983, p. 32116
65 *African Concord*, 13 November 1986, p. 10.
66 Both Samora Machel and his predecessor, Eduardo Mondlane, were active guerrilla leaders. This was about to create a trend in Mozambican leadership that the country's president must have some experience as a military leader.
67 The disagreement between the Frelimo party and the Catholic Church dated back to the war of liberation, when the party believed that the church took sides with the Portuguese.
68 Vines, *op. cit.*, p. 120.
69 *ibid.*, p. 121.
70 *African Research Bulletin*, April 1990, p. 9635.
71 *African Research Bulletin*, August 1990, p. 9775.
72 *African Research Bulletin*, September 1990, p. 9803
73 *Keesing's Record of World Events*, January 1991, p. 37951
74 *Keesing's Record of World Events*, February 1991, p. 37993.
75 See Chissano's reaction in *African Concord*, November 1991, p. 16.
76 See *African Confidential*, 14 August 1982.
77 *African Concord*, 20 July 1992.
78 *African Research Bulletin*, p. 10660
79 *African Confidential*, Vol.33, No. 16 of August 14 1992 provides a fairly detailed account of the events that led to the signing of the agreement.

4. Zimbabwe

1 During my visits to Matabeleland in March and April 1990, most of the people with whom I talked told me that they held this belief.
2 ZAPU actually tried to persuade ZANU to join ZAPU and fight the election jointly. It was even said that Nkomo sent a ZAPU delegation to Mugabe to appeal to him that they should operate on a joint ticket.

NOTES

3   For a detailed account of the process of military integration, see Michael Evans, "Gukurahundi: The Development of the Zimbabwean Defence Force, 1980—1987", *Strategic Review of Southern Africa*, Vol.X, No. 1, May 1988.
4   Virtually all former ZIPRA combatants I discussed with during my field trip to Zimbabwe held this belief.
5   Personal interviews.
6   Interview with former ZIPRA combatants. Held between February and May 1990 in Zimbabwe.
7   Michael Evans, *op. cit*.
8   Discussions with ex-ZIPRA members of the ZNA during my first visit to the country in 1990.
9   *Zimbabwean Defence Force Magazine*, Vol.1, No. 1 (Nov. 1982), p.8.
10 Gukurahundi is the Shona word for the wind that separates the dirt from the real substance.
11 Personal interviews conducted in Zimbabwe.
12 This speech was delivered at the burial of a ZIPRA nurse, Jane Matiba. See *Sunday Mail* (Harare) 6 July, 1980. This speech will remain a significant document for future researchers working on the ZANU/ZAPU split in post- independence Zimbabwe.
13 The clashes took place twice in Entumbanne, and once each in Matoko, Coneramma and Chitinguisa respectively.
14 For the Prime Minister's account of the clash, see, Hansard (Zimbabwe),
12 February 1981, column 1923-6.
15 I got this feeling from the discussions I had with ex-ZIPRA guerrillas during my visit to Zimbabwe in the spring of 1990.
16 For more on this, see Richard William, "Conflict in Zimbabwe: The Matabeleland Problem", *Conflict Studies*, No. 151, 1983.
17 It is possible that the government discovered the caches much earlier, but considered it indiscreet to act, as the military integration exercise was going on, and the government could not predict what would be the reaction of the ZIPRA guerrillas to any punishment of Nkomo. There is even documentary evidence to this effect. See *Africa Contemporary Record*, Vol.XIV, 1981/82, pp. B863-9. It was reported that the government discovered ZAPU arms cache carried in from Zambia through Chirundu. These arms according to the report, were removed and there was no official announcement made. When ZAPU discovered this, the party was said to have stopped carrying arms in through Chirundu.
18 These were the publicised ones, although the government announced further discovery at the Castle Arms Hotel in Bulawayo.
19 As of the time, Chinamano was then the Minister of Transport and the Vice President of ZAPU; Msika was the Minister of National Resources

and Water Development and also the Secretary General of ZAPU, while Mtuta was the Deputy Mines Minister.

20   About 52 ZAPU properties worth about Z$20 million were confiscated by the government.

21   Three days later, General Walls denied, through his lawyers, that he had arranged or attended any meeting between Nkomo and the officials of the South Africa Security Force. He also denied allegation that he had planned or was taking part in any activity detrimental to the Zimbabwean government. See *Keesing's Contemporary Archives*, June 1982, p. 31551.

22   After independence, one of the most important determinants of Zimbabwean foreign policy was the liberation war experience. Against this background, the Mugabe government was initially cold to all the countries that supported ZAPU during the liberation war. As the Soviet Union was the most important ally ZAPU had, the establishment of relations with Zimbabwe was somewhat difficult, and it only came after Moscow had made "certain pledges".

23   *Financial Times* (London) 16 February 1982.

24   This was largely true, as both sides considered it wise to keep some arms to meet what could be outcome of the Lancaster House-organised election. It should be mentioned that both ZANU and ZAPU suspected that there could be attempts to rig the elections in favour of Muzorewa.

25   *Herald* (Harare), 8 April, 1983.

26   The Emergency Powers made provision provision for the government to detain without trial. When Masuku's health was failing, he was released in March 1986. He died the following month. Dabengwa was not released until December 1986.

27   This is indicative of the relationship between Zimbabwe and Zambia immediately after the former's independence. As Zambia had supported Nkomo's ZAPU during the liberation war, the relationship between the two countries was initially cold.

28   See Prime Minister's Question Time in Hansard (Zimbabwe), July 13 1983, column 395—5.

29   This is the time usually regarded as the beginning of the dissident activities in Zimbabwe. There is however a claim by Wilf Mbaya, a South African based Zimbabwean journalist that the dissident operation had started since 1980. See "Ndebele Rebellion Gathering Force" *The Star*, Johannesburg, 23 July, 1980.

30   See *Zimbabwe: A Chronology of Dissidency*, Ministry of Information (Post and Telecommunication Publication, Harare, 1984).

31   This revelation was made by the dissidents who accepted Government's offer of amnesty at the end of unrest in 1987.

32   Some of the people I discussed with during my visit to the dissident

NOTES

affected areas of Zimbabwe told me this. However, a place where this is documented is the African Watch Report on Zimbabwe titled "Zimbabwe: A Break With The Past? Human Right and Political Unity".

33 After independence, the government passed the Firearms Recovery law to bring arms in individual hands under control. It is however obvious that not much success attended this effort at the initial stage.

34 The kidnappers were later caught, tried, convicted and were hanged. They confessed that the tourists were killed the day following their capture.

35 *Gayigusu* in Shona means grinding the bush. Apart from him, there were some other dissidents who attained notoriety in their own right. One of such was a man called Gwasela, who had more than 50 murder cases to answer for. Gwasela became a household name in Zimbabwe during the dissident operation, and as would be expected, a lot of myth surrounded his name. For example, he was believed to have magical powers with which he could disappear at will. This power was said to have been given to him by a witch doctor whom he later killed to prevent him from turning back later to withdraw the power. Gwasela was later killed by the government force, but Gayigusu survived the period of dissidency and was later granted amnesty.

36 Those found guilty of the murder were later hanged. One of them was one Phinas Ndlovu, who was believed to have led the attack.

37 These were the Police quoted figures, quoted from David Martin and Phyllis Johnson, *Destructive Engagement: Southern Africa at War* (Harare: Zimbabwe Publishing House, 1986), pp. 54 & 63.

38 Those accordingly marked down for retribution suffered unprintable punishment and could be killed.

39 Gathered from discussions with people in Matabeleland.

40 See especially the one made on 13 July 1983.

41 Throughout the unrest, the government claimed that it had "proof" linking Nkomo to the activities of the dissidents, but this was never disclosed. The only proof that could be used was the evidence of one Sango — the man who killed the six tourists. Sango claimed in court that he was instructed by Nkomo to kill the tourists. However, the court had no difficulty in dismissing him as an unreliable witness, as he was in the habit of changing his evidence at will. For example, at one point he said the tourists were alive and were still living in Zambia, whereas they had been killed more than six months earlier.

42 When the Prime Minister was asked what would be the punishment for anybody who provide food to the dissidents under duress, he said the circumstances would be understood. However, the circumstances under which assistance was offered made no difference to the soldiers that operated in the region.

43 Colin Legum, *The Battlefronts of Southern Africa* (Africana Publishing

Company, London, 1988), p. 252.
44 *Herald* (Harare), 28 August 1981.
45 Moorcraft, *op. cit.*, pp. 297—312.
46 Personal interview
47 David Martin and Phyllis Johnson, *Apartheid Terrorism: The Destabilization Report*
48 Stephen Ellis and Tsepo Sechaba, *Comrade against Apartheid: The ANC and South African Communist Party in Exile* (James Currey, London, 1992), pp. 109—110.
49 *ibid.*
50 Terence Ranger, "Matabeleland Since the Amnesty", *African Affairs*, p. Vol. 88, No. 351 p. 161.
51 Actually, the 5th Brigade became involved in the Matabeleland operations in January 1983. Before this time, a military force led by Lieutenant Colonel Lionel Dyke, of the former Rhodesian Army, led the military operations against the dissidents.
52 For an elaborate account of the human rights violation during this period, see "Zimbabwe: Wages of War", Lawyers Committee for Human Right Report.
53 Interview with former ZANLA members in the ZNA.
54 Personal interview with Professor Banana, July 1991.
55 An example of this, according to him, was the closing down of shops in Matabeleland.
56 *Hansard* (Zimbabwe), August 22 1984, col. 1087.
57 Nkala remained in Mugabe's cabinet until he was found guilty of corruption by the Sandura Commission of Inquiry which investigated the Willowgate Car Sale scandal in 1988 and was forced to resign.
58 For more on Nkomo's account of his escape, see his memoir *The Story of My Life* (Methuen, London, 1983).
59 *Hansard* (Zimbabwe), 19 January, 1983, column 872.
60 See *Hansard*, 15 March, 1983. This was published in the *Herald* (Harare), 16 March 1983.
61 *Keesing's Contemporary Archives*, July 1983, p. 32242.
62 *ibid.*
63 *Hansard* (Zimbabwe), 3 March, 1983.
64 Another "unusual" thing about Senator Todd's mild criticism was that it was reported by the *Herald*, the government's newspaper.
65 Williard Chiwewe, "Unity Negotiation", in Canaan Banana (ed), *Turmoil and Tenacity : Zimbabwe 1980—1990* (College Press Harare, 1990).
66 As of the time, Nyagumbo was ZANU's Secretary for Administration and a member of the party's Political Bureau, Munangagwa was the Minister of State (Security) in the Prime Minister's Office, while Zvobgo was also

NOTES

a member of the party's Politburo.
67 For a most comprehensive account of the debate on this, as well as other, see, Williard Chiwewe, "Unity Negotiation", in Banana, *op. cit.*
68 *ibid*, p. 261.
69 *ibid*.
70 Didimus Mutasa, "The Signing of the Unity Accord — A Step Forward in Zimbabwe's National Political Development, in Canaan Banana, *op. cit.*, p. 290.
71 *Parade* (July 1988), p. 11.
72 *ibid*.
73 *Parade* (July 1988), p. 13
74 Two of them, Never Maziri and Phumuza Ndlovu, represented their constituencies. See *Parade* (February 1990), pp 18-20.
75 During the first Congress meeting of the new party, a ZANU member — possibly unintentionally — shouted "Pamberi ne ZANU na va Mugabe; pasi ne ZAPU" (Forward with ZANU and Mugabe, down with ZAPU).
76 Welshman Ncumbe, "The Post-Unity Period: Developments, Benefits and Problems", in Canaan Banana, *op.cit.*, p. 309.
77 Those found guilty include senior minister for Political Affairs, Maurice Nyagumbo; Minister of Higher Education, Dzingai Mutumbuka; Minister of Industries and Technology, Callitus Ndolvu; Minister of Defence, Enos Nkala; Minister of Political Affairs, Frederick Shara and the Governor of Matabeleland North, Jacob Mudenda. All the Ministers later resigned from their posts and one of them, Maurice Nyagumbo, later committed suicide.
78 Shortly after independence, he was arrested and detained for leading an attack which resulted in the death of a white farmer. He was, however, freed on technical grounds. Tekere was later accused of anti-party activities, and he was relieved of his Ministerial duties and of his position as the party Secretary-General.
79 Welshman Ncumbe, *op. cit.*, p. 322.

5. Ethnicity

1 Books that emerged during this period include; Frederick Barth (ed), *Ethnic Groups and Boundaries: The Social Organisation of Cultural Difference* (Little Brown, Boston, 1969); and Glazer and Moyniham

(eds), *Ethnicity: Theory and Practice*, (Harvard University Press, Cambridge MA 1975).
2   Stephen Ryan, *Ethnic Conflict and International Relations* (Dartmouth Publishing Company Ltd., Aldershot, 1990), p. xiii
3   As quoted from Engeen Rosens, *Creating Ethnicity: The Process of Ethnogenesis* (Sage Publication, London, 1989), p. 12
4   Nancie Gonzales "Conflict, Migration and the Expression of Ethnicity: Introduction", in Nancie Gonzales and Carolyn McCommon (eds), *Conflict, Migration and the Expression of Ethnicity* (Westview, Boulder, 1989), p. 8.
5   Stephen Ryan, *op. cit.*, p. 12
6   Nigeria presents a good example in this regard. There are many "Unity Schools" built in all the states in the country to bring together people from all the ethnic groups in the country, while there is an obligatory one year "national service" for all university graduates to live and work in states outside that of their origin.
7   A recent work that discusses ethnicity is Eghosa Osaghe, "A Re-examination of the Concept of Ethnicity in Africa As an Ideology of Inter-State Competition", *African Study Monographs*, 12, (1), (June 1991).
8   The *Mfecane* is the Zulu word used to describe the violent military outburst that engulfed the whole of southern Africa in the 19th century. It was one of the greatest military occurrences in the sub-region, during which Shaka, the Zulu king, embarked on a remarkable series of conquests to form a large kingdom which was to last for sixty years after his death in 1828. The Ndebele leader who emerged during the turmoil was Mtwalikizi, and he led his people away from the war zone to the place named Bulawayo, meaning "The place of the persecuted". Bulawayo remains till date, the capital of the Ndebeles. For more on the *Mfecane*, see, J.O. Omer-Copper, *The Zulu Aftermath: 19th Century Revolution in Bantu Africa* (Longman, London, 1966).
9   These were Joseph Msika (Natural Resources and Water Development), Clement Mucahchi (Public Works) and George Silundika (Post and Telecommunication). Nkomo was for the Home Affairs Ministry.
10 Discussion with people in Bulawayo in March 1990.
11 I gathered these feelings during my interviews with the people in Matabeleland.
12 Personal interview.
13 Perence Shiri was later seconded to the Air Force of Zimbabwe, becoming its first Black Commodore and Deputy Commander. He is presently the Commander of the Air Force of Zimbabwe.
14 Discussions with people in Matabele province of Zimbabwe.

NOTES

15 Keith Somerville, *Angola, Politics, Economic and Society* (Frances Pinter, London, 1986), p.58.
16 *ibid.*, p. 60
17 Foremost in this regard is Fred Bridgland in his celebrated book on Savimbi.
18 Alex Vines, *Renamo Terrorism in Mozambique* (James Currey, London, 1990), p. 84.
19 *The New Yorker*, 22 May 1989, p. 70.
20 For more on this, see Alex Vines, *op. cit.*, especially chapter four of *The Domestic Dimension to the Renamo Crisis*.
21 I was able to see and read one of these during my visit to Chiredze in March 1990. The leaflet written in a rather poor English language, alleged that Mugabe decided to maintain his position on RENAMO in order to sacrifice the people living on the border towns, and asked the people whether they thought Mugabe would not have negotiated if the affected areas are those where he had ethnic and political support.

6. Economic Cost

1 Joseph Hanlon, *Apartheid's Second Front: South Africa's War Against Its Neighbours* (Penguin, Harmondsworth, 1986).
2 Joseph Hanlon quoted the former Head of South Africa railways Dr Jacobus Loubser, who coined the phrase "transport diplomacy"; academic Den Geldenhuy who rated ports and railways as the most important economic weapon; and the Head of African Institute in Pretoria, G.M.E. Leistner, who considered transport as the most effective retaliatory measure against South African neighbours.
3 Guy Arnold and Ruth Weiss, *Strategic Highways of Africa* (Julian Friedman Publishers, London, 1977), p. 21.
4 *Africa Analysis*, 28 May 1993, p. 4.
5 Carolyne McMaster, *Malawi: Foreign Policy and Development* (Julian Friedman, London, 1974), p. 124—5.
6 *ibid.* p. 91—3.
7 There is a detailed expose of the opposition to the creation of the dam in

Cabora Bassa and the Struggle for Southern Africa, A World Council Churches Publication.
8 Martin and Johnson, *op. cit.*, p.14
9 David Martin and Phyllis Johnson, *Apartheid Terrorism* (Commonwealth Secretariat, London, 1989).
10 *ibid.*
11 *African Confidential*, Vol. 33, No. 16 (14 August 1992).
12 These figures were taken from Naigzy Gebremedlin, "The Environmental Dimension of Security in the Horn of Africa", *Life and Peace Review*, No. 1, 1991.
13 Joseph Hanlon in the appendix to his book *Beggar Your Neighbour*, has broken down the issue of South Africa's destabilization under several detailed sub-headings.
14 Virtually all published works put this at between $10 and 15 billion.
15 *The Citizen*, 20 July 1987.
16 *ibid.*
17 *African Confidential*, 4 March 1988.
18 *The Guardian*, London, 24 February 1987.
19 *Southscan*, 20 January 1988.
20 *The Windhoek Advertiser*, Windhoek, 6 June 1988.
21 ibid.
22 Mr Chalmer, a white member of the Zimbabwean parliament, said there was a 25 per cent reduction in tourism. See Hansard of the Zimbabwean parliament, 26 July 1983. This was neither confirmed nor denied by the authorities.
23 *Index on Censorship*, Vol. 21, No. 4, 1992, p. 23.

7. Conclusion

1 The most recent in this regard is Guy Arnold, *South Africa: Crossing the Rubicon* (Macmillan, London, 1992).
2 See *West Africa*, 16—22 November, 1992, p, 1981.
3 *Africa News on Human Right and Democratic Development International Society for Human Rights*, Vol. 1, No. 1, 1993, p. 2.
4 *African Research Bulletin* (May 1993), p. 10994
5 "Angola: Restarting the Economy", *African Confidential*, Vol. 33, No. 18, (13 November 1992).
6 *Index on Censorship*, Vol. 21, No.4, (April 1992), p. 23.

NOTES

7   Discussion with a relief worker in Mozambique.
8   *West Africa*, 14—20 November 1992, p. 2146
9   *ibid*.
10 Quoted by *West Africa*, 29 November—5 December, 1993, p.2172.
11 Her reaction was quoted in, Chris Simpson "Angola: Another Year of Bloody War", *African Topics* (Nov—December, 1993), p. 16.

APPENDICES

APPENDIX 1

Text of the Unity Agreement signed Between ZANU and ZAPU in Zimbabawe in December 1987

1. That Zanu (PF) and PF Zapu have irrevocably committed themselves to unit under one political party;

2. That the unity of the two political parties shall be achieved under the name Zimbabwean African National Union (Patriotic Front), in short ZANU(PF);

3. That Comrade Robert Mugabe shall be the First Secretary and President of ZANU(PF);

4. That ZANU(PF) shall have two Second Secretaries and Vice Presidents who shall be appointed by the First Secretary and President of the Party;

5. That ZANU(PF) shall seek to establish a socialist society in Zimbabwe on the guidance of Marxist-Leninist principles;

6. That ZANU(PF) shall seek to establish a one-party state in Zimbabwe;

7. That the leadership of ZANU(PF) shall abide by the Leadership code;

8. That the present leadership of PF Zapu shall take immediate vigorous steps to help eliminate and end the insecurity and violence prevalent in Matabeleland;

9. That ZANU(PF) and PF ZAPU shall convene their respective

APPENDICES

Congresses to give effect to this agreement within the shortest possible time;

10. That, in the interim, Comrade Robert Gabriel Mugabe is vested with full powers to prepare for the implementation of this agreement and to act in the name and authority of ZANU(PF);

11. That, in the interim, Comrade Robert Gabriel Mugabe is vested with full powers to prepare for the implementation of this agreement and to act in the name and authority of ZANU(PF).

APPENDIX 2

Mozambique's "12 Principles" for Peace

1. We are faced with an operation of destabilization which should not be confused with a struggle between two parties.

2. The operation has been mounted through brutal acts of terrorism which provoke immense suffering falling, above all, on the population and their property. Hundreds of thousands of people have already died. Many economic and social infrastructures in the country have been destroyed or paralysed, impeding the normal life of citizens and turning millions of people into displaced persons.

3. The aim is to put an end to this inhuman situation. The first action should be to stop all terrorist and bandit actions.

4. Afterwards, conditions should be created for all Mozambicans citizens to lead normal lives in such a way that they can participate, on the one hand, in the political, economic. social and cultural life of the country, and on the other hand, in the discussion and definition of the policies which will guide the country in each of these aspects (political, economic social and cultural).

5. These policies are established by national consensus, formulated through a process of consultation and debate with the people or social groups involved. The principal laws relating to land, health and education, were approved after consultation with the people. The on-going revision of the constitution has been taking place through a debate which aims at introducing growing factors of democratic participation in the working of the state. Religious institutions are being consulted in the process of the preparation of legislation on religious liberties.

APPENDICES

6. Dialogue will aim at clarifying these positions and giving guarantees of participation in it to all individuals, including those who until then had been involved in violent acts of destabilization.

7. This participation and enjoyment of rights applies immediately to the processes which are already underway regarding the affirmation of the principles defined in the Constitution in relation to:
(a) the protection of individuals and collective liberties; (b) the protection of human rights; (c) the protection of democratic rights.

8. Individual and social liberties, such as freedom of worship, freedom of expression and freedom of assembly are guaranteed. They should not be used against the general interests of the nation. They should not be used to destroy national unity, national independence and the integrity of persons and property. They should not be used to propagate tribalism, racism. regionalism or any form of divisionism or sectarianism. They should not be used for the preparation of perpetration of acts punishable by law, such as robbery, assassination or aggression. They cannot be used for the preparation or perpetration of violent acts against the State and the Constitution, such as secessionist movements or coup-detat.

9. Policy or constitutional changes or revisions, or changes or revisions to the political laws of the country, where in many cases debate or consultation with the citizens has already accrued or is in process can be brought and should be brought only through the ample participation of all citizens.

10. It is unacceptable for a group to use intimidation or violence to impose themselves on the whole society. It is anti-democratic to alter the constitution and the principal laws of the country through the violence of a group.

11. The normalisation of life and the integration of those until now

involved in violent actions of destabilization implies, in general way, their participation in economic and social life through suitable ways agreed by them and guaranteed by the government.

12. The acceptance of these principles could lead to a dialogue about the modalities foe ending violence, establishing peace and normalising life for all in the country.

APPENDIX 3

Renamo's "16 Points" Condition for Peace

1. Since 1964, the Mozambican people have been dying everyday, victims of war.

2. It is therefore essential that all true nationalists and lovers of peace, whether members of political organisations or not, should make effort, mobilising for a purpose the means at their disposal to find a genuinely Mozambican and African solution, which will bring enduring peace and stability.

3. The Mozambican people need freedom. It is from freedom that peace, stability, prosperity and individual respect and dignity derive.

4. The principle must dominate that the people are sovereign and have the inalienable right to elect their representatives who serve their expectations and who respect their secular traditions.

5. Renamo is a political force which is active on the Mozambican political scene. Any solution for peace must take this reality into account as well as the traditions, culture, level of development and realities of the present moment.

6. It is not Renamo's intention to change the existing order in Mozambique through armed force. The armed struggle only serves as the last resort in the defence of the people against the denial of their rights and against their oppression.

7. Renamo will never agree to military force being used to impose a leadership or political options against the will of the

people.

8. None of the parties to this conflict have anything to gain from the continuation of this war. Only the people see suffering increasing everyday.

9. A stop must be put to verbal and insulting attacks both by those who are fighting against us as well as those outside who are/have a direct or indirect interest in the problem. Look to the future and not the past.

10. Propaganda against Renamo does not change the political and military reality in Mozambique, and neither will it facilitate national reconciliation.

11. The presence of foreign forces brought in by Frelimo do not (sic) bring peace and well-being for the Mozambican people. We in Renamo see this presence as an obstacle to peace, besides signifying an insult(?) to our dignity and the loss of national sovereignty and independence.

12. For the resolution of the present conflict, Renamo takes into account the neighbouring countries and other interests in the region.

13. Renamo publicly declares that it will do everything in its power to ensure that the present negotiation process continues and finally results in peace.

14. Renamo defends the people, the reasons for its existence and its struggle, with intransigence. It is opposed to any act which violates the people's physical or moral integrity, such as massacres, pillaging etc.

15. Renamo is a guerrilla force, whose survival depends only on the people, and for this reason it is naturally against any act of atrocity (sic) which puts at risk the life of the people. The reason for its existence.

APPENDICES

16. Renamo wants: genuine negotiations leading to national reconciliation without winners or losers followed by constitutional reforms; to join forces to form a new Mozambique, where our brotherhood may be affirmed through free debate of ideas and by consensus; a new Mozambique where the armed struggle will never again become the last and only resort for the solution of our problem.

APPENDIX 4

Text of the Amnesty Law declared by the Frelimo Government in Mozambique for the Renamo Rebels

The war which is being waged against us from outside our borders is characterised by cruel and barbaric acts of terrorism, in the perpetration of which Mozambicans working for anti-Mozambican interest have also taken part. They have concentrated especially on civilian targets - women, children and old people, and on the social and economic infrastructure.

The strong feeling of revulsion which such actions have aroused among our people has been shared by the international community. Even among those who have been used as instruments by the foreign enemies of our people, there are some who have become aware of the true and express designs of this struggle, which aims to destroy the people themselves.

There are others who, having been abducted and forcibly trained by the enemy, have been turned, against their will, into the allies of the indignity and into the denigrators of the people.

With the objective of encouraging those who want to abandon their life of crime and who aspire to peaceful life among the Mozambican nation, the present amnesty is declared, as a way of allowing them to reassume their places in family and society.

This measure of clemency follows a principle which is already a tradition of the Mozambique Liberation Front (FRELIMO) and which springs from the deep conviction that man is able to change himself, and that our society is able to change man. It is part of an attempt to achieve peace, but a real and enduring peace, which will protect the independence, national sovereignty and territorial integrity of our

APPENDICES

country, respecting the dignity and the character of our people, guarding their achievements and guaranteeing the well-being and happiness of all Mozambicans. Because of this, the law which follows establishes the principle of the reintegration of those individuals who voluntarily give themselves up, taking the necessary steps for public health, employment, and making other adequate provisions.

Thus, using the powers granted under Article 44, Clause (i) of the Constitution, the People's Assembly decrees:

ARTICLE 1

EXTENT OF THE AMNESTY

1. Crimes against the security of the people and the People's state, covered by Law no.2/79 of 1 March are amnestied, when committed by Mozambican citizens who in whatever manner have fought against or have promoted violence against the Mozambican people or state, inside the country or abroad on condition that they voluntarily give themselves up.

2. The amnesty also applies to those who, before the date when the present law comes into force, have voluntarily given themselves up to party or state bodies.

ARTICLE 2

PRESENTATION OF BENEFICIARIES

1. Those who wish to benefit from the present amnesty may give themselves up, either directly, or through others, to any Party or State body.

2. They may give themselves up through members of the Mozambican Red Cross, or through members of any other legally-recognised social organisation.

3. In foreign countries, they may give themselves up through the

diplomatic and consular representatives of the People's republic of Mozambique, either directly or through recognised international organisations which, in this case, will make contact with the Mozambican Government.

ARTICLE 3

RECEPTION AND SOCIAL REINTEGRATION

1. Wherever necessary, the Government will organise reception centres with sufficient, basic and healthy conditions for the reception, organisation and social reintegration of beneficiaries of the amnesty.

2. Social reintegration will be accomplished by creating conditions in which those covered by the present measure may contribute to national reconstruction by doing socially useful work.

3. In order to create the employment referred to in previous clauses, the Government may mobilise the support and eventually the participation of international organisations.

ARTICLE 4

DEADLINE FOR PRESENTATION

The deadline for presentation under the present law expires on 31 December 1988.

ARTICLE 5

DATE OF COMING INTO EFFECT

The present law comes into effect immediately.

APPENDIX 5

Main Clauses of the Rome Peace Agreement Between the Mozambican Government and Renamo.*

1) The Government of the Republic of Mozambique will reach agreement with the Government of the Republic of Zimbabwe on the means for concentrating Zimbabwean forces along the zones known as the Beira Corridor and the Limpopo corridor, at a maximum distances of three kilometres outside the farthest edges of those corridors. This limit can be changed at the proposal of the Joint Verification Commission, referred to in paragraph 3, according to criteria to guarantee more secure and efficient verification. The Zimbabwean troop concentration in the above-mentioned corridors will begin at the latest fifteen days after the signing of the agreement and will be completed before a deadline of twenty days after the date of beginning the concentration.

1.1) The Government of the Republic of Mozambique will inform those negotiating of the maximum number of Zimbabwean troops who will remain in the corridors.

1.2) Zimbabwean troops are not allowed to take part in offensive military operations while the concentration is taking place.

2) To facilitate the peace process in Mozambique, the Renamo will stop all offensive military operations and attacks along the Beira and Limpopo corridors, within the areas agreed in paragraph 1.

3) A Joint Verification Commission is established to supervise the strict implementation of this agreement. It includes three civilians and military representatives each nominated by the Government of Mozambique and Renamo, whose names will

be given to the mediators within seven days of the signing of this agreement. The Government of the Republic of Zimbabwe may also nominate three representatives to the Joint Verification Commission.

3.1) The mediators or their representatives will also be members of the Joint Verification Commission, which they will chair. Eight countries, to be agreed between the assenting parties, will also be members.

3.2) The Joint Verification Commission will be based in Maputo. It will submit regular reports to the negotiating sessions, or at the request of one of the assenting parties.

3.3) The Joint Verification Commission may establish sub-committees with the same membership, to verify the implementation of the agreement on the ground.

3.4) The members of the Joint Verification Commission will enjoy diplomatic status. The Government of the Republic of Mozambique and Renamo will guarantee the safety and the free movement of the members of the Commission and its sub-committees, as well its representatives, in any areas covered by this agreement.

3.5) The Joint Verification Commission will work out the security measures for its members in due course. The Government of the Republic of Mozambique will furnish offices for the Joint Verification Commission, as well as the necessary supplies for its work.

3.6) The Joint Verification Commission will be sworn in within fifteen days of the signing of this agreement and will begin work at once. It will supervise the implementation of the agreement for a six month period, renewable if necessary by agreement between the assenting parties.

3.7) The Joint Verification Commission will submit the basic principles of its work to the negotiating session for approval as soon as it has been sworn in.

3.8) The delegations of the Republic of Mozambique and the Renamo ask the Italian Government and other member countries of the Joint Verification Commission to try at both the bilateral and multilateral levels, to secure the necessary funding and technical support for the efficient operation of the Joint Verification Commission set up by this agreement.

4.) The assenting parties agree to avoid any activity which might directly or indirectly violate the spirit or the letter of this agreement. In case any unusual occurrence of a military nature is noted, which could prejudice the implementation of this agreement, the mediators may, at the request of one of the parties, take practical steps to identify and resolve the problem.

4.1) The Government of the Republic of Mozambique and Renamo, believing that the signing and implementation of this agreement will make a significant contribution to the strengthening of the climate of confidence necessary for dialogue, renew their commitment to the further analysis of the remaining agenda points, aimed at achieving peace in Mozambique.

5.) This agreement comes into force on the date of signing.

APPENDIX 6

UNITA's Twelve Point Peace Plans

A 12-Point Peace Plan to end the civil war in Angola was adopted by UNITA in 1989. The Plan was put in the form of 12 Questions.

1.) Should we sign a cease-fire?

Decided: UNITA should sign a cease-fire, but both sides must release all political prisoners under the supervision of the International Red Cross and similar organisations.

2.) Should a cease-fire be supervised?

Decided: It should be supervised by countries like Nigeria, Morocco, Togo and other African countries. (Later at a press conference, Unita leader, Jonas Savimbi, suggested Portugal might be included.)

3.) What do you think of reconciliation between UNITA and the MPLA?

Decided: There must be reconciliation, leading to a government of national unity as a transitional stage.

4.) Who should mediate?

Decided: Only one country should mediate. (President Mobutu Sese Seko of Zaire was approached after the Congress and accepted)

5.) Should UNITA insist on free and fair election and democracy or is a compromise acceptable?

Decided: No Compromise. UNITA must insist to the end of free elections.

APPENDICES

6.) Should Savimbi go on exile?

Decided: Absolutely not.

7.) Should UNITA and the MPLA integrate and also FALA and FAPLA (their respective armies)?

Decided: No form of integration is acceptable.

8.) What do you think of MPLA's policy of amnesty and clemency?

Decided: Both must be rejected. There must be reconciliation instead.

9.) What do you think of the MPLA's view that there is no need for a new constitution?

Decided: There can be no peace or reconciliation unless a new constitution is written.

10.) In spite of UNITA's flexibility, the MPLA and its friends remain intransigent. What should UNITA do?

Decided: UNITA must go fighting until the MPLA accepts.

11.) What if the MPLA's intransigence leads to all help for UNITA being cut?

Decided: UNITA must go on fighting until Angola's sovereignty and liberty have been achieved.

12.) If the MPLA's intransigence and UNITA's response lead to UNITA being cut off from all help, for how long in your opinion can UNITA continue to resist?

Decided: UNITA must resist to the end.

SELECT BIBLIOGRAPHY

Abegunrin O., *Economic Dependence and Regional Cooperation in Southern Africa: SADCC and South Africa in Confrontation*, New York: Edwin Mellen Press, 1992.

Abrahamse L., "Current Trend in Southern Africa", *South Africa International* (January 1978).

Akinbinu F., *Mozambique-South Africa Relations*, Unpublished M.Sc thesis, University of Ife, 1985.

Akinrinade O., *Africa and the Commonwealth: The Impact of an International Organisation in Foreign Policy Making*, Unpublished Ph.D. thesis, University of London, 1988.

Alao A., *African Conflict: The Future Without the Cold War* London: Brassey Publisher (For the Center for Defence Studies), 1993.

------- *The Defence and Security Implications of the Liberation War on Zimbabwe, 1980-1987*, Unpublished Ph.D. thesis, University of London, 1992.

Aluko. O., and Shaw T.,(eds) *Southern Africa in the 1980s*, London: George Allen and Unwin, 1985.

Ascrow A., *Zimbabwe: A Revolution that Lost its Way ?*, London: Zed, 1983.

Anglin D., Shaw T., and Widstrand C., (eds) *Conflict and Change in Southern Africa*, Waashington: University Press of America, 1978.

Arnold G., *Southern Africa: Crossing the Rubbicon*, London: Macmillan, 1992.

BIBLIOGRAPHY

Azeredo M., "A Sober Commitment to the Liberation: Mozambique and South Africa 1974-79", *African Affiars*, Vol 79, No. 317, 1980.

Banana C., (ed) *Turmoil and Tenacity: Zimbabwe 1980-1900*, Harare: College Press Ltd., 1989.

Barrat J., "Detente in Southern Africa", *The World Today*, March 1975.

---------, "Southern Africa: A South African View", *Foreign Affiars*, October 1976.

---------, *Eyes on the Eighties: The International Political Outlook for Southern Africa*, Braamfontein: Souther African Institute of International Affiars, 1979.

Barber J., "Zimbabwe: The Southern African Setting" *The World Today*, October 1988.

Barber J., and Barrat J., *South Africa's Foreign Policy: The Search For Status and Security, 1975-1988*, Cambridge: Cambridge University Press, 1990.

Bender G., *Angola Under The Portuguese* London: Heinemman, 1978.

Bloomsfield R., (ed) *Regional Conflict and US Policy: Angola and Mozambique*, Algonac: World Peace Foundation, 1988.

Bowman L., "South Africa's Southern Strategy and Its Implications for the United States, *International Affiars*, 47, January 1971.

Bratton M., "Development in Zimbabwe: Staregy and Tactics", *Journal of Modern African Studies*, 19, 1987.

Bridgland F., *Jonas Savimbi: A Key to Africa*, Edinburgh: Mainstream Publisher, 1986.

---------- *The War For Africa: Twelve Months that Transformed A Continent*, Gibralter: Ashanti Ltd. 1991.

Brittain V., *Hidden Lives, Hidden Death: South Africa's Crippling of a Countinent*, London: Faber and Faber, 1988.

Burchett W., *Southern Africa Stands Up: The Revolutions in Angola, Mozambique, Zimbabwe, Namibia and South Africa,* New York: Urizen Books, 1978.

Callaghy T., (ed) *South Africa in Southern Africa: The Intensifying Votex of Violence,* New York: Praeger, 1983.

Callinico A., *Southern Africa After Soweto* London: Pluto Press, 1977.

Campbell H., "Nkomati Before and After: War Reconstruction and Dependence in Mozambique", *Journal of African Marxist*, October 1984.

Carter G., *Which Way is South Africa Going,* Bloomington: Indiana University Press, 1980.

Cater G., and O'Meara P., *South Africa in Crisis* Bloomington: Indiana University Press, 1977.

-------- and ---------., (eds) *Southern Africa: The Countinuing Crisis*London: Macmillan, 1979.

Chan S., *Exporting Apartheid: Foreign Policy in Southern Africa, 1978-1988,*London: Macmillan, 1990.

-------- *Kaunda and Southern Africa: Image and Reality in Foreign Policy,*London: British Academic Press, 1992.

Christe I., *Samora Mache: A Biography,* London: Panaf, 1989.

Clough M., *Changing Realities in Southern Africa: Implications for American Foreign Policy,* Berkeley: Institute of International Studies, 1982.

Crocker C., "South Africa: A Strategy for Change" *Foreign Affairs,* No. 9, 1980-81.

BIBLIOGRAPHY

Dalcanton C., "Vorster and the Politics of Confidence", *African Affiars*, 75 1976.

Davis R., "South Africa Strategy Towards Mozambique Since Nkomati" *Transformation*, 3, 1987.

------- and O'Meara D., "Total Stategy in Southern Africa: Analyses of South Africa's Regional Strategy Since 1978", *Journal of Southern African Studies*, Vol 11, No. 11, April 1985.

El-Khawas M., and Cohen B., (eds) *The Kissinger Study on Southern Africa: National Security Memorandum, 31*, Westport: Lawrence Hill, 1976.

Evans M., "Gukurahundi: The Development of Zimbabwean Defence Force 1980-1987", *Strategic Review of Southern Africa*, Vol. X, No. 1, May 1988.

Fauset P., "Roots of Counter-Revolution: The Mozambique National Resistance", *Review of African Political Economy*, No 29, July 1984.

Frederikse J., " The Long Awaited Peace Still Seem far Away", *Moto*, March 1985

Garba J., *Diplomatic Soldering*, Ibadan: Spectrum, 1987.

Geldenhuys D., "The destabilisation Controversy: An Analysis of a High-Risk Foreign Policy Option for South Africa" *Politikon* 2 1982.

Grundy K., *Confrontation and Accomodation in Southern Africa: The Limit of Independence*, Beckeley, University of California Press, 1973.

Grundy K., *The Militarisation Of South African Politics*, London: Tauris, 1986.

Guelke A., "Southern Africa and the Super Powers" *International Affiars* 56, 1980.

Hallet R., "The South African Intervention in Angola in 1975-76",

African Affiars,Vol. 77, No. 308, July 1978.

Hanlon J., *Apartheid's Second Front* Harmondsworth: Penguin, 1986.

--------- *Begger Your Neighbour*, London: James Currey, 1986.

--------- *Mozambique: The Revolution Under Fire*, Lomndon: James Currey, 1984.

--------- *Mozambique: Who Calls The First Shot* London: James Currey, 1991.

Hodder-William R., "Conflict in Zimbabwe: The Matabeleland Problem", *Conflict Studies,* No 151, 1983.

Hoile D., *Mozambique: A Nation in Crisis,* London: Clardge press.

Holness M., *Apartheid's War Against Angola* New York: Center Against Apartheid, 1983.

Hull G., *Pawns on a Chessboard: The Resource War in Southern Africa* Washington: University of America Press, 1981.

Isaacman A., "The Malawian Connection" *African Report,* Nov/Dec 1986.

--------- and Isaacman B., "South Africa's Hidden War" *African Report* Nov/Dec 1987.

Jaster R., *South Africa and Its Neighbours: The Dynamic of Regional Conflict,* Adelphi papers 209, Summer 1986.

Jenkins S., "Destabilisation in Southern Africa", *The Economist,* July 1983.

Johnson R., *How Long Will South Africa Survive?* New York, Oxford University Press, 1977.

Legum C., *Southern Africa: The Year of the Whirlwind,* London: Rex

BIBLIOGRAPHY

Collins, 1979.

-------- *The Battlefront of Southern Africa* New York: Africana Publishing Press, 1988.

-------- " The Soviet Union, China and the West in Southern Africa", *Foreign Affiars*, July 1976.

------- et al, (eds) *Africa in the 1980s: A Continent in Crisis,* New York: McGraw-Hill, 1979.

Lemarchand R., (ed) *American Policy in Southern Africa: The Stakes and The Stance* Washington: University Press of America, 1981.

Leornald R., *South Africa at War,* Craighall: AD Donker, 1983.

Macara M., "The Political Sociology of racial Dominance: Rhodesia 1860-1965" *Unpublished Ph.D. thesis, University of Rhodesia*, 1974.

Machel S., *Sowing the Seeds of Revolution*, Harare: Zimbabwe Publishing House, 1991.

Malan T., "New Dimensions in Southern African Economic Relationship", *ISSUP Strategic Review*, March 1983.

Mallaby S., *After Apartheid*, London: Faber and Faber, 1992.

Mandaza I., (ed) *Zimbabwe: The Political Economy of Transition* Darker: Cordessia Press, 1986.

Martin D., and Johnson P., *Apartheid Terrorism,* London: Commonwealth Secretariat Press, 1989.

---------- and --------- *Destructive Engagement: Southern Africa at War,* Harare: Zimbabwean Publishing House, 1986.

Martin R., Regional Security in Southern Africa *Survival,* September/October 1987.

Maier K., "Stalingrad Waits in the African Bush", *Christian Science Monitor*, march 1988.

Mawani M., "Nkomati False Dawn", *New Africa*, October 1984.

Maxwell K., "Portugal and Africa", in Gifford P., and Louis W., *The Transfer of Power In Africa*, New Haven: Yale University Press: 1982.

McMaster C., *Malawi: Foreign Policy and Development*,London: Julian Friedmann, 1974.

Meredith M., *The First Dance of Freedom: Black Africa in the Post War Era*, London: Hamish Hamilton, 1984.

Metrowich F., *South Africa's New Frontiers*, Sandton: valiant, 1977.

Minter W., "Correspondence in Southern Africa" *Review of Books"* June/July 1989.

---------- *Operation Timber: Pages from the Savimbi Dossiers*, Trenton: A.W.P., 1968.

Mondlane E., *The Struggle For Mozambique*, London: Penguin

Msabala I., and Shaw T., (eds) *Confrontation and Liberation: Regional Direction after Nkomati Accord*, Boulder: Westview, 1979.

Nana J., "The Political and Staregic Implications of the Nkomati Accord on the Frontline States", *Unpublished M.Sc. thesis, University of Ife*, 1985.

Newsum A., and Abegunrin O., *United States Foreign Policy Towards Southern Africa: Andrew Young and Beyound*, London: Macmillan, 1987.

Nolutshungu S., *South Africa in Southern Africa: A Study of Ideology and Foreign Policy"*, Manchester: Manchester University Press, 1975.

Norval M., *Death in the Desert: The Namibian Tragedy*, Washington:

Selous Foundation Press, 1977.

Osaghe E., "A Reexamination of the Concept of Ethnicity in Africa As An Ideology of InterState Competition" *Africa Study Monography*, 12 June 1991.

Ranger, T., "Matabeleland Since the Amnesty", *African Affiars,* Vol 88, No 351, April 1989.

Rotberg, R., *Suffer the Future: Policy Changes in Southern Africa*, Cambridge Mass: Harvard University Press, 1980.

-------- and Barrat J., (eds) *Conflict and Compromise in Southern Africa* Lexington Mass: Lexington Books, 1980.

Salaita J., "The Miliitarization of the SADCC States As a Consequence of South Africa's Total stategy and its Socio-economic and Political Implications" *Unpublished Paper.*

Seidman A., *The Roots of Crisis in Southern Africa* Trenton: African World Books, 1985.

Seiler J., (ed) *Southern Africa Since the Portuguese Coup* Boulder:Westview 1980.

Shaw T., "International Organisations and the Politics of South Africa: Towards regional Integration or Liberation", *Journal of South African Affiars*Vol. 3, No 1, Oct. 1976.

-------- "Southern Africa: Cooperation and Conflict in an International Sub-system" *Journal of Modern African Studies, Dec, 1974.*

-------- *and Kenneth A., (eds) Cooperation and Conflict in Southern Africa* Washington: University Press of America, 1977.

Shevchenco *Breaking with Moscow*, New York: Ballantine Books, 1975.

Sommerville K., *Angola: Politics, Economics and Society*, London:

Frances Pinter, 1986.

------------ "The USSR and Southern Africa Since 1976", *Journal of Modern African Studies*, 22 (1) March 1984.

Soremekun F., *Angola: The Road to Independence* Ife: University of Ife Press, 1984.

Spence J., "Detente in Southern Africa: An Interim Assessment", *International Affiars*, 53, London January, 1977.

-------- "South African Foreign Policy: The Outward Movement" in Potholm C., and Dale R., (eds) *Southern Africa in Perspective*, New York: Fress Press, 1971.

-------- *The Soviet Union, The Third World and Southern Africa* South African Institute of International Affiars

-------- "South Africa's Military Relation With Its Neighbours" in Baynham S., (ed) *The Military Power and Politics in Black Africa"* London: Croom Helm, 1986.

Stockwell J., *In Search of Enemies*, London: Andrew Deutsch, 1978.

Swift K., *Mozambique and The Future*, London: Robert Hale and Co., 1975.

Vine A., *Renamo: Terrorism in Mozambique*, London: James Currey, 1991.

Wolfer M., and Bergerol J., *Angola in the Frontline* London: Zed Press, 1983.

INDEX

Addis Ababa, 42
Afghanistan, 26, 32, 69
Ambriz, 16
ANC, 4, 7, 29-31, 47, 59-65, 141, 142, 150
Angola, 1-9, 11, 13, 15, 17, 18, 19, 20-37, 39, 41-45, 47, 49, 62, 67-71, 83, 110, 111, 118, 120, 153, 154
Arusha, 61

Bade, 56
Bakongo, 3,
Ben-Ben, General, Arlindo Chenda, 42
Benguela, 17, 22, 25,35,43, 130
Benguerir, 24
Bie, 33, 35, 118
BMATT, see British Military Advisory and Training Team
BOSS, 49
Botswana, 6, 18, 80, 128
Brazzaville, 37
Britain, 25, 57, 58, 72, 73, 92, 93
British Military Advisory and Training Team, 56, 85
Bulawayo, 87, 89, 92, 106

Cabinda, 20, 29, 33, 41, 43, 62, 132, 133, 146
Cahama, 28
Caiundo, 28
Carlucci, Frank, 72
Catholic Church, 39, 75, 76, 100, 104
Caxito, 43
Chalker, Lynda, 74
Chicoa, 7
Chingunji, 32
Chioco, 7
CIA, 3, 23, 26, 69, 71
CIO, 45, 46, 97
Citizens for America, 26, 55
Constructive Engagement, 30, 31
Crocker, Chester, 30, 31
Cuando Cubango, 27, 33, 35, 118
Cuba, 3, 17, 21, 34, 36, 37,

41, 141
Cuito Cuanavale, 32-36, 42, 176, 141, 142
Cunene, 27, 28, 33, 118
Cuvelai, 28

Dabengwa, Dumiso, 87, 89-91, 95, 96, 114
de Klerk, President F. W., 38, 43, 140, 141, 142
de Klerk, Gert, 43
Dhalakhama, Alfonso, 47, 48, 50, 66, 73, 74, 76-80, 121, 147
Domingo Raul, 78
dos Pasos, Luis, 41
dos Santos, Maecelimo, 4
dos Santos, Wilson, 32
dos Santos, President Eduardo, 38-40
du Troit, Wyanand, Petrus, 29
Dumbutshena, Enock, 107

ed Fugit, 78
El Salvador, 20
Emocha, 133
Empadeni, 104
Encounter Overland, 92
Essexvalle, 87
Estoril, 40
Evora, 39

Fifth Brigade, 100
FLEC, 41, 146
Freedom Inc, 71,
Frontline States, 2, 56, 61, 62, 83, 150

Gabon, 44
Gayigusu, 93,
Gbadolite, 38
Geneva, 37, 83
Gorbachev, Mikhail, 141
Gorongosa, 56, 65, 79
Gukurahundi, 86
Gulf Oil, 20

Harare, 11, 12, 54, 78, 87, 106, 107, 111, 122, 128, 144
Heritage Foundation, 51, 71
Holland, 58
Honwana, Fernando, 67
Huambo, 33, 42-44, 118

Iran, 20
Irangate, 71

Jadin, 51
Jamba, 25, 26, 33, 34, 38, 40, 43
Johnson, 97,
JVC, 79

Kafunfo Diamond Mines, 26
Kalanga, 111
Kambona, Oscar, 72
Katanga, 19, 130
Kuwait, 20

Lancaster House, 10, 12, 46, 72, 83, 84, 88, 96, 97, 138
Laos, 26
Lonrho, 80, 136
Luanda, 15, 16, 20, 40, 42, 43, 119, 133

# INDEX

Lusaka Accord, 28, 62

Magua, 7
Malawi, 51, 52, 54, 56, 67, 128, 128, 129, 131, 135
Martin, 51, 97
Maseko, Javen, 85
Massinga, 69
Masvingo, 111
Matabele, 88, 89, 95, 98, 101, 115, 116, 176, 132
Mbundu, 3, 110, 119
Meiring, General George, 28
Middle East, 24, 26, 69
Miller, 20
Minter, 50
Moyo, Jonathan 144
Mozambican Christian Council, 75
Mozambique, 1, 4, 6-13, 153, 15, 18, 45, 46, 47, 49, 51-57, 58-66, 68-76, 78-81, 83, 86, 97, 105, 110, 121, 123, 124, 127-144, 146-148, 149, 150
Mugabe, Robert, 5, 10-12, 54, 55, 67, 72, 77-80, 82-86, 88-91, 94, 96, 99, 100, 102, 104, 106, 107, 112, 114-117, 122, 123, 135, 140, 150, 151
Mutara, 56

Nakala, 51, 54, 56, 128, 129
Namibia 2, 7, 8, 11, 15, 19, 28, 30, 31, 36, 37, 39, 43, 44, 68, 140, 142, 144, 150
Ncumbe, Welshman, 106, 144
Ndau, 121-124
Ndebele, 5, 84, 86, 96, 98, 99, 105, 110, 111-117, 120, 121, 123, 124, 143
Negage, 43
New York, 37
Nicaragua 26, 71
Nigeria, 18,
Nkomati Accord, 57, 59, 61-66, 69, 71, 74, 141, 150
North Korea, 85
Nova, 56, 128
Nyanga, 73, 93
Nyerere, Julius, 52

Ogaden war, 21
Ovimbundu, 118-120

Philippines, 20
Portugal, 7, 15-17, 19, 39, 40, 42, 44, 58, 60, 74, 130

Raffaelli, Mario, 78
Reagan Doctrine, 26
Red Beret, 66
Regulos, 48
Renamo 11, 157, 45, 46-60, 62-66, 68-80, 82, 105, 110, 111, 121-123, 127-129, 131-137, 139, 140, 142, 144, 147, 148, 150, 157, 176
Roberto, Holden, 3
Rome, 74, 78-80
Rowland, "Tinny", 80
Rucana, 37

SADCC, 13, 79, 127, 128
SADF, 15, 24, 28, 29, 34-36, 47, 60, 64, 65, 88, 142
Sandura, Justice Wilson, 106
Sanguiba, 18
Senegal, 20, 24
Shona, 5, 12, 93, 111, 112, 114-116, 120, 122, 124
Simango, Uria, 4
Sithole, Ndabaningi, 107, 122, 123
South Africa, 2, 3, 5-13, 18, 19, 22, 24, 25, 27-29, 30-32, 34-37, 43, 46-49, 51, 52, 54, 56, 57, 58-71, 78, 89, 89, 92, 96-98, 126-130, 134, 135, 139, 140, 141-145, 150, 151, 176, 177
Soviet Union, 3, 18, 21, 22, 23, 32, 38-40, 61, 68, 70, 71, 89, 141-143
SWAPO, 11, 13, 19, 27-31, 35, 36, 62,

Tanzania, 18, 51, 61, 75, 130, 131
Tazara, 130
Tete, 7, 51, 129
Texeira de Sousa, 17

UDI, 4, 7, 8.
Uige, 43
Ululu, 147
UNHCR, 54, 131
UNITA, 2, 3, 18, 19, 22-44, 71, 74, 82, 110, 118, 119, 120-122, 127, 132-136, 139, 140, 142-146, 153.

United States, 3, 21, 22, 25, 26, 30, 33, 51, 68-72, 107, 112, 142, 143, 146
UNOMOZ, 80, 81
USAID, 69
Ustinov, 70

van Dunem, 32, 143
Victoria Falls, 26, 92, 136
Viljoen, Constand, 29, 64

Xangongo, 28

Yugoslavia, 58, 169, 144

Zaire, 15, 17-22, 33, 34, 38, 39, 42, 44, 130
Zambezi, 6, 66, 67, 129
Zambezia, 51, 133
Zambia, 17, 20, 22, 44, 61, 67, 127, 130, 131
ZANLA, 5, 10, 12, 46, 54, 83-86, 90, 91, 98, 114
ZANU, 5, 9, 10, 12, 32, 55, 83, 84-86, 91, 98-103, 105-107, 110, 112-118, 122, 123
ZAPU, 5, 7, 10, 12, 13, 32, 83, 84, 84-86, 87, 89, 89, 90-93, 95, 99-105, 106, 110, 112-115, 117, 118, 122,
Zimbabwe, 1, 4, 5, 6, 9-13, 15, 32, 44, 45, 52-57, 61, 66-68, 73, 75, 77, 82-98, 100, 101, 105-108, 110-112, 118, 120-124, 127-132, 134-136, 138-140, 143, 145, 148,

INDEX

176.
ZIMOFA, 57
ZIPRA, 5, 12, 83, 84-87, 88, 89-93, 95, 96, 97, 105, 110, 113-116, 123, 124, 163
ZUM, 55, 106, 107, 123
Zumbo, 7

www.ingramcontent.com/pod-product-compliance
Lightning Source LLC
Chambersburg PA
CBHW052040300426
44117CB00012B/1903